"A detailed look into both the appeal of conspiracy theories and the effects that they can have on society writ large."

—*InsideHook*, "The 10 Books You Should Be Reading This September"

"Enormously powerful, clearheaded, and convincing."

—*The Straight Dope*

ALSO BY SARAH KENDZIOR

The View from Flyover Country

Hiding in Plain Sight

our common life. . . . If *They Knew* was a concept album, it would unite multiple musical genres."

—*Chicago Tribune*

"An eye-opening look at the forces behind those attempting to undermine democracy, create political division, and protect the criminal and political elite from prosecution and responsibility. You will walk away with a greater understanding of how Washington really works, and, along with informing you, it may also scare you a little."

—*Town & Style*

"Her writing raises points worth discussing and dissecting, in ways that can make readers stop and think and come up with conclusions that may make sense—but aren't always easy to accept."

—*St. Louis Post-Dispatch*

"Kendzior chooses her examples of embedded crime with the skill of a brain surgeon, attempting a reverse lobotomy on a mostly comatose nation."

—*Wall Street on Parade*

"Deftly dissects the tangled truths behind the conspiracies that intertwine American and international politics, business, and criminality, with a style reminiscent of Ronan Farrow's *Catch and Kill* or Bob Woodward's recent books. . . . Kendzior's compelling and urgent prose will speak to readers who are working to make sense of the current political and social landscapes."

—*Booklist*

"A sharp dissection of a culture of lies, secrets, and conspiracies—including 'the original conspiracy theory: American exceptionalism.' . . . A provocative, pointed challenge to all Americans to dig harder for the truth."

—*Kirkus Reviews*

"Eye-opening . . . Kendzior's deep dives into recent scandals are illuminating."

—*Publishers Weekly*

THEY KNEW

**How a Culture of Conspiracy
Keeps America Complacent**

SARAH KENDZIOR

FLATIRON
BOOKS
NEW YORK

www.flatironbooks.com

Designed by Steven Seighman

The Library of Congress has cataloged the hardcover edition as follows:

Names: Kendzior, Sarah, author.
Title: They knew : how a culture of conspiracy keeps America complacent / Sarah Kendzior.
Description: First edition. | New York : Flatiron Books, [2022]
Identifiers: LCCN 2022020887 | ISBN 9781250210722 (hardcover) | ISBN 9781250857880 (ebook)
Subjects: LCSH: Conspiracy theories—United States. | Social conflict—United States—History—21st century. | United States—Social conditions—21st century. | United States—Politics and government—21st century.
Classification: LCC HV6275.K426 2022 | DDC 303.60973—dc23/eng/20220711
LC record available at https://lccn.loc.gov/2022020887

ISBN 978-1-250-87860-1 (trade paperback)

Our books may be purchased in bulk for promotional, educational, or business use. Please contact your local bookseller or the Macmillan Corporate and Premium Sales Department at 1-800-221-7945, extension 5442, or by email at MacmillanSpecialMarkets@macmillan.com.

First Flatiron Books Paperback Edition: 2024

10 9 8 7 6 5 4 3 2 1

For my children, and for our country

CONTENTS

AUTHOR'S NOTE

I wrote this book in 2021: between the coup plot and the war, between delta and omicron, navigating the mix of chaos and inertia that defines our era. 2021 is a year that will be remembered in history—if the future is lucky enough to have history—as pivotal, much like 1918 and other years that make or break the world. *They Knew* discusses the difference between a conspiracy and a conspiracy theory, two terms that those in power want us to believe are inseparable so that we remain ignorant of the past and passive about the future. 2021 brought a reexamination of the United States as a country built on conspiracy, and *They Knew* is a reboot of the historical record. It is not comprehensive and it is not conclusive, and that is a good thing. Whatever happens between the time I wrote this and the time you read it, I hope you are still left with the freedom to make up your own mind.

—February 22, 2022

They regarded it, not as a foreshadowing of evil in the future, but as the fulfilment of an evil already presaged.

—Herman Melville, *Moby-Dick*

Nobody saw it coming.

—American folk saying

THEY KNEW

DEATHS OF DECEPTION

n northern Arkansas there is a town called Eureka Springs, where no streets meet at a right angle. The town is built into the bedrock, captive to ancient geology, its buildings carved into curving cliffs and its trees erupting through layers of sloping sidewalks. There are no traffic lights in Eureka Springs because there is no clear way to turn, no bearings to get, no center to hold. You can enter the ground floor of a building and walk a straight line out the back door only to discover you have just left that side's fifth floor. The topography dictates your journey: renames it, replaces it. It's reassuring in this day and age, such reliable disorientation. No one comes to Eureka Springs for certainty anyway. They come for the magic and the ghosts.

Before the pandemic hit, every December my family would drive from St. Louis, Missouri, to Dallas, Texas, to celebrate Christmas with my sister and her family. Every year we would stop in Arkansas and spend a night in Eureka Springs. The official reason was to break up the ten-hour drive, but the real reason was to stay at the Crescent Hotel, and the reason we wanted to stay at the Crescent Hotel was that it's haunted. This is not our opinion, but the hotel's calling card. Since 1886, the Crescent has loomed over Eureka Springs, attracting travelers seeking miracle cures in the town's waters, which are said to possess magical healing powers. In the nineteenth and early twentieth centuries, the famous and infamous passed through as the Ozarks became a gangsters' paradise and a politicians' retreat. The hotel changed hands and identities: a luxury resort, a women's conservatory, a junior college. Then the Great Depression hit and it became a place where people literally died of false hope.

In 1937, a con artist named Norman Baker arrived in Eureka Springs with a new mark in mind. Born in the Mississippi River trade town of Muscatine, Iowa, in 1882, Baker grew up rich and spent his formative years getting wealthier through fraud. In the 1920s, he traveled through a shell-shocked America still reeling from the Spanish Flu, scouring the landscape like a vulture preying on pain. An aspiring politician, former carnival barker, and skilled demagogue, Baker gained a massive audience spouting conspiracy theories through the newly popular medium of radio. He operated a station in Muscatine that he called "KTNT," which stood for "Know the Naked Truth." Muscatine was at this time a fledgling Midwestern media mecca. Mark Twain had worked at its newspaper, before being accosted by a local with a knife who insisted he call him the son of the devil or be killed, at which point Twain decided to leave town.[1]

Throughout the late 1920s, Baker warned his audience that evil cabals ruled the United States. He assured his listeners that he could expose the evildoers, so long as they kept on listening. His 10,000-watt broadcasts extended far beyond Muscatine, reaching over one million homes.[2] Off the air, Baker consulted with a team of vicious lawyers he had hired to threaten the public officials and journalists investigating his numerous criminal offenses, which ranged from obscenity to libel to theft.

But Baker's cruelest crime was making ordinary people believe he could save them. In 1929, as the stock market crashed and America lurched deeper into despair, Baker proclaimed himself a medical genius. In December, he started a print magazine, *The Naked Truth*, and put a photo of himself on the cover alongside the proclamation CANCER IS CURED. In 1930, he set up a hospital in Muscatine, called it the Baker Institute, and staffed it with people who had minimal medical expertise. He peddled a cancer treatment that consisted of little more than seeds, corn silk, carbolic acid, and water, though he did not tell that to his audience.

He branded this tonic "Secret Remedy #5." Baker's secrets earned him $444,000 in 1930 alone, the 2021 equivalent of $7.2 million.[3]

Baker was an opponent of vaccines. He told his followers that doctors recommending vaccines were part of a nefarious government plot. He claimed that doctors knew how to cure cancer, but refused to do it because it afforded them no financial gain, unlike his own selfless actions.[4] Baker was vicious in his denunciations, but his audience liked it. In a time of economic misery and political instability, it felt good to have an enemy, and Baker's confidence was its own lure. Throughout the early 1930s, tens of thousands of desperate Americans gathered together at rallies to hear him speak. Baker assured them that one day cancer would disappear, like a miracle. They drank his treatment down like Kool-Aid-flavored hydroxychloroquine, and thereby sealed their own demise.

Within a year, the American Medical Association had caught on to Baker and sought to shut down his operation, seeing him as a merchant of death. "The viciousness of Mr. Baker's broadcasting lies not in what he says about the American Medical Association but in the fact that he induces sufferers from cancer who might have some chance for their lives, if seen early and properly treated, to resort to his nostrum," they wrote in 1931.[5] Baker responded by claiming that the American Medical Association had sent armed assassins to kill him. He then unsuccessfully sued the AMA for defamation.

These were classic Baker tactics—accuse your opponents of an outrageous crime and sue them early and aggressively. But this time, he failed. He lost his radio license and his institute and gained an arrest warrant. He fled to Mexico, where he purchased a border radio station and broadcast to his audience that he would continue to live above the law. After a few years of lying relatively low, he returned to the United States in 1937. He served one day of prison time in Iowa, for practicing medicine without a license, and set off for Eureka Springs.

You can make a lot of money peddling lies on the road. But you can make even more when you settle in one place, forcing your victims to pay to come to you. By the time Baker arrived in northern Arkansas in

July, the local economy had collapsed. The Crescent Hotel was a vacant Victorian behemoth from which one could gaze down at the town's past glory and current decay. Eureka Springs officials welcomed the flamboyant radio star, hoping his prowess for publicity would reverse their misfortune. And so, the scam, and the deaths, began anew.

Under Baker's management, the Crescent Hotel was transformed into the Baker Hospital and Health Resort. His descriptions of his medical ingenuity became as outrageous as the hotel's décor, which now included purple hallways (to match his trademark lavender tie) and a calliope mounted on the roof. Baker posted ads in newspapers throughout the United States claiming his cancer cure required no operations, radium, or x-rays, but could be achieved by a simple injection of his special serum. He photographed rows of jars of tumors he claimed were removed from cured patients and announced: "We have hundreds of specimens like these. Actual cancer specimens and laboratory data proves all. All specimens are preserved in alcohol."[6]

Americans read Baker's advertisements and believed them. They sent their sick to the Crescent Hotel to be cured by the famous doctor, so charismatic in his white suit, so full of confidence in his followers, and so full of condemnation for all who questioned him. They wanted to believe, and clearly there was nothing to fear—if there were, someone would have stopped him by now, right? Americans showed up riddled with disease and swallowed Norman Baker's cures and lies.

In June 2018, in another life, I drove with my husband and children from Missouri to Rocky Mountain National Park. We traveled freely and blithely, stopping at restaurants and tourist traps on a whim. The phrase "Mask up, kids, we're going to the gas station!" had not yet entered our vocabulary. We were unconcerned with pandemics and were contending only with the usual problems of economic decline, rising autocracy, rampant gun violence, disinformation warfare, climate catastrophes, systemic racism, and endemic corruption. This time is what we refer to now as the good old days.

The summer of 2018 felt like a hinge on which the country swayed between democracy and autocracy, a demarcation as precipitous as a knife's edge. I lived on that edge, as a journalist who spent every day documenting the downfall but also dealing with its practical ramifications as a mother and as an American. In 2018, the respectable thing for journalists to do was deny the possibility of authoritarianism in America, but I was never very good at being respectable.

It is very bad in America to be right too early. It is considered a sin in journalism to tell the public what you have learned in real time, both because you are going against the tide of profit motive, but mostly because it destroys plausible deniability for the corrupt and powerful. My dire warnings were echoed by political officials only when it was too late for them to act. In 2015, I warned that Donald Trump would win the presidential election. In 2016, I warned that Trump was a career criminal who would rule the United States like a Central Asian kleptocrat. In 2017, I warned that if action was not taken immediately, Trump would purge institutions and pack courts so that the damage to America would last decades—if America lasted at all.

I was growing weary of my own unheeded warnings. I worried about the inability of people in my country to discern between a "conspiracy theory," in the pejorative sense, and an actual ongoing conspiracy.

On television, the news alternated between Trump's firehose of lies and a parade of feel-good institutionalists whose reputations for justice were buoyed by anticipation instead of deed: the Federal Bureau of Investigation's James Comey and Robert Mueller, House Speaker Nancy Pelosi, "the intelligence community," "the steady state," "the players behind the scenes." The descriptions of the heroes in wait became more amorphous as the crimes became clearer and the punishments smaller. Liberal pundits declared that secret saviors would rescue America from Trump. Trump crowed that he would rescue America from a cast of rotating villains. On each side, everyone told everyone else to shut up and "trust the plan."

The severity of that from which Americans needed to be rescued—deep, entrenched corruption; the unchecked dismantling of our most basic civic protections; the cavalcade of catastrophes that awaited us in the form of climate change if action were not taken—was ignored or cloaked in spectacle. That Trump's illicit actions obviously required enablers from the very institutions he proclaimed his enemies—the FBI, Wall Street, the Democrats, the media—made for awkward discussions. It was easy for liberals to designate Trump as an anomalous villain, an American exception to American exceptionalism. It was easy for right-wingers to designate Trump an anomalous hero, a restorer of America's unmanifested destiny.

It was harder for all of them to explain how this con artist had risen to establishment glory despite his decades of documented criminal acts and illicit foreign ties. On the whole they ignored the darkness that lay behind that "Teflon Don" moniker and continued to cover up his crimes with his scandals. It was easier not to think about it—safer, too. Whether you are the criminal or the captive, there are few things more disconcerting than learning that the rescue crew is in on the plot.

By the summer of 2018, I was worn from the hype and dreading the day when my own conclusion—that this was a transnational crime syndicate masquerading as a government—would be accepted, because it is the kind of concession elites make only when the expiration date for democracy has passed.

I decided to hit the road: not so much for my own sake, but for my children's, to show them proof of life in a dying nation and that not all big American ideas are bad. That year, my children were ten and seven years old and had not known any America other than one of looming threats and broken promises. A nation that adults cloaked in a veneer of "exceptionalism" but that they, as children, could see clearly, because they had not been trained to avert their eyes. My children knew their homeland was on the decline but didn't dwell on it. Like other kids, they preferred the world-building game Minecraft, where they veered, much as I did in day-to-day life, between "survival mode" and "creative mode." They did not see the Trump era as any more aberrant than I had seen the Reagan era as a child of the 1980s. Decline was America's natural trajectory, paved during their parents' childhoods and passed down to their own. The president was a liar and no one had a steady job and the earth was on fire and it had never been otherwise. My children learned early that the world keeps turning as it burns.

I wanted them to see that America had beauty as well, and that people had sought to preserve it—for their generation and any that followed. I wanted them to see mountains and wildlife and conservation in action, and I wanted them to watch other Americans enjoying these sights too, regardless of from where they came or for whom they voted. The national parks were both a break from America and its finest embodiment, a liminal space of past and possibility.

But I had additional fixations, and when it came time to choose a place to stay in Estes Park, I made a reservation at the Stanley Hotel, the place that inspired Stephen King to write *The Shining* when he stayed there in the 1970s. I couldn't help myself: I was a sucker for King and a sucker for a horror story, and so we wandered the floors and took pictures of the fabled room 217 (237 in the movie, but I was a purist). I made the kids pose like the doomed ghost sisters at the end of a hallway and they rolled their eyes and laughed. The Stanley capitalized on *The Shining* and advertises itself as haunted, but nothing about it felt scary. We were play-acting, a family of four on a last-chance road trip, contemplating buying a big wheel tricycle and seeing if the staff would let my son ride it down the halls. (We asked; they would not.) When we went to the bar to drink like Jack Torrance the radio was playing "Don't Stop Believing" by Journey. The only thing this hotel killed was the mood.

We fell asleep in a clean and unremarkable room, and when I woke up, the sky had turned red. There were wildfires sweeping through Colorado. You could see them coming down the mountains, you could smell the smoke choking the air, you could hear the alerts from your phone, warning you to get out, to run from this place, because death was coming.

America is a ghost story, I thought as we packed our bags. And we are the ghosts.

In December 2019, we made our final trip to the Crescent Hotel, turning down a state road past a shuttered church with a sign out front that said PEACE ON EARTH—CLOSED. Eureka Springs is a pilgrimage paradox, a progressive oasis in a mostly conservative state that attracts artists and hippies and LGBT southerners seeking freedom from Republican rule. It is also an evangelical mecca, embodied by the towering Christ of the Ozarks statue that gazes from the mountains, surrounded by re-created biblical structures and a venue for performances of the Passion Play. The two dominant subcultures of Eureka Springs, deemed irreconcilable opposites in national discourse, coexisted in relative peace—in part out of economic necessity; in part because complex communities can never be reduced to binary politics; and in part, perhaps, because a town built on miracles and lies forces everyone to believe in the impossible.

The Crescent is isolated from the rest of the town on a mountaintop overlooking a church teeming with turkey vultures. Every year the hotel decks itself out for Christmas, and my kids would go into the backyard and marvel at the elaborate lights and homemade holiday displays built by locals. In 2019, however, there was a new sight: a faint hole in the ground, and a sign stating that hundreds of bottles containing what appeared to be human remains had been unearthed that spring. The bottles matched the description of the ad Norman Baker had posted in 1938, claiming he had excised the tumors of cancer patients with his miracle potion and preserved them in alcohol. Over eighty years later, a landscaper had unearthed them with a backhoe while breaking ground for an archery range.

No one is clear how many people died in the Crescent Hotel under Baker's supervision, but there is a morgue in the basement where Baker and his staff would store the corpses. To see it, you need to take the ghost tour. My family had been to the hotel several times, but never taken the tour, as I felt my youngest child was too young to know what happened there. As 2020 approached, I felt there could be nothing on that tour more shocking than what he heard every day on the news, so we signed up. Our family descended the stairs into the morgue and saw the jars of newly discovered specimens on the wall. I flinched but felt relief: this was evidence. This was confirmation of the crime, a reminder that wealthy criminals—even master con artists—could be stopped. In 1941, Baker was apprehended by federal authorities. He spent the 1940s in a Missouri penitentiary following a federal conviction for fraud, before eventually moving to South Florida in the 1950s and dying of cirrhosis of the liver.

How novel: a criminal demagogue had been caught and constrained in his own lifetime, left unable to harm anyone else. But it did not take away the cruelty of what he had done. In the Crescent Hotel, people had been left to die in agony and their bodies were disposed of as if they were nothing. There was a palpable heaviness to the place, an unresolved anguish that seemed to manifest in the air itself, a sense of buried memories that is maybe what people mean when they talk about ghosts.

Every ghost story is at its heart a story of grief. But was there a worse way to die, I wondered, than alone and betrayed, at the mercy of a career criminal who markets your demise as his own victory, who sells your sham salvation to lure more victims into his lair? There is no crueler elixir than false hope. The hotel advertised more conventional tales of misfortune as evidence of its paranormal draw—guests falling off balconies, accidents of unlucky workers—but its tenure as a criminal's cancer ward was the one that horrified me on a visceral level. Deaths of humiliation and desperation and abandonment, all avoidable if they had not fallen for the con: what if, what if, what if.

It was the question not only of their time, but my own. By 2019, it felt like something new and dark had been unleashed: something beyond just the predictable pain of politics and the catastrophes of climate change, something evil and unmoored. I had nightmares that left me shaken but I felt relief because those dark dreams were still less frightening than either my intuition or the news. I welcomed nightmares; nightmares end. What

I witnessed when I was awake—a sense of impending dissolution, of hard-hewn plots coming to a head—had no clear resolution or expiration date.

I was grieving the future, I realized with a start.

In 2018, I had published a book, *The View from Flyover Country*, on how the breakdown of institutions and social trust had set the stage for American autocracy. That book was a collection of essays written between 2012 and 2014, when the concept of America losing its status as a sovereign democratic nation seemed laughable to most. In 2019, I had written another book, set for publication in 2020, *Hiding in Plain Sight*, in which I exposed several decades of transnational organized crime, the political and media elites who abetted it, and the deteriorating conditions that fostered this catastrophe and exacerbated it in turn.

I had hoped that my documentation of national crises would help people solve them. But in the end, I did not deliver much beyond the truth, an increasingly useless currency in the land of the conned and complicit. It's a currency I cling to anyway, because truth cannot be stolen. Hidden, but never stolen. Like buried evidence, it works its way out of the earth.

In the summer of 2019, I was so certain that Americans would lose the ability to move freely by *Hiding in Plain Sight*'s April 2020 publication date that I wrote the book as if the travel restrictions had already happened. "We still had the freedom to travel, and there is so much to see," I wrote about our 2018 drive out west, perplexing copy editors with my conflicting tenses: but it proved an accurate summation. By December 2019, I was sure this would be our last road trip for a long while, though I still did not know the precise nature of the disaster that loomed. I convinced my husband we should blow some money and get the Crescent's biggest room.

The hotel calls it "The Governor's Suite," in honor of nineteenth-century Arkansas governor Powell Clayton, but it was also the office and accommodation of Norman Baker. When Baker owned the Crescent, he had sealed the room with bulletproof glass and kept his submachine guns inside. Those were gone, but the old-fashioned décor remained, shoddy and beautiful excess, like living inside a cover-up. I would gaze out the window at the mountains and think about how this was the same view Baker saw when he lied to his patients. I would listen to the vultures hiss and wonder if he had heard the same sounds when he catalogued his bodies and collected his cash. I never wondered what made Baker commit atrocities, because the answer is the same for every serial abuser: people let him. Ordinary people saw that he was committing exceptional crimes, and they let him get away with it. Here I refer not to the unwitting sick who clung to him for a cure, but of the witnesses who were aware he was killing people and stayed silent. Those who might have questioned his criminality, but failed to stop it. They knew.

Those are the people who haunt me, the enablers, those who could have saved human lives and did not. Had they even made a conscious choice, I wondered? The famed scholar of fascism Hannah Arendt wrote: "The sad truth is that most evil is done by people who never make up their minds to be good or evil." A refugee from Nazi Germany, Arendt made this observation after witnessing some of the cruelest political violence in world history. But it was the banality of evil that haunted her— not the brazen depravity, but the quiet moral rot. The way evil travels like a disease, infecting people who breathe it in and absorb it into their system, only to breathe it out and infect others. Are they aware that they've contracted it? Would they rid themselves of it if they had the chance? Or is it too frightening to confront when it's a part of yourself, too enjoyable when it's a weapon you wield?

On Christmas Eve, we left Eureka Springs and drove south through Arkansas toward Texas. Bald eagles flew above us in a cloudless deep blue sky and we pulled over to stare. My daughter took a photo of one landing on a treetop, its white wings outstretched, its talons poised to grasp a branch. One of my earliest memories as a 1980s schoolchild was learning that the bald eagle was both America's national symbol and an endangered species. My fellow Americans had hunted and poisoned our national symbol nearly to death before I was born. Even as a kid I thought this was a little too on the nose, and I remember my class laughing when the teacher broke the news. It was the kind of laugh a child makes when adults have screwed up so badly that we couldn't get in trouble for mocking the idea that they were in charge.

But to my surprise, as I grew up, the bald eagle reemerged. Conservationists had acted to protect it and officials had passed laws to ensure their efforts mattered. By the time I was a teenager in the late 1990s, the bald eagle had fallen off the endangered species list and been downgraded to "threatened" status. By the time I became a mother, in 2007, the bald eagle was neither endangered nor threatened but living the elusive American dream: free and safe at once. By then I had moved to Missouri, prime eagle migration territory, and started to seek them out. Every winter my children and I would drive up and down along the Mississippi River, looking for flocks and nests. I didn't tell my children the bald eagle had almost gone extinct. I didn't want them to know yet that such a rebound was an anomaly in our era of climate catastrophes. I told them seeing a bald eagle in the wild was good luck, because that's what it felt like to me. Telling a child to believe in luck felt more honest than telling them to believe in promises.

We drove on to Oklahoma, passing through the Cherokee and Choctaw reservations. The reservations always opened a conversation with the kids about why Native Americans lived on special pieces of land. As a child, I had grown up in New England, where I was told that Europeans were welcomed by Squanto, first friend of the Pilgrims; then told that the Indians had mysteriously relocated by the time the United States was founded; then told that the Americans had to kill some Indians but that was okay because all wars have winners and losers and Americans are meant to be winners; then told that it was mass slaughter but it evened out because the Indians who survived got casinos. This did not make sense to me even at the time, but I accepted it then because no one told me there were tribes of Native Americans still residing in my country in large numbers, fighting for their rights.

At the time, I had no idea that white Americans' broken promises had determined their fate. I had heard the joke that the United States was cursed because it was built on a giant Native American burial ground. I did not know until I was older that this was true and that history was buried there with it.

By the evening we had crossed from Oklahoma into Texas, and as we approached Dallas, the traffic thickened. It was a shock to sit in traffic after living in St. Louis, where decades of abandonment meant you never had to wait in line. Highways snaked around Dallas's suburban sprawl, giving us views of housing developments hopeful and haphazard, vibrancy devoid of vision.

My sister is a Texas transplant, having moved there after her husband's fourth job transfer. As a millennial, she was simply grateful he was employed. His first job out of college was at Enron, where he worked for a month before Enron's massive corruption scheme collapsed and took the economy with it, inaugurating the first recession of our adult lives. For years my sister and her husband bounced around America to the rhythms of disaster capitalism. She rented her first apartment at a discount because it overlooked the giant hole where the World Trade Center once stood. She couldn't afford anything else, she explained, and tried not to think about the air she breathed. Now she and her husband lived in a suburban Dallas home they bought after the housing crash that kicked off the second major economic downturn of our adulthood. I have trouble remembering the year my sister moved to Dallas because I think of it as "during the recession" but the recession started in 2008 and didn't end until 2020, when it turned into a new recession caused by a global plague.

While on a summer visit to Dallas in 2017, I decided to see Dealey Plaza, the site where John F. Kennedy was assassinated. I wanted to sit on the grassy knoll; I wanted to stand on the sidewalk where the limo had passed; I wanted to look through the book depository window. I needed to see it to believe it and the only way to believe it was to see it from all sides. The former book depository building now housed a JFK assassination museum where I was greeted by a sad-eyed man who told me not to enter unless I liked being deceived. He handed me a pamphlet he said would guide me to the real story of who killed JFK, a complex tale he offered to expand upon for a small fee.

His printed pamphlet felt quaint, since this was 2017, and the current president floated in a sea of impunity buoyed by social media lies. I wondered how long this man had been handing out pamphlets, how many decades he had spent obsessing over this crime. "Jack Ruby isn't what you think he is," he informed me. He was in his late sixties, a baby boomer scarred by a childhood of televised tragedy. I could relate to that feeling so I thanked him for his information, but I entered the museum anyway.

When I was in second grade, my teacher told our class we were in for a treat. We knew what it was because we had spent weeks preparing: it was the day of the launch of the Challenger, the first shuttle to send a teacher into outer space. The teacher's name was Christa McAuliffe and she had dark curly hair like my mom, who was also a public school teacher, and I kept wishing my mom was a cool astronaut teacher instead of a boring regular one. My teacher lined us up and escorted us into the gym, where a television had been wheeled in for the occasion, and we sat cross-legged on the floor to watch the event with the other kids.

We shrieked in delight as the Challenger soared into the sky and then we stared, confused, at an explosion of flames. I had never seen a space shuttle launch and did not know what I was witnessing until a teacher turned it off and herded us back into our classrooms and told us the astronauts had died. I felt deep irrational guilt for wishing my mother had been on the shuttle and began to cry.

When I told my mother about it later, she said that when she had been thirteen years old, an announcement came over the middle school intercom saying that the president had been shot. My mother had loved John F. Kennedy, who she thought was movie-star handsome and hopeful and kind, like an American president should be. Her eighth-grade teacher, unsure of what to do, continued to teach the day's lesson until class was officially dismissed, and my mother remembers that the most—the way they were supposed to just sit there like the world hadn't ended. Then the long walk home, the shocked faces and tears, the uniformity of confusion and grief. Learning who Lee Harvey Oswald was and watching Jack Ruby murder him on television. That detail shocked me, that my mother had also watched a person die on TV. It felt obscene that TV was allowed to do that.

Inside the JFK assassination museum, I saw the exhibits through my mother's eyes: it was impossible not to. Residual grief had sealed my view of the event, because the only thing I trusted was that it had caused enormous pain. There had never been a time when I felt I knew the full truth about the JFK assassination or thought it was possible to learn it. When I was twelve, Oliver Stone had made his JFK conspiracy movie based on a JFK conspiracy book; by the time I was a teenager, the shooting was parodied on *Seinfeld*. The murder and the mythology had long been commodified past the point of recognition, but the grief remained among those who lived through it, clouding the eyes of even the hardest cynics. Whether those eyes were clouded with tears or rage or suspicion varied, but I had never met anyone alive in 1963 who did not have an intense, immediate recollection of where they were when JFK died.

I did not understand this kind of collective grief until I was older. In the 1990s, I joked that O. J. Simpson's white Bronco chase was my generation's "where were you when" moment, only for the Twin Towers to fall and then the global economy and then American democracy and then a series of catastrophes so rapid and relentless that I forgot what it was like for there to only be one at a time.

There's no way to drive through America without hitting a conspiracy or a crime. I've driven through all forty-eight contiguous states and for a time, my mental geography was demarcated by places known best for mass shootings: Jonesboro, Littleton, Paducah, Newtown. I would drift along the highways, trying to remember how I knew that town, and be jolted into recollections of senseless violence. Eventually the mass shootings became so numerous that I lost track. An American town known for a massacre became just another town.

In the summer of 2021, the route I used to drive between St. Louis and Dallas became the Covid Corridor. Late 2019 was the last time we would drive it clean: no masks, no contagion, no towns now synonymous with plague comeback tours. In the summer of 2021, officials told us the pandemic was departing, but it rose again in the Ozarks, the same region where Norman Baker deceived cancer victims into paying for their own deaths. In southwest Missouri, in northern Arkansas, in northeast Oklahoma, in eastern Texas, people were dying of the delta strain. The dying did not want to be vaccinated and their refusal led coastal pundits to declare that my state merits a bitter end. "Everyone stupid enough to live in Missouri deserves to die!" strangers would tell me daily on social media, unaware that they are rooting for my elimination far more blatantly than any Trump-voting Missourian ever did.

Because we are mere "red states"—in reality, gerrymandered hostage states run by hard-right Republican legislatures that disregard the public will—the D.C. elite decided to play horse-race politics with our plague. Pundits and politicians blame the refusal of some in "red states" to take the vaccine on partisanship, despite the fact that most people are unaffiliated voters, and that the group with the highest rate of vaccination is white boomers, which is in turn the most likely demographic to vote for Republicans. Outsiders blame Fox News, they blame Facebook, they blame the lies of Republican officials, and while all these entities deserve a great deal of blame, this judgment does not strike at the core of what has happened here, which is an epidemic of disillusionment and distrust so vast it stretches into paralysis.

What is happening in Missouri is the result of having been lied to so many times about matters of life or death that the desire to die on your own terms outweighs the desire to get tricked into choosing it. What is happening here is the aftermath of predatory big pharma dynasties like the Sacklers swooping into your state and promising you relief in the form of opioids, assuring you they are safe, and leaving your community addicted and decimated while they laugh and profit off your pain and seek permanent immunity in the courts.[7] What is happening here is recognition that if something were indeed wrong with a new and experimental vaccine, there would be no recourse and no justice, because political officials do not care if you die. What is happening here is abandonment as a way of life, from the streets of St. Louis to the hills of the Ozarks, and the knowledge that making a wrong move in a broken healthcare system is a gamble too expensive to take. What is happening here is not only people falling for conspiracies but remembering the times their loved ones had faith in the system and faith made a fool of them, at the cost of their survival.

When reporters ask Missourians why they will not take the vaccine, one of the most common answers is that they are not opposed to it on principle, but are waiting to see if it is safe. I know this feeling. I got vaccinated when I was deemed eligible but I did not like it or fully trust it. I simply hated covid more and chose the vaccine over covid. It was a lot like voting in a presidential election.

The crisis, of course, is that there is no such thing as a loner's plague. The choices of one affect all. Missouri is in the center of the country: where the rust belt meets the bible belt, where north meets south at a gateway to the west, where a plague variant born in Joplin gets its kicks on Route 66 as it spreads to St. Louis and beyond. Missouri is a magnet for opportunists, where operatives from around the world ply politicians with dark money and corporations ply people with guns and drugs. We are a petri dish for the end of the American experiment and we spawned a new plague variant just when the rest of the country thought they were safe.

In 2021, the relentlessness of covid only exacerbated distrust formed by decades of predation and institutional rot. Desperate people from a broken country run by liars and besieged by con artists were suddenly confronted with a matter of life and death. Some fell for stories that prompted them to make a choice that cost them their life and jeopardized the lives of others. Some died from not making up their minds at the speed of a transforming plague. Some made a sincere and rigorous effort to find the truth, only to wind up deceived again, and that deceit pushed them harder into confusion.

Skeptical of past deceptions by authorities and frustrated by conflicting advice, they formed their own theories. These are theories, mind you, not facts, and everyone has the right to form theories—in a flailing democracy, one could argue, that right becomes a duty. The danger comes when questions are mistaken for answers and theories are mistaken for facts.

Here we land in the murky territory of conspiracy theory, a term that is used both to describe a vast array of behaviors and to make you not want to talk about any of them in public. The rest of this book breaks down the phenomenon in detail, but the pejorative assumptions surrounding the term should be discarded. When abuse by authorities is both rampant and downplayed, a culture of distrust will emerge as a consequence. Conspiracy theories are the midway point to truth, the fork in the road between enlightenment and delusion. Conspiracy theories are what you end up with when people bury past sins and build over the graves and one day somebody finds bones in the earth.

A conspiracy theory is not the same thing as a conspiracy. Conspiracies are portrayed as elaborate and rare, but they are common and often simple in their basic goals, if not the execution. A conspiracy is an agreement of powerful actors to secretly carry out a plan that protects their own interests, often to the detriment of the public good. The mafia is a conspiracy, the drug trade is a conspiracy, white-collar crime is a conspiracy. War and espionage operations rely upon conspiracy. The American Revolution was a conspiracy. Conspiracy is baked into the founding of our nation.

Conspiracies depend on obfuscation and insularity. Conspiracy theories, on the other hand, are morally neutral and easily accessible. They can be weaponized as propaganda by conspirators, or they can be sincere expressions of the search for truth. Conspiracy theories are group projects open to all: they are perversely democratizing in a country that has lost transparency and trust.

That the state of the union is suspicion is not new. It is as old as the original conspiracy theory: American exceptionalism. Our famed "rugged individualism" was often a by-product of institutional abandonment or a defense mechanism to prevent oneself from being a mark. What has changed over the centuries is the means, not the men. Nearly one hundred years ago, in the aftermath of a global pandemic and a war, Americans in my part of the country fell for a career criminal media personality who convinced them to pay to die for his sins. In 2016, a man very much like Norman Baker was declared the President of the United States, and the world felt the consequences of his skilled exploitation of uncertainty and pain.

These are the "confidence men," otherwise known as "con men." Confidence men are an American institution, different from other American institutions—like representative government or the rule of law—mostly in their endurance. When everything else collapses, they remain, and prosper. They sell you lies that are pleasant to believe because the lies assuage your fears or promise to vanquish your enemies. Conspiracy theories, in contrast, are not pleasant to hear. They deepen your fears and erode your trust—but, crucially, that can include your trust in the confidence men or other powerful actors. This opens the door to consequences and accounts for some of the derision heaped upon the term. A conspiracy theory is often a critical inquiry that powerful people do not want you to make.

The best criminal conspirators know this and invent their own conspiracy theories as a preemptive weapon to disarm their marks. They cover big lies with small lies and bury grains of truth in each. When confidence men hold the reins of the law, you are left reeling in the mire. You are trapped in a psychic Eureka Springs, where the floor you are on changes depending on which door you enter, where a twisted landscape that you did not create determines your destination. The only reliable compass in twenty-first-century America is a moral one.

We live in a country where the mantra of the powerful is "Move on from the dead." Move on from the reasons behind assassinations and wars and genocides and pandemics and deaths of despair. Move on and do not look too hard at who is responsible, because that may spur reevaluation and recourse. Move on and don't ask questions, because questions challenge impunity. Move forward, because justice is divisive to the unjust. The idea of moving forward taps into optimism, which used to be an effective means of public placation. But it's 2021 now, we are paralyzed in a plague now, we mourn the future more than the past now, and there is nowhere to move but into the realm of memory, where we seek to make sense of old ghosts.

The collapse of democracy, rule of law, and climate at once leaves us with one lesson: the truth may hurt, but the lies will kill you.

2

THEORIES OF CONSPIRACY

n March 2021, my husband and children and I headed to my sister's house in Dallas to celebrate Christmas. I hadn't seen any family members who lived outside St. Louis in the fifteen months since the plague began. We drove the ten hours in one shot, stopping briefly at a truck stop in Oklahoma where grackles perched on gas pumps screamed as we darted inside with our black masks on like a family of bandits. My parents had been vaccinated, which meant the deep fear I had held for over a year—that we would catch it, not know it, and kill each other accidentally—was supposed to be gone. Things were opening up, I was told, as we drove past giant American flags lowered to half-staff to mark the three mass shootings that had happened in the last forty-eight hours of things opening up.

As a full-time prognosticator of doom—that is, a twenty-first-century realist—I was relatively prepared for the pandemic when it hit hard in March 2020. For years, I had kept a stockpile of canned food and emergency supplies in my basement in case of tornadoes, a routine occurrence in Missouri. But the stockpile grew along with my fears about climate change, and expanded again with the election of Donald Trump and his administration's flirtations with cyberattacks and war. The stockpile increased further when Wuhan shut down in January and I watched Chinese doctors pleading in online videos for the world to save itself, warning that their government was not telling the full story.

When I showed friends photos of my burgeoning bunker, they were amused by my seeming paranoia. As February 2020 brought news that the virus had hit American shores, they reconsidered, but fretted about doing a big supermarket run because they "didn't want to look like a crazy conspiracy theorist." Everyone says this before they run out of toilet paper.

I was prepared for the pandemic on a material level, but not on a psychological level. There is no way to be prepared for mass death playing out every second on a rectangular screen you carry in your pocket and relentlessly refresh. The plague arrived after years of encroaching autocracy and after decades of elite criminal impunity, shattered institutional trust, and widespread economic despair. One of my biggest worries in March 2020 was that most Americans would not be able to afford to buy extra food and supplies to ride out the pandemic storm, because most Americans do not have more than four hundred dollars in savings.[1] I did not know that this particular storm would come in infinite waves.

Covid slashed through what was left of both the safety net and the social fabric. As a child of the Reagan era, I spent my life watching that safety net unravel—and had fallen through it a few times myself. I had lived my life on the defense, navigating collapsing terrain and clinging to crags of stability. In 2020, it was the loss of the mundane, reliable rhythms of American life that jolted me most.

Covid stole lives and covid stole time. It pushed us inward both physically and psychologically, exacerbating an already fractured sense of reality and meaning. Covid revealed actual conspiracies by malicious actors, spurred conspiracy theories by a frightened population bereft of reliable data, and was weaponized by propagandists seeking to use conspiracy theories to annihilate compassion. By 2019, the United States was experiencing the predictable disorientation of an accelerated push from a deeply flawed democracy into a mafia-state autocracy. The country felt seeded with dread no matter your political persuasion, and the chaos was exacerbated by social media churn that altered our perception of an external world that we could no longer venture out to see for ourselves. By March 2020, there were few things left tying Americans together. By the end of that year, even those things were suddenly, terrifyingly, gone. The markers of time went missing: we were traveling a road with no milestones.

We lost ritual and we lost cohesion. This happened on both a national and a personal level. There could be no more weddings, and most horrifically for the bereaved, no funerals. There were no graduation ceremonies. There was no excited drop-off of children on their first day of school. There were no birthday parties or anniversary get-togethers. There were no summer blockbuster movies and no fall TV season. There were no celebrity-packed awards shows to mock or stadium-filled sporting events to cheer. There were no tours or festivals or carnivals or fairs. The odds that you would share a public space with people very different from yourself and enjoy the same experience—that crucial, often unconscious reminder of your shared humanity—became slim.

There were no big holiday celebrations, at least not without risk. The reason we were driving to Texas in March to celebrate Christmas was that Christmas 2020 had been canceled due to the plague, along with July Fourth and Thanksgiving and Halloween and everything else that had reliably marked the passage of time. Now we inhabited a zeitgeist with no *zeit* and too much *geist*. Simple comforts and escapes, traditions that tied us to childhood memories and gave us a sense of continuity in the despair, had vanished. The pandemic left us with only one national pastime: politics. And that meant we were held together by a web of lies.

The word "conspire" comes from the Latin *com* and *spirare*, meaning "to breathe together." I thought of this throughout 2020, as propagandists exploited a conspiratorial culture to shape public health while actual conspiracies—theft of medical supplies, threats to silence officials, data deletion, coup plots—flourished. *They breathe together*, I would think, looking at the Trump administration's coronavirus team—a collection of wealthy lackeys formerly under federal investigation or associated with white-collar crime, none of whom had a background in public health—*so that other Americans can't.*

I wrote parts of this book in the summer of 2021, watching a blood-red sun caused by West Coast wildfires thousands of miles away set over St. Louis streets filled with the deceived and the dying. I am trying to imagine if, by the time you read this, the following individuals will be indicted or be working as cable news commentators. My money is on the latter, since the people who analyze actual criminal conspiracies these days are often the same people who participated in them, accomplices rewarded by the media with lucrative television and book deals. There is no "If I Did It" anymore, only bidding wars for criminal confessions and reputational rehab for merchants of death. The world is a white Bronco and the highway never ends.

Most of the people whom Donald Trump appointed to handle the pandemic were survivors of his revolving-door aspiring autocracy. They were among the few who lasted all four years, lackeys bound through nepotism and links to white-collar crime. His daughter Ivanka Trump and son-in-law Jared Kushner, who engaged in kleptocratic ventures and illicit foreign activity both before and during their federal appointments.[2,3] Stephen Miller, a white supremacist who designed the administration's migrant abuse camps, and his wife, Katie, a White House official who aided him in this endeavor. Secretary of Commerce Wilbur Ross and Secretary of the Treasury Steven Mnuchin, Wall Street corporate raiders with decades of shady ties to foreign oligarchs.[4,5] The newer staffers included Mark Meadows, who, in March 2020, became Trump's fourth chief of staff—a position that was the Trump administration equivalent of Spinal Tap's drummer—and went on to try to overturn the election results that winter. Michael Caputo, a former public relations agent for Vladimir Putin who became the head of communications for Health and Human Services in April 2020 and labeled scientists as "seditionists."[6]

These are not people you put in charge if you want to end a plague. They are people you put in charge if you want to profit off a crisis or if you get off on the idea of mass death. This had always been true of Trump, a self-described fatalist who had long expressed his desire for destruction.[7] "When bad times come, then I'll get whatever I want," he told Barbara Walters in a 1980s interview.[8] In 2014, he told Fox News, "You know what solves it? When the economy crashes, when the country goes to total hell and everything is a disaster. Then you'll have a [laughs], you know, you'll have riots to go back to where we used to be when we were great."[9] Trump's initial reaction to 9/11 was that the collapse of the World Trade Center made his own buildings look taller.[10] Trump's initial reaction to the 2008 economic collapse was joy at his potential to profit.[11]

"Life is what you do while you're waiting to die," Trump, then a real estate tycoon filing for bankruptcy, told *Playboy* magazine in 1990. "You know, it is all a rather sad situation."

"Life?" the interviewer asked. "Or death?"

"Both. We're here and we live our 60, 70, or 80 years and we're gone. You win, you win, and in the end, it doesn't mean a hell of a lot. But it is something to do—to keep you interested."[12]

Mass death did not mean a lot to Trump, but it kept him interested, and it was a rather sad situation. Trump's lifelong penchant for annihilation set the tone of the administration. But it was put into action by more skillful bureaucrats, who saw in the chaos an opportunity for grift. His coronavirus dream team proceeded to do the following, among other acts: hijack personal protective equipment meant for hospital workers, threaten governors and mayors trying to enforce public health and safety initiatives, fabricate data about the virus and how it spreads, and peddle fake remedies, including telling Americans to inject household cleaners and other random chemicals. (A few Americans did, and died.)[13]

The Trump administration was not unique in its horrific handling of the pandemic. Every kleptocracy played a variation on the theme: Boris Johnson's UK, Vladimir Putin's Russia, Narendra Modi's India, Jair Bolsonaro's Brazil. Trump was part of an axis of autocrats who rose to prominence preying on pain for profit, and the plague only accelerated their preexisting agendas.

My initial fear when the pandemic hit was that autocratic leaders would use the crisis as a pretext to strengthen authoritarian rule, as dictators have done throughout history. I could relate to the protesters concerned about losing civil liberties despite my own opposition to the politicians they claimed to adore. But the opposite occurred: instead of an exploitable crackdown, we got criminal negligence. Officials saw that it was cheaper to let the masses die out on their own, especially when the plague hit hardest the groups whom they saw as undesirable and expendable: Black, Latino, Native American, disabled, impoverished Americans, and other marginalized communities. Covid is but a prelude for how states will handle the era of catastrophic climate change. It is a test run of what happens when powerful elites deem the public disposable without even feigning a pretense of concern. It is a dark omen of our lost leverage.

The malice of state officials was initially labeled incompetence because the idea that this appalling outcome could be seen as desirable was too much for a desperate public to take. But along with rapacious officials, plutocrats and oligarchs lunged at opportunities to redistribute wealth to themselves, and the disproportionate death toll of citizens from marginalized communities pleased white supremacists and the eugenicists aligned with them. Pharmaceutical companies earned record profits with each new variant, and refused to waive their patents. Many firsthand witnesses waited to speak the truth about covid until it became clear that a timed reveal of hoarded knowledge would make them rich. The reporter Bob Woodward, who had helped bring down Richard Nixon in a distant era when exposure facilitated accountability, withheld what Trump told him about covid's deadly nature in February 2020 until his book on the crisis was released in September 2020.[14] By that time, tens of thousands of Americans who could have used Woodward's information in February were dead.

Americans could not count on the federal government. They could not count on much of the national media, and they usually could not count on state officials. These included Republican officials whose apathy to human suffering spurred nicknames like Death-santis (Governor Ron DeSantis of Florida) or the Parson Plague, named for my governor, Mike Parson, who replaced the previous Missouri governor, Eric Greitens, after Greitens resigned for corruption and for having a sex blackmail dungeon. Other gubernatorial failures included Democrats like New York's governor Andrew Cuomo, son of former New York governor Mario Cuomo, who was investigated for letting nursing home residents get infected and die as he earned millions on a book lauding his handling of the covid crisis while dodging his own sex crime lawsuits.

The investigation of Cuomo's handling of the pandemic, like the investigations of everyone on Trump's corrupt covid crisis committee, brought no charges, despite the offenses taking place in the open. No wealthy official was ever held accountable for their role in facilitating mass death. They are members of a protected bipartisan class, unpunishable elites bound by nepotism and wealth whose impunity became even starker as ordinary citizens struggled for basic survival—and for answers.

By 2020, Americans could no longer count on accurate information from the Centers for Disease Control, which the Trump administration defunded and banned from using phrases like "evidence-based" or "science-based" in 2017.[15] In 2018, National Security Advisor John Bolton eliminated the National Security Council pandemic response team, and then quit in 2019 to make millions on a memoir, documenting crimes he had witnessed but did not stop.[16] (Bolton refused to testify to Congress during Trump's first impeachment, preferring to profit off his book that revealed the inner workings of the Trump administration.)

In March 2020, the CDC was run by Nancy Messonnier, sister of Rod Rosenstein, the then-deputy attorney general who helped bury the findings of the Mueller probe before going on to work for Israeli spyware company NSO, which is used by dictators around the world to track and assassinate dissidents,[17,18] in one of many examples of siblings occupying transnational positions of power. In February, Messonnier had announced that "Disruption to everyday life might be severe" and was replaced at Trump's press conferences by the newly appointed coronavirus response coordinator, Dr. Deborah Birx, who nodded dutifully as Trump and his lackeys lied about both the threat and the cure.

Birx was joined at press briefings by Dr. Anthony Fauci, who told Americans on March 8, 2020, not to wear masks despite masks being the most effective preventive measure in Asia, then told Americans to wear masks in April as the virus was raging.[19] At the time of this writing, Fauci remains committed to his recitation of incoherent advice and excessive self-praise. Over the summer of 2021, as I looked to the White House for advice on how to protect my children from the delta strain raging in Missouri, I landed instead on a bizarre video of pop star Olivia Rodrigo reading worshipful tweets praising Fauci as he sat next to her, basking in his own glow.[20]

The explicit sadism of the Trump administration may have been gone, but the priority of optics over transparency remains in its successor. President Joe Biden's pandemic response is overseen by coronavirus response coordinator Jeffrey Zients, a multimillionaire business tycoon with no experience in public health, and by CDC director Rochelle Walensky, who had to apologize to disabled Americans for her cavalier response to the prospect of their deaths.[21]

The Biden administration is also advised by Zeke Emanuel (older brother of President Barack Obama's chief of staff Rahm Emanuel), who served as an interim member of the Biden COVID-19 response team and now issues guidance from the sidelines. The elder Emanuel became notorious in the Obama era for his belief that people over the age of seventy-five are of minimal utility to society[22] and for other stances that seemed to advocate eugenics.[23] Nicknamed "Doctor Death," Zeke Emanuel was erroneously deemed a proponent of "death panels" by Republicans who wanted an excuse to block Obamacare. Yet a decade later when their fears about Emanuel's ghoulish outlook were finally proven valid, the GOP had adopted the same horrific rhetoric themselves.

Then there was the gaslighting. In July 2021, President Biden told Americans that vaccinated people cannot spread covid as his vaccinated White House staffers announced that they had been infected anyway. This is an ongoing pattern. We see disaster coming with our own eyes, but the people who are tasked to stop it do not see us, not enough to find us worthy of the truth. In 2021, I had a "covid guy"—a sociologist with medical expertise who breaks down Missouri public health information on Twitter in a clear way, because no one else is doing it.[24] I should not have to have a "covid guy," but there was no one overseeing public health in the Missouri state legislature since the last health director stepped down after he was caught tracking the menstrual periods of Missouri girls and women on a secret spreadsheet.[25] This is life in the Wild Midwest, and it is increasingly the model for life in the United States as a whole.

I could go on and on, reliving the horror movie of 2020 and its bad actors and preventable plots, and 2021, which emerged like a second-rate slasher sequel playing to an exhausted and jaded audience, but there is no need. Many books about covid have been written and many more will follow, books that position the authors as heroes or frame a plague as a partisan game or simply chronicle an era that most of us want to forget.

I used to wonder why the 1918 Spanish Flu faded from public consciousness, why there were so few works of art depicting it or inspired by it, but now I understand. Who would want to remember the particular combination of grief, terror, and loneliness that a plague inspires—its senseless silent slaughter? The way it makes the future feel impossible, the present endless, and the past irrelevant? There is something particularly awful about the intersection of plague and government corruption, where the urge to block out the horror battles the duty to document it. The desire to forget is as overwhelming as the obligation not to.

There is one takeaway here for the purposes of this book, one conclusion that should satisfy everyone in its ability to flatter no one, which is: *of course people will flock to conspiracy theories when nearly every powerful actor is lying, obfuscating, or profiteering off pain.* This has always been true to an extent, but it was predominant in 2020 and 2021, as a global plague, digital technology, and an utter failure of moral leadership converged to create an information vacuum that people were desperate to fill or have filled for them.

A rise in conspiracy theories is inevitable when collective trauma is combined with a lack of transparency and a history of state abuse.

Conspiracy theories are rarely entirely true or entirely false. Instead, they inhabit the uneasy world of unknowns, where people from disparate backgrounds grab at fragments of information to piece together a glimpse of a shared reality. By 2020, "we the people" had been left on our own. There were still medical researchers trying to provide evidence and advice—as well as doctors and nurses saving lives and decent state and local actors struggling to keep their communities safe—but the bottom had dropped out on institutional trust, and deservedly so. The top levels of authority had long been seeded with profiteers, perverts, and professional propagandists.

The decades-long entanglement of state crime, white-collar crime, and corrupt mass media had birthed a system where public health information was wielded as a weapon to manipulate the masses, instead of giving them the information they needed to survive. For criminal elites and their accomplices, a pandemic was seen as an opportunity instead of a crisis. The survival of the masses was deemed incidental at best, undesirable at worst. The brazenness of this cruelty came as a shock to middle- and upper-class white Americans, who had not previously been treated as disposable in the unabashed way they were now, unlike marginalized groups who had long faced institutional apathy to their suffering. The ranks of the betrayed had grown. Our new common ground was the dirt kicked in our faces.

The real American exceptionalism is the shrinking of a protected class into an infinitesimal slice of the population, who lecture and swindle the rest of us from their gilded retreats. It's not partisan these days. It's barely American, in the sense that it does not intend to benefit the welfare of the American people. But it is indeed exceptional.

A conspiracy is a form of betrayal. Conspiracy theorists feel betrayed because important information has been withheld and because information is not just a matter of power, but of status. To be believed is an act of power that you cannot control. People therefore search for evidence that will overwhelm the power of those who deny the truth and force it into the light. A conspiracy theory, when rooted in a sincere desire to find and expose the truth, is a refusal to move on from betrayal. Conspiracy theories are expressions of grief and memory.

This type of evidence-gathering is not solely the domain of conspiracy theorists. It is what historians, detectives, and human rights activists do. It is what investigative journalists and state officials are supposed to do, but frequently do not, because the professional incentive is to remain compliant in order to receive access to the conspirators or maximize a personal payout. The conspiracy theory label is slapped on both hostile actors who seek to deceive and honest actors who seek to enlighten, with the commonality being that they all tread uneasy ground, the kind of ground that, when split, opens the door to hell.

The definition of "conspiracy theory" is extraordinarily malleable. When verified, a conspiracy theory is recast as "investigative journalism" or "unburied history" and, in some cases, a legal slam-dunk. Watergate, Iran-Contra, the CIA's MKUltra mind control experiments, the aborted 1960s false flag Operation Northwoods, and other US government plots were all, at some point, labeled wild conspiracy theories—until they were investigated and proven real. Many examples of systemic sexual abuse by the wealthy—Harvey Weinstein's use of the Israeli mercenary spy group Black Cube to track and silence dozens of Hollywood actresses he assaulted while countless witnesses stayed silent, for example—sounded unbelievable until painstakingly revealed as true. Systemic sexual abuse in the Catholic Church was deemed a conspiracy theory until it became documented with heartrending evidence. Thanks in large part to fossil fuel corporations, climate change was dismissed as a conspiracy theory for decades, long after it had been documented by scientists, and today it is only acknowledged as real by most political officials now that it is too late to stop it.

The greatest advantage all these individuals and institutions have is not that people do not want to know the truth about what they have done, but that they do not want to believe it.

People are understandably afraid to hear the worst about the people and organizations whose job it is to protect them. This embrace of denial has accelerated despite (or perhaps because of) ample evidence of elite criminality available in the public domain. Trump and his cohorts' long-standing dealings with the mafia and the Kremlin—a saga exhaustively documented over multiple decades—is often labeled a conspiracy theory by those terrified by the national security ramifications of it being real. Centuries of state abuse of Black and Native Americans—the torching of Tulsa's Black Wall Street in 1921; the 1985 MOVE bombings of Black citizens, including children, in Philadelphia; the ongoing unearthing of mass graves of Native Americans—were dismissed as conspiracy theories until people from those communities gained the structural power to publicize them and found an audience willing to listen. It is notable that as knowledge of these atrocities increases among white Americans, other white Americans seek to ban this history from being taught in schools.

Both conspiracy theories and actual conspiracies revolve around questions of preexisting power dynamics and the potential to shift them. Who to believe, who controls information, whose pain matters, what constitutes evidence: these questions form the nexus of the crisis of belief. Today truths are not self-evident. Propaganda and disinformation operations aim to divert people away from the search for the evidence and toward easy answers and echo chambers.

Similarly, the sneering dismissal of conspiracy theories in favor of uncritical acceptance of institutionalist narratives is aimed at protecting the powerful, bolstering the reputation of the disdainful as a "rational actor," and again directing people away from the search for accurate information. The mantra of the "rational actor" is Occam's Razor—the belief that the simplest explanation is the correct one—but this belief not only falls apart when examining an actual criminal conspiracy, it enables the criminals by making a mockery of the spirit of inquiry. In the twenty-first century, American democracy slit its wrists on Occam's Razor, and no one answered for the blood.

One of the most common techniques used to keep inquisitive minds in check is to state that a conspiracy is, by definition, impossible. Skeptics claim conspiracies cannot exist because no complex organization can keep a secret. When challenged, they are forced to concede that exceptions include law enforcement, intelligence, religious groups, and organized crime. They must then acknowledge that the institutions tasked with investigating conspiracies are at times the originators of them. They must then admit that the two main industries framing an exposed conspiracy as either a lunatic lie or a certified truth are the media and public relations: industries that are easily influenced by wealthy elites when they are not simply stocked with their own peers.

Skyrocketing income inequality over the last few decades has turned the industries tasked with accountability—politics, law, and media, to name a few—into pay-to-play fields that require expensive credentials and inherited wealth to enter. This has changed who can participate and whom these industries seek to protect. When the social circles and incentives of the powerful overlap, when those circles narrow over decades so that nepotistic ties or purchased merit become the buy-in to both the crime and the cover-up, a culture of conspiracy grows, and with it a culture of elite criminal impunity. The refusal to accept this as fair will get you labeled a "conspiracy theorist": a pejorative preemptive strike meant to silence and smear.

"If you're down at a bar in the slums, and you say something that people don't like, they'll punch you or shriek four-letter words," scholar Noam Chomsky observed in a 2007 interview about cover-ups of institutional corruption. "If you're in a faculty club or an editorial office, where you're more polite—there's a collection of phrases that can be used which are the intellectual equivalent of four-letter words and tantrums. One of them is 'conspiracy theory.' [It's part of] a series of totally meaningless curse words, in effect, which are used by people who know that they can't answer arguments, and that they can't deal with evidence. But they want to shut you up."[26]

As institutions are packed and purged, the court of public opinion has become the most fertile ground from which to judge the powerful. But it is slippery terrain both for those seeking the truth and those seeking to suppress it. Never before has information moved so freely and quickly. Never before has the original source of a piece of information been so difficult to track. The goal of conspirators today is not only to protect themselves but to vilify the search for truth, and force you to destroy your reputation if you pursue it publicly.

Then there is the matter of what you find. For a researcher with integrity, exposing a conspiracy is a depressing pursuit, because the truth hurts and it is painful to share it. The boundaries between good and evil have always been blurrier than many wanted to admit. Good people can do bad things, honest people lie when they see other honest people lying, virtuous people turn vile under threat, upstanding citizens fall in line when frightened. We live in the gray area. The gray area terrifies people because it means the villain could be anyone around them. It means that the villain could, one day, be you. It is not surprising that many hearing the bad news would rather retreat into their illusions and attack the messenger.

The desire to understand the worst of humanity requires conviction that is hard to maintain without feeling contaminated by what you find. At the heart of it all are issues of trust and power, and vulnerability is where trust and power meet. A conspiracy theorist is vulnerable: at best, willing to debunk and expose the machinations of power; at worst, easily manipulated by hostile actors. Because conspiracy theories are emotionally potent, they can easily be weaponized by malevolent actors to mislead the public further. This places any individual who dares to question a conspiracy and retain their professional reputation in a dangerous position.

To be vulnerable in the twenty-first century is not only to be vulnerable in public but in a way that can be preserved online for eternity. Digital content can be removed from its original context and weaponized. Past words can be repurposed to stoke bad-faith interpretations. Past actions can be selectively described to incite mobs. Your reputation is determined by abuse and algorithm, and if you are targeted by a media-savvy malevolent actor, you will be left gazing at a funhouse mirror reflection of yourself for the rest of your life. Everyone is famous for fifteen minutes and then they never see themselves again.

Surveilled vulnerability makes people hesitant to raise questions and eager to embrace groupthink. An already anxiety-inducing experience—to ask questions about the powerful and know you may be sickened by what you find—is made worse by not knowing who is watching you ask but knowing for sure that someone is. Surveilled vulnerability makes everyone the prey, and it is here that weaponized conspiratorial narratives are the most dangerous. For the powerful and their armies of media and PR flacks, rumors are buried under piles of money and lawsuits. For actual criminal conspirators, rumors are a blessing, a way to muddy the waters. But ordinary people travel through separate, unprotected territory.

The vilest manifestation of this inequity is when victims of a horrific crime—for example, a mass shooting—are labeled "crisis actors" by propagandists seeking to alter the narrative or cause chaos. The victim's family endures not only the agony of their actual loss but the cruelty of those who claim it did not even happen, or who insist that their loved one was a player in a vendetta. To propagate these narratives about ordinary people, especially children, is to side with the powerful at the expense of the victims—and maybe that's part of the appeal for those who spread the lies.

Viral dehumanization is a grotesque, uniquely twenty-first-century phenomenon. The dynamics of fame have been transferred to people who do not have the resources to battle defamation.

Conspiracy theories can be weaponized not only to torment victims of violence but to spur violence against individuals or entire populations. This is not new. Weaponized rumors have been used to stoke slaughter and genocides for thousands of years, made easier today by the global speed of technology, the breakdown of institutions, and the increasing pressure to see yourself not as a person but as a brand. Economic stability, family safety, and psychological well-being all rely on your ability to navigate a panopticon of propagandists and provocateurs. "Power is impenetrable," wrote social scientist Elias Canetti in his 1960 book, *Crowds and Power*. "The man who has it sees through other men, but does not allow them to see through him."[27]

Canetti's book was once considered a landmark study of political manipulation by powerful demagogues. Nowadays it comes across as a depiction of everyday life in the digital era. We struggle to be honest yet impenetrable, to walk hand in hand through a minefield, to be followed but not stalked. This has created a state of what many deem hypervigilance but what I call twenty-first-century rational living. "There is no such thing as paranoia; your worst fears can come true at any moment," the journalist Hunter S. Thompson proclaimed in the 1990s, about a decade before he shot himself, and he was right.[28]

I am a writer who studies conspiracies by the powerful. I began my career exposing a conspiracy created by the authoritarian government of Uzbekistan, which had fabricated a terrorist group in order to justify slaughtering hundreds of protesters in 2005. I continued my work exposing conspiracies involving my own government, and in my decades of writing I have never had to issue a retraction or disavow a prediction. I am a lifetime independent voter in the Democratic-majority city of St. Louis in the Republican-majority state of Missouri, which means I live at the center of an America that does not hold. I do not belong to any parties or groups. I have refused to define myself, but I am forthright in my beliefs. As a result, a diverse array of furious strangers have taken it upon themselves to define me.

For over a decade, I have been the subject of innumerable rumors spread by both angry powermongers and random obsessives. Sometimes

I wait for my stalkers to find each other and cancel each other out, like when the people who thought I was a CIA agent found the people who thought I was a Kremlin agent and gave up forming a coherent lie. (Now *that's* mutually assured destruction!) I have also been accused of running an international drug cartel; being a member of Hamas, the Yakuza, the Irish Republican Army, Hezbollah, and Al Qaeda; being kidnapped and held in a "black site" and then partnering with my captors to brainwash the United States; launching separatist movements in at least six countries; serving as an undercover espionage agent with my partner, Beyoncé Knowles, with whom I protect the *real* Tupac Shakur, who is not dead but is working for Vladimir Putin; being a time-traveler, a psychic, and a witch; and leading a number of cults, including the Blue Öyster Cult, which would have been a vastly superior career move.

Most of these accusations burned briefly and died out, in part because the people creating them implicated so many other random people in the same deranged plots. But the false narratives did not disappear before I was stalked by people who read them, not before my family members were threatened with violence, not before a number of other frightening things occurred that I am still not up for writing down.

I am well aware of the danger of false narratives spread by malevolent actors. Where I may depart from other scholars and journalists is that I believe an equal danger lies in dismissing what are deemed "conspiracy theories" out of hand, instead of interrogating the power dynamics and motivations behind them and parsing out the grains of truth. The old adage that "the greatest trick the devil ever pulled was convincing the world he didn't exist" holds up all too well for our time.

In 1835, Nathaniel Hawthorne published one of the earliest American horror stories, "Young Goodman Brown." Brown is a Puritan in Salem, Massachusetts, who secretly decides to attend a Satanic vigil only to discover that everyone he knew and trusted had decided to do the same. Every trusted figure in the village—the minister, the deacon, his catechism teacher, and, most traumatically, his beloved wife, Faith—had gathered in the forest under the cover of night to initiate new converts into their demonic clan. They were joined by townspeople shunned by day as degenerates. "It was strange to see, that the good shrank not from the wicked, nor were the sinners abashed by the saints," noted Brown.[29] No one was what they seemed, not even his pointedly named wife, whom he had cherished for her steadfast purity. Brown woke up the next morning wondering if it had been a terrible dream. But he is haunted by it all the same, and lives out his remaining years in a state of suspicion.

"A stern, a sad, a darkly meditative, a distrustful, if not a desperate man, did he become," writes Hawthorne in the concluding paragraph. The ending is ambiguous. Is Young Goodman Brown a victim of his own paranoia? Or is he reacting with understandable horror to others' evil and deceit?

In March 2019, I stood at the gravestone of Nathaniel Hawthorne's great-great-grandfather, John Hathorne, one of the few judges in the Salem Witch Trials who never repented for his role in the baseless prosecutions. My children and I were in central Connecticut visiting my parents, and I had decided to take them to Salem for a day to show them the sites, to teach them how easily mobs and law and morality can be manipulated. The closest Judge Hathorne came to recriminations for his abuses of power were the ruminations of his descendant a century and a half after the fact. Now the lessons of that descendant's prose seemed to have been forgotten in my own conformist and corrupt era nearly two centuries later. History was a feedback loop of unlearned lessons and reverberating lies.

My family had arrived in Salem in the midst of rapid and disconcerting political developments. On February 27, former Trump lawyer Michael Cohen had testified to Congress that his boss was a crime lord who had him threaten hundreds of people into compliance. On March 8, district judge T. S. Ellis III, after being threatened to the point that he had to have armed security,[30] declared the indicted Trump campaign manager Paul Manafort, who had once run a group nicknamed "the torturers' lobby," to be a person who had "led an otherwise blameless life" and gave him a small sentence of forty-seven months instead of the decades expected for his litany of offenses. On March 11, Speaker of the House Nancy Pelosi abruptly declared impeaching Trump "not worth it" regardless of what crimes he committed.[31] On March 24, Attorney General Bill Barr, known since the early 1990s as the "Cover-Up General" due to his willingness to bend the law for criminal Republicans,[32] lied about Mueller's unreleased report and declared Trump exonerated, a claim the media promptly echoed. Mueller would not debunk these lies for several months, allowing them to slither and breed in the American consciousness.

All of these developments pointed in one direction: we were living in a rapidly consolidating mafia state, one that operated according to threat instead of according to law, and our institutions were too corroded or complicit to combat it. This was the outcome I had warned of, to no avail, for several years, based on the preponderance of evidence in the public domain and my decades of studying how kleptocracies and autocracies emerge. I had sought to avoid this outcome by warning of it in advance, but ran up against two major obstacles: the decades-long corruption of institutions by criminal operatives, and the refusal of institutionalists who claimed to oppose these individuals to admit the extent of the rot. To describe the conspiracies at play in the most straightforward terms was to "be conspiratorial," because the depravity on display was not supposed to be so brazen. That brazenness indicated not only extreme corruption, but confidence that the opposing side would not or could not disrupt their plans.

Liberals and Republican "Never Trumpers" highlighted the corruption of the Trump administration, but rarely conceded that their own side lacked the fortitude to confront it. Initially, it did not seem that this would be the case: The Democrats had gained control of the House in the 2018 midterm elections by running on a platform promising accountability. On March 4, 2019, Democrats on the House Judiciary Committee released a list of eighty-one people and institutions related to Trump administration corruption whom they sought to investigate through congressional hearings and testimony.[33] As of spring 2022, only one of the people on that list, Michael Cohen, has ever been made to take the stand in public. The leading force behind the push to hold Trump's cohort accountable, Representative Elijah Cummings, who oversaw Cohen's hearing, died in October 2019 after facing harassment from Trump over the summer.[34] The investigations Cummings led—which included Michael Flynn's illicit attempt to engineer the 2016 election and the influence Black Cube held over US politics, among other salient topics—died with him.

The Democrats under Pelosi had no more interest in holding the current crime cult accountable than they had its previous iterations under prior Republican administrations whose crimes they had excused. The crises under those administrations often involved Trump administration and campaign staff: the 2008 financial collapse (Steven Mnuchin, Wilbur Ross, and other Wall Street predators), the treacherous war in Iraq (John Bolton), the failure to prevent the 9/11 attacks or protect citizens in the aftermath (Robert Mueller, Rudy Giuliani), the Iran-Contra affair (Bill Barr), Watergate (Trump mentors Roy Cohn and Roger Stone), and so on. For four decades, elite Democrats and Republicans had worked to uphold a continuum of institutionalized corruption, with the Trump administration being only its most overt manifestation. By the end of 2019, Pelosi had to be dragged by other Democrats and the general public to impeach Trump on brand-new charges—the shakedown of the president of Ukraine, Volodymyr Zelenskyy, and a series of threats Trump made to US public officials.

These illicit acts, committed in the summer of 2019, gave Congress the opportunity to ignore Trump's decades of criminality and Kremlin ties and disregard other offenses he committed while president—offenses, like obstruction of justice or conspiracy to tamper with an election, that had much more of a direct effect on citizens than the intimidation of the president of Ukraine. Avoiding the broader context of Trump's corruption allowed both parties to circumvent conversation about institutional failure—that is, their own failure to investigate him and his criminal partners decades earlier. In December 2019, Trump was impeached by the House for abuse of power and obstruction of Congress. In February 2020, he was acquitted by the Senate.

Many people have forgotten the first impeachment of Trump, because the coda of the hearings was the emergence of a global plague and the encore was a violent attempted coup.

But the most important aspect of the first impeachment was arguably the initial refusal of House Democratic leadership to do it. They first refused to hold public hearings, and then, once they agreed to hold them, they insisted on limiting the scope. Their timidity paralleled that of the Mueller investigation, but the impeachment hearings were even more of a betrayal of the public since the boundaries of hearings are much looser than those of a legal investigation by a special counsel. Given the opportunity to put on official record much of what was in the public domain, elected officials chose obfuscation over accountability. The American public assumed there must be a good reason for the intransigence, but there was not. I felt like I was back in Hawthorne's Salem, learning the worst lesson of the witch trials: the public will bow to authority, no matter how corrupt, if they believe that authority is curtailing a greater threat—even if the complicity of the authority becomes increasingly explicit. The longing for a legal system to combat an almost otherworldly evil overrides the public's ability to see the man-made evil right in front of them.

On April 10, 2019, I published a short essay on the website for my podcast, *Gaslit Nation*, of the dire implications of delayed hearings and treating threats to all Americans as partisan matters. I am including excerpts here because chronology and context are essential to understanding actual conspiracies as well as the propaganda that emerges in their wake. "Who knew what and when?" is a central question that citizens should ask when their government is carrying out a conspiracy. "Was this crisis predictable and preventable, and if so, who let it happen?" is another.

We stand in favor of impeachment. This was previously not a controversial view, as Trump has committed a multitude of impeachable offenses, including but not limited to: violating the emoluments

clause; obstruction of justice; ordering unconstitutional imprison-
ment of migrant families; abusing the pardon power; high crimes
and misdemeanors; conspiracy against the US; and conspiracy to
illegally influence the 2016 election.

Trump has committed these crimes in plain sight and confessed
to some of them, like obstruction, on television. These are not merely
constitutional violations but severe threats to national security and
public safety that require immediate action—investigation and indictment as well as impeachment.

Impeachment is not a snap of the fingers producing an instant
result. It is a process of hearings in which officials present evidence of
crimes and deliberate in a public forum, removed from media bias.
Americans these days tend to exist in information silos, but hearings,
from [James] Comey to [Michael] Cohen, have brought our country
together to bear witness. Hearings give the public information long
withheld from them and shift expectations of accountability. We see
parallels with Watergate, in which much of the republic was uncon-
vinced of the severity of Nixon's crimes until hearings began and
they learned the full details.

The public has the right to information and to make up its own
mind. Our media is largely sponsored by dictators or dictated by
sponsors. It is critical that officials present evidence to the public
directly.

This is not a partisan issue: it is a matter of public safety. Trump's
supporters have as much right to the truth as do Trump's opponents.
We are Americans, and we are in this together.

Pelosi, however, does not appear to see herself as in it together
with us—she sees herself as above it. She sees Trump as a partisan
matter, not an urgent public threat. She does not understand that
we are already divided as a nation, and that truth and transparency
are the salve. She is replicating the mistakes made by the Obama
administration (and by the FBI and Comey) when they withheld the

truth about Trump and Russia from the American public due to their fear of seeming "divisive" or angering Mitch McConnell.

The GOP has been hijacked by a transnational crime syndicate masquerading as a government. This is not a secret. We have seen the indictments and we have seen the panicked protectiveness of Trump by the GOP even when they are confronted with his most severe and obviously illegal infractions.

The Republicans created this situation: they long ago abdicated their duty through corruption and capitulation. If the GOP were to impeach Trump, they would effectively impeach themselves, since they are caught in Trump's web of criminality. (Michael Cohen, for example, was the deputy finance chairman of the Republican National Committee.) But when Pelosi makes a bipartisan resolution that she knows is impossible the standard for following rule of law, she continues the very abdication that the GOP initiated—and in doing so, aids in their complicity.

Supporters of Pelosi believe there must be a secret message or a secret plan behind her statement, but there is very likely not. (We will be delighted if we are wrong and there is, since we are thinking first and foremost about the welfare of the American people.) Some have said the point of Pelosi proclaiming Trump "not worth it" is to wound his ego—as if Trump cares what Pelosi says. All Trump cares about is money, power and being immune from prosecution. Impeachment hearings actually threaten all three of these things. Attempted jibes do not. The message Pelosi conveys when she says Trump is "not worth it" is that it is not worth holding him accountable for crimes that have resulted in the loss of human life and the ongoing destruction of our nation.

Pelosi may not have intended for this to be her message, but that is how many received it. She hurled a grenade into progressives and wounded many with her words. She may think we can vote Trump out, but she has hurt that very cause. We have heard from younger voters and voters from marginalized groups who no longer want to vote for the Democratic candidate because her flippant dismissal of impeachment has led them to believe that the two parties are the same. They are not the same: one party is an existential threat, and one party is deeply flawed. But we demand that the Democrats confront our grim reality head on—that there may not be a 2020, that there may not be free and fair elections, and that every day is damage done. It may be a partisan game for Speaker Pelosi, but for the rest of us, and for this country, it is a matter of life or death.

It is critical that the stakes are made clear. Refusal to impeach sends the message that the situation cannot possibly be that dire—it if were, the Democrats would move to impeach, right? This is the same disastrous miscalculation that gave us an unpunished cadre of criminals from Watergate, Iran-Contra, the War on Iraq, and the 2008 financial crisis—criminals who are working with the White House right now! This is not a comparative study; this is literally the same people committing crimes over and over without repercussions. We would not be dealing with this crisis if officials had acted with conscience and conviction earlier, and brought these criminal elites to justice.

Let us be clear: we do not think that, if the House impeaches Trump, the GOP-dominated Senate will convict. We also do not think that if the Senate, by some miracle, impeaches Trump, that he will leave. Trump has made it clear he will not leave office even if the will of the people demands it in an election, and even if the will of Congress demands it in impeachment. Trump is an aspiring autocrat, and the GOP is seeking a one-party state.

So what is the point of the House impeaching Trump? An informed public is a powerful public, and hearings are the best way of informing the people on what the White House has done. Impeachment sends a message about who we are as a country and what we will accept and abide.

The rule of law demands action. Refusing to take action is normalizing atrocity. Lawlessness must be confronted regardless of the *outcome, as a matter of principle and conscience. Fighting only the battles that you know you will win is a sure way of ensuring you lose. Preemptive surrender, in a rapidly consolidating autocracy, is permanent surrender. The American people have suffered enough under Trump; they should not have to suffer due to Pelosi's capitulation as well. We all deserve better than this.*

In late fall 2020, homebound in an effort to avoid the plague raging yet again in St. Louis, I did a paint-by-number of Edvard Munch's *The Scream*. This activity—a rote replication of a painting of an agonized man with his hands on his ears and his mouth gaping in horror—is what it felt like to rehash the points I made in the above essay for years on end. No matter how much I laid out the roots and depth of the crisis of entrenched corruption, even writing two bestselling books about it, many Americans did not want to believe it—that we could be that bad or that officials could be that weak and corrupt. Dumbstruck by the audacity of complicity, Americans were further encouraged to embrace delusions of competence by people who had the authority to clarify what was happening, but refused to do so.

Powerful actors feign shock to avoid accountability. Lawmakers and pundits often deem the events that followed that 2019 essay—the Capitol attack, the threats to public officials, the series of revelations about institutional corruption—as "shocking." But it was all predictable, and therefore preventable. Even in that short essay, the future is apparent: Trump not conceding the election and refusing to leave office, the Democrats refusing to investigate and stop obvious crimes, the Republicans committing and abetting obvious crimes, the continued fracturing of Americans into information silos, the knowledge that if these crimes were not confronted they would lead to bigger, more horrific crimes that endangered human life. I had a bird's-eye view of a downward spiral. Complacency, careerism, conformity, corruption, complicity, conspiracies, collusion, cults, covid.

There is no satisfaction in being right about terrible things. That's what many miss about the people who investigate conspiracies: in the end, we would rather be wrong. We would happily be mocked as hysterics and alarmists if it meant everyone could avoid the fate we foresee. When our theories involve the theft of the future, there is no benefit, not even financial, in scaring everyone senseless. This applies to my fellow realists labeled scaremongers: the climate scientists, the epidemiologists, the scholars of authoritarian states. We would love it if things were not as bad as we claimed. We would be delighted if officials were accountable and honorable and acted to prevent crises in time. We would like more time, in general. Even as I write, I half expect this book to never see the light of day because I don't fully expect to see the light of day myself. The light of day is an eclipse.

Why bother then? Because the truth matters, doing the right thing for its own sake matters, and we owe it to the next generation to try to protect them from the hell we inherited. Refusal to examine past sins has broken the American present. We are told to move on, but there is no moving on without accountability, and there is no accountability without the truth. In this era, confronting the truth means delving into terrain that the respectable often scorn, because it can be outrageous and revolting and weird. A panorama of paranoia is the new American landscape, and all you can do is navigate it, "conspiracy theorist" label be damned. In a repressive political climate, the truth will not necessarily set you free. But it may at least free your mind to reexamine the past and avoid repeating its mistakes in the future.

And in some cases, to learn the history—the terrible history—about your country for the first time.

3

EPSTEIN WASN'T THE FIRST

The QAnon narrative involves cabals of pedophiles corrupting the federal government. . . . It is entirely fictitious.
                                              —*Politico*, September 4, 2020[1]

On January 18, 1982, *The New York Times* published a piece called "Have Names, Will Open Right Doors," about a man with the inside track on everyone in Washington, D.C.[2] His name was Craig Spence and he was a former ABC News correspondent turned Republican political operative. But above all, he was a power broker for the elite. "There seems to be an inexhaustible demand in Washington for the sort of thing Mr. Spence offers," the *Times* wrote. "To unravel the mysteries of the capital, special-interest groups, both foreign and domestic, retain lawyers, consultants, lobbyists and public relations specialists by the score, although few cut as broad a swath."

Spence had become well known for the lavish parties he held in his home in D.C.'s opulent Kalorama neighborhood. Attendees included State Department officials, ambassadors, and celebrities. He was friends with US senators and former presidents, in particular Richard Nixon, and with members of the Washington press corps. Spence conducted his affairs with a level of secrecy at odds with his flamboyant public persona:

even the phone number of his consulting firm was unlisted. His connections into the worlds of business, politics, and media merged not only in his parties but in his practice.

Sometime in the late 1970s, Spence hired D.C. journalists employed by mainstream outlets to research American political officials on the side. He told the journalists he was using their work to brief corporate clients, who he said were multinational companies and Japanese businessmen. (Spence kept no public record of his clients.) He asked the journalists to provide him "a summary of the subject's career, political views, and personal interests and habits." This arrangement thrived until four of the journalists learned to their shock that the Department of Justice had registered them as foreign agents—because Craig Spence, their employer, was a foreign agent himself.

A foreign agent for whom? That was the big question, the one powerful people spent the 1980s avoiding. Who was Craig Spence, really, and whom did he serve? There was less than a decade to find out, because on November 12, 1989, Spence was found dead in the Boston Ritz-Carlton hotel at age forty-eight, clad in a tuxedo with three dollars in his pocket and a newspaper clipping by his side. The clipping detailed legislative efforts to protect CIA agents who were called to testify before the government.[3] Spence's death was deemed a suicide, though the details of how he did it are murky. His final act was to scrawl in black marker on the hotel mirror: "Chief, consider this my resignation, effective immediately. As you always said, you can't ask others to make a sacrifice if you are not ready to do the same. Life is Duty. God bless America. To the Ritz, please forgive this inconvenience."[4,5]

Who was "Chief"? What was the work from which Spence "resigned"? Over thirty years later, it is still unclear. But between his introduction to the public via the *New York Times* profile and his sudden death, a disturbing narrative emerged. In late June 1989, the newly formed paper *The Washington Times* began a series of exposés on Spence that would run for months. The first, published on June 29, claimed that the purpose of Spence's parties, which he had been holding since the late 1970s, was to entrap US and foreign government and business officials in a sexual blackmail operation. Spence "bugged the gatherings to compromise guests, provided cocaine, blackmailed some associates and spent up to $20,000 a month on male prostitutes" for the attendees. As a result, Spence had fallen under federal investigation for "credit-card fraud, illegal interstate prostitution, abduction and use of minors for sexual perversion, extortion, larceny, and related illicit drug trafficking and use of prostitutes and their clients."[6] *The Washington Times* procured copies of hundreds of credit card statements of Spence's clients to verify their claims, and printed excerpts of the documents alongside the articles.[7]

Henry Vinson was the owner of the D.C. escort service whom Spence hired on a monthly basis. On June 29, 1989, Vinson told *The Washington Times* that he feared the investigation into Spence was going to be derailed by high-level administration officials. He said that Spence had been giving late-night tours of the White House to clients and prostitutes, including a midnight tour on the Fourth of July—a detail later corroborated by other outlets.[8] In his 2014 memoir, published decades after his release from prison—he was indicted for his role in the operation—Vinson claimed that Spence, along with Lawrence E. King Jr., an Omaha businessman with close ties to the Reagan administration who was arrested in 1988 for financial crimes, operated an "interstate pedophile network that flew children from coast-to-coast." He said Spence told him the operation was for the purpose of blackmailing the powerful, and that Spence admitted all rooms in his home were bugged with surveillance devices. Vinson added that King seemed "obsessed with the subject of murdering children."[9]

The federal investigation into Spence came on the tail of an investigation into King. In addition to being indicted in November 1988 on forty counts of embezzlement, fraud, and tax evasion, King—the former vice chairman of the National Black Republican Council and a prominent GOP political operative in the Reagan era—spent the late 1980s being investigated in Nebraska for child trafficking. King was accused of abducting boys from Omaha and forcing them into prostituting themselves to political officials nationwide.[10,11] The case was shrouded in rumor and violence.[12] On July 11, 1990, the lead investigator, Gary Caradori, died in a plane crash shortly after gathering testimony for the prosecutor. A documentary about King's case, *Conspiracy of Silence*, was scheduled to air on the Discovery Channel in 1994, but was abruptly dropped, only to emerge in a grainy online version decades later.[13] In the documentary, several Nebraska state politicians as well as alleged victims of the operation said they had been threatened with violence for discussing the case and labeled conspiracy theorists and liars. In 1990, twelve days after Caradori's death, a grand jury convicted King of financial crimes but acquitted him of the sex abuse charges. The King case became known as the Franklin Scandal, named after Omaha's Franklin Community Federal Credit Union, which he had defrauded.

Both King and Spence were part of mainstream Republican circles, speaking at or hosting GOP conventions and galas. On June 30, 1989, *The Washington Times* revealed more of the guests who had attended Spence's parties. They included William Casey, the director of the CIA from 1981 to 1987; right-wing ideologue Phyllis Schlafly; and Joseph diGenova, who was a US Attorney for the Reagan administration. DiGenova would go on— with his wife, Reagan deputy assistant attorney general Victoria Toensing—to work with mafia-affiliated oligarchs and serve as Donald Trump's legal advisor in both of his impeachment trials.[14] (In 1989, diGenova stated he had never participated in any illicit activity at Spence's gatherings.)[15] Numerous interviewees confirmed that Spence's house had two-way mirrors used for surveillance. One interviewee, an anonymous businessman, said Spence told him that the CIA intended to "doublecross Spence," kill him, and "make it look like a suicide."[16]

The Washington Times also identified Spence as a good friend of Roy Cohn, the notorious lawyer and GOP operative who had represented Joseph McCarthy and the leading families of the New York City mafia before going on to mentor Donald Trump and his future campaign advisors, Paul Manafort and Roger Stone. Cohn, who died in 1986, was rumored to have operated his own sexual blackmail operations from the 1950s onward.[17] According to New York attorney John Klotz, Cohn used a suite in the

Plaza Hotel (before the Plaza was purchased by Trump in 1988) to record powerful officials sexually abusing trafficked children and use the footage to compromise them.[18] Among those who may have been ensnared in a blackmail operation involving both Cohn and the organized crime figures with whom he associated—like Cohn's colleague Lewis Rosenstiel, a bootlegger turned entrepreneur connected to Meyer Lansky's syndicate[19]—was FBI head J. Edgar Hoover.[20] Hoover spent the initial three decades of his forty-eight-year tenure claiming that the mafia did not exist and therefore the FBI could not investigate it.[21] Like Spence, Cohn straddled the worlds of organized crime, media, and law enforcement all too well.

On June 30, 1989, the resignations began. The first to go was Paul Balach, an aide to Reagan administration labor secretary Elizabeth Dole, the future North Carolina senator and wife of future presidential candidate Bob Dole.[22] Balach's resignation was followed by that of Reginald deGueldre, a White House guard who admitted he did late-night White House tours for Spence in exchange for a Rolex watch. Reagan White House personnel officer Charles K. Dutcher resigned after admitting he had used Spence's services.[23] *The Washington Times* confirmed that US Attorney General Jay B. Stephens was overseeing the investigation of the Spence operation and added that Stephens's own former White House colleagues were implicated.[24] Lt. Gen. Daniel Graham, former head of the Defense Intelligence Agency, noted that Spence's operation may have been infiltrated by the KGB, meaning that what had likely begun as a domestic blackmail operation had possibly been penetrated by foreign intelligence.

On July 31, 1989, Craig Spence was arrested at the Barbizon Hotel in New York after calling the police and claiming that he had been robbed at gunpoint. When the police arrived, they found Spence with a twenty-two-year-old man, a small amount of cocaine, and an illegally procured pistol—the latter a felony. The police released Spence on his own recognizance. *The New York Times* was one of few outlets to cover the incident, making a brief note of the federal investigation of Spence's involvement in the D.C. prostitution ring. They made no mention of his role as an elite power broker that they had highlighted in their profile of him seven years before.[25]

The framing was not unique: the full story of Craig Spence was being suppressed by the mainstream media, to the point where outlets like *The Washington Post* wrote about the strangeness of their own suppression. In an August 1 article called "The Bombshell That Didn't Explode," the *Post* compared the Spence saga to Watergate and noted that many D.C. journalists felt it merited more coverage than major papers were giving.[26] *The Washington Times*, a conservative outlet with a reputation for salaciousness, had been publishing a steady stream of Spence stories for a month, but they did so alone. The reluctance of other outlets to follow up did not rest on the veracity of the claims, but on fear of powerful officials combined with careerist conformity.

"We can get a little too stuffy," explained Stephen Hess, a senior fellow at the Brookings Institution, when asked about the lack of coverage. "In some way, that's a classic story. It's just that the press has become so professional that we have a class structure built in now and we look down our noses at yellow journalism—the kind that Hearst and Pulitzer made their reputations with."[27] The editor of the *Los Angeles Times* admitted that the reason they had not covered the potentially momentous Spence story was that *The New York Times* and *The Washington Post* were not covering it. The news industry was locked in an ouroboros of obfuscation.

The refusal to cover the Spence case was part of a growing refusal of major outlets to delve deep into elite political corruption—a departure from the investigative journalism that ruled the 1970s and prompted realignments and resignations. In 1987, *The Washington Post*, *The New York Times*, and *The Wall Street Journal* all declined to cover the emerging Keating Five scandal and the corresponding savings and loan crisis. Instead, the scandal was exposed by the obscure mortgage trade journal *National Thrift News*.[28] *National Thrift News*'s September 1987 report set in motion a series of investigations and hearings that, in 1989, brought down dirty financier Charles Keating as well as the five senators who protected him. The mainstream outlets later claimed that the Keating scandal was "too complicated" to report and added that they were afraid of being sued.[29]

Similar hesitancy emerged around reporting of the Iran-Contra affair, another Reagan-era crisis buried by the mainstream press until it became too big to ignore. In a 1993 speech, Robert Parry, the reporter who first broke the story of the Reagan administration's illicit arms sales to Iran to fund Nicaraguan right-wing militants, explained how media and government elites in the 1980s—and in the decades that followed— prevented dark truths from being told.[30,31]

"Obviously for a long time the [Oliver] North network was just a 'crazy conspiracy theory,'" Parry recalled. "And then the idea that Bush was involved was a 'crazy conspiracy theory,' and the idea that there was a cover-up was a 'crazy conspiracy theory,' and I'd seen all these conspiracy theories actually turn out to be true."[32]

In 1985, Parry broke the Iran-Contra story in the Associated Press, only to find that his editor was an associate of Iran-Contra mercenary Oliver North and that the AP would no longer publish his investigative pieces on the crisis. Over the ensuing years, he joined and quit multiple publications in his quest to get his reporting out.[33] His struggle reflects the shifting media mores of the time, which saw smaller publications increasingly breaking the stories that most seriously threatened political power. That the Craig Spence case would first appear in *The Washington Times*—a seven-year-old paper then owned by Sun Myung Moon, the leader of a Korean messianic religious movement—instead of a more established outlet is in keeping with the political media culture of the 1980s.

Prior to Spence's arrest, *The Washington Post* had taken a stab at covering his criminal case—in the Styles section. On July 18, they ran a piece portraying Spence, a well-connected power broker under federal investigation, as a social climber whom Washington's elites either never liked or hardly knew. DiGenova, newsman Ted Koppel, and a number of US intelligence officials stated that while they had attended Spence's parties, they had no clue about that whole prostitution blackmail operation thing.

In August 1989, *Washington Post* managing editor Leonard Downie Jr. described their July 18 story as "a very interesting, sophisticated, classic Style story on a very interesting Washington phenomenon" and added, "I'm sorry we had it second, but none of us had Craig Spence on our screen."[34]

To which Spence remarked: "I had the world at my house, and now they don't know who I am."[35]

On August 9, Spence declared in a *Washington Times* interview that he had spent his life cultivating contacts at the highest levels of government and now believed his own death was imminent.[36] He claimed his apartment had been rigged with the help of US intelligence, and stated that Donald Gregg, a national advisor to then vice-president George H. W. Bush who was implicated in the Iran-Contra affair, had helped arrange his White House tours with prostitutes in attendance.[37] (Gregg denied this allegation.) Prior to his tenure in the Reagan White House, Gregg had worked under CIA director and Spence party guest William Casey during their attempts to stonewall the 1970s Church Committee and Pike Committee congressional investigations of improper CIA activity.[38] These investigations included an examination of the CIA's use of "love traps"—surveilled areas where illicit sexual activity would take place—to ensnare targeted officials.[39]

Allegations of Reagan administration offenses were not sufficiently investigated by officials of the George H. W. Bush administration, most notably Bill Barr. In the early 1990s, Barr became known as the "Cover-Up General" due to his role in burying the Iran-Contra case, the related Bank of Credit and Commerce International (BCCI) money-laundering scandal, the Inslaw/PROMIS software scandal, and more.[40] Barr's path to becoming Bush's attorney general, and therefore having the power to bury these cases, was unusual.

During a forty-eight-hour period in April 1991, two senators who had investigated Reagan-era state crime—John Tower, a former senator from Texas who led the Tower Commission on Iran-Contra in the 1980s before becoming chair of Bush's Presidential Intelligence Advisory Board; and John Heinz of Pennsylvania—died in two separate plane crashes.

Heinz's widow, Teresa Heinz, went on to marry Massachusetts senator John Kerry, who led the investigation into drug running in Iran-Contra. (The Kerry Committee's 1,166-page report, released in 1989, was largely ignored by the media until it was revived by journalist Gary Webb in the mid-1990s; in 2004 Webb was found dead in his apartment of an alleged suicide caused by two gunshots to the head.)[41] Bush's attorney general at the time of the plane crashes, Dick Thornburgh, quit to run for Heinz's vacant Senate seat. On August 10, 1991, Bill Barr, who had been serving as deputy attorney general, was announced as the new attorney general, and he remained in the position until the end of Bush's term.[42] In 2019, he returned as Trump's attorney general to bury Special Counsel Robert Mueller's probe into Russian election interference, the investigation into Jeffrey Epstein's alleged suicide in prison, and other alleged criminal plots.

In the final interview before his death, Spence said: "All this stuff you've uncovered involving call boys, bribery, and the White House tours, to be honest with you, is insignificant compared to other things I've done. But I'm not going to tell you those things, and somehow the world will carry on."[43]

And carry on it did. Days after Spence's sudden suicide, US Attorney Stephens ended the investigation into Spence and his operation, despite the objections of several members of Congress. On November 12, 1989, Rep. Helen Delich Bentley testified to the House of Representatives that she was worried that Spence had compromised US security. "I bring this to the floor today, Mr. Speaker, because I am frankly puzzled that these stories are out in print, both in Japan and in America, and there seems to be no official investigation into what to me are very grave charges."[44]

No US officials followed up. Spence had had names, and the door to his case was closed.

If you followed, even on a superficial level, the Jeffrey Epstein sex crimes and blackmail operation, you would immediately recognize parallels between Epstein and Spence. An enigmatic, wealthy, and well-connected man rises to prominence advising political and media elites—Spence in the 1980s, Epstein in the 1990s. He lives in a lavish home rigged with surveillance equipment, which he uses to entrap political figures in sexual blackmail operations allegedly linked to multiple governments and foreign intelligence services. He never reveals the origin of his wealth, the extent of his illicit activity, or who funded or benefited from his actions. He is arrested on a smaller charge, and within months of the arrest, dies in a strange suicide that curtails further investigation of his crimes.

If you followed, on a closer level, the Jeffrey Epstein case as it played out over multiple decades, you'd notice parallels in the media coverage as well. Both Epstein and Spence were introduced to the public with puff pieces portraying them as wealthy insiders beloved by their highbrow social circles. As their criminal connections were revealed, media outlets pivoted from praise to making light of their illicit acts, which included trafficking and abusing minors. Even the literary allusions used to soften their image were the same; both were repeatedly compared to Jay Gatsby.[45,46] As the charges became more serious and implicated powerful officials, coverage largely receded until a smaller publication—*The Washington Times* for Spence, the *Miami Herald* for Epstein—forced their cases back into the spotlight. During the time each man allegedly carried out his sexual blackmail operation, federal officials delayed or dropped investigations into their illicit activity, and never explained why.

Where the Spence and Epstein cases diverge is in the manner of the cover-up. The corrupt and powerful used to bury their crimes with silence. Now they do it with noise.

The life and death of Craig Spence was disappeared through a near-uniform media and political blackout. There were no mainstream books, few follow-up articles, and no congressional hearings. Much of the coverage from the time is not easy to find today. *The Washington Times'* 1980s articles, for example, are not in its publicly available archive. Spence is a ghost of history, a specter at the edges of a storm. I was a child when Spence carried out his operation, and I was in my thirties when I first heard about it, despite studying government corruption for my entire life. In 2017, I discovered Spence while researching Epstein, and was startled both by the similarities between the two men and by the fact that I had never heard of Spence. At the least, his case seemed like memorable tabloid fodder—the kind of salacious story a ratings-hungry media usually embraces—and likely indicative of something darker and more dangerous. It surprised me that reporters old enough to have remembered the Spence case unfolding in real time never brought it up in the context of Epstein or other sex crime cases involving members of the United States government.

Then again, until 2019, few media outlets were willing to discuss Jeffrey Epstein either—at least not in truthful and therefore negative terms. Beginning in the early 2000s, Epstein, aided by the powerful public relations agency of Howard Rubenstein, became the subject of flattering media profiles portraying him as a man of wealth and taste whose proclivity for raping underage girls was dismissed as a charming affectation. The publicity glow dimmed only slightly following Epstein's 2006 arrest for unlawful sex acts with a minor. That Epstein was a pedophile rapist and trafficker had become public knowledge by the end of that decade, but it did not seem to bother the wealthy New Yorkers with whom he socialized.[47] In 2011, Epstein registered as a level three sex offender and continued to be invited to high society parties and policy conferences. Rarely were Epstein's crimes portrayed as the horrors they were; nor was his broader trafficking operation investigated much, either by journalists or by law enforcement.

The Epstein coverage puts to rest the theory that American mainstream media is guided primarily by ratings and profit. For decades, outlets worked against their own financial interests, shielding the public from a blockbuster case involving spies, celebrities, politicians, and rape. With brave exceptions, the prerogative of the media tends to be the protection of the powerful, at the expense of victims.

Even the 2016 presidential election, which featured a candidate, Donald Trump, whom a woman claimed in court had raped her when she was thirteen years old after she had been forced to work for Epstein, did not elicit deeper coverage. (That woman's attempt to hold a press conference about her alleged rape in November 2016 was canceled due to death threats.)

In the 2000s, Epstein had taken Bill Clinton for rides on his plane, nicknamed the "Lolita Express." Epstein's criminal partner, Ghislaine Maxwell, was a guest at Chelsea Clinton's wedding in 2010—meaning that both 2016 presidential candidates, Donald Trump and Hillary Clinton, had at the least an acquaintance with Epstein, though Clinton was never accused of abuse by an Epstein victim. In January 2015, both Bill Clinton and Donald Trump were listed in Epstein's black book, which was published on the website Gawker.[48] Roughly one year later, Gawker was sued out of existence by right-wing tech billionaire Peter Thiel. In November 2018, the *Miami Herald*'s Julie K. Brown published a long, detailed investigation of the Epstein criminal operation based on interviews with dozens of survivors. She had to fight both officials and editors to get her investigation published. Her reporting, published at the height of the 'me too.' movement, made the reticence to cover Epstein recede somewhat. It also prompted a wave of lawsuits by women who had been abused by Epstein and Maxwell.

On July 6, 2019, Epstein was arrested on one count of sex trafficking of a minor and one count of conspiracy to commit sex trafficking. The arrest spurred anticipation that the high-level participants in his operation may finally have to discuss their alleged offenses under oath. This testimony never came to pass. On August 10, Epstein allegedly committed suicide in prison, but there were no witnesses or video recordings of the death. In an amazing coincidence, the prison guards fell asleep and the prison cameras all malfunctioned at the precise moment he hung himself in his cell. The suspicious circumstances of the "suicide" on top of the claims that Epstein was dead—and thus unable to threaten people—spurred a brief cavalcade of coverage.

Suddenly there was no longer a paucity of reporting on Epstein, but a flood of conflicting narratives. The truth became buried in an explosion of articles, memes, and theories posted in the aftermath—a blitzkrieg of innuendo that does a disservice to his victims by making a mockery of his crimes.

Epstein is a linchpin in a network of high-power corruption and abuse for which there has been almost no accountability. While trafficking children, he partnered with players in multiple industries that are frequently the subject of widespread anxiety over their rising power and diminished sense of responsibility toward the public good: government, technology, media, national security, higher education. He spent decades with Ghislaine Maxwell operating a trafficking operation in which hundreds of children were raped by powerful men from around the world. Among the men accused of abusing girls procured by Epstein and Maxwell are Trump, Prince Andrew, Alan Dershowitz, and Ehud Barak. (All have denied the accusations, though Prince Andrew has entered into a confidential settlement with an accuser.) Powerful men who have associated with Epstein include Clinton, Steven Pinker, Harvey Weinstein, Larry Summers, and Bill Gates. This is an abbreviated list limited to some of the most high-profile and well-documented examples: Epstein and Maxwell had their tentacles everywhere.

Epstein was brought into the realm of the global elite by Donald Barr, the father of Bill Barr and headmaster of New York's prestigious Dalton School, who in 1973 hired a twenty-year-old Epstein to teach math. (On the side, Donald Barr wrote science fiction novels about fascist intergalactic pederasts.)[49] Epstein's relationships with Dalton parents gave him connections to players in high finance. He struck up partnerships with CEOs like Victoria's Secret's Les Wexner, who was later accused of being a participant in Epstein's trafficking operation and who hired Epstein to handle his money; and in higher education, where Epstein partnered with Harvard and MIT faculty who were aware of his crimes and pocketed his donations anyway.[50,51] Epstein was obsessed with "transhumanism"— the belief that mankind could be improved through genetic engineering and other technology—and sought to impregnate twenty captive women at a time at his New Mexico ranch due to his belief in his own genetic superiority. Epstein was a eugenicist, but his elite friends did not care, just like they did not care that he was a serial rapist and trafficker.[52] They cared about his money and their secrets.

But they knew—they all knew. In 2006, Epstein was arrested after over forty women came forward claiming that they were part of an international underage sex crime ring to service the wealthy and powerful. In 2007, US Attorney for South Florida Alex Acosta worked with the FBI, then headed by Robert Mueller, and Epstein's lawyers, Alan Dershowitz (who went on to defend Donald Trump) and Ken Starr (who had previously prosecuted Bill Clinton), in a plea deal to give Epstein a mere eighteen-month sentence for soliciting, molesting, and raping underage girls. Epstein never spent a day of his sentence in prison, and in 2009, he was granted early "release" from his pseudo-confinement. He returned to making forays to his private island in the Caribbean on which he had built a gold-domed temple with secret doors and an underground lair.[53]

The US government granted Epstein immunity from all federal charges, but would not say why, and his victims were not informed of this secret deal until 2019. Acosta, who in 2017 became Trump's secretary of labor, said that White House officials told him that Epstein "belonged to intelligence and to leave it alone." He never specified to which country's intelligence Epstein belonged.[54] US judges and prosecutors sealed the evidence of his crimes, blocking them from journalistic scrutiny. Epstein's arrest in July 2019 prompted hope that the truth would finally emerge during trial—a trial that never happened because Epstein was proclaimed dead in August.

In 2018, I began writing *Hiding in Plain Sight*, a history of a multi-decade, transnational criminal operation in which Epstein played a significant role. I finished it one month before Epstein's arrest in July 2019, and spent that August rewriting the chapter on Epstein as long-withheld information about his trafficking and blackmail operation came to light. As a result, I recorded my final moment of fleeting faith in American accountability, the only part of the book that does not hold up today: "I am updating this chapter one week after Epstein's mysterious death," the pre-plague, pre-coup, pre-apocalypse me wrote, "with new information confirming my worst suspicions by the hour. I hope that by the time you read it, the women who were brave enough to tell their stories will have seen some justice. I anticipate that what people learn about Epstein in the years to come will have significant geopolitical implications if the full extent of his illicit activity is revealed and accomplices brought to trial."[55]

There was, of course, no justice. To the extent that there were significant geopolitical implications, they can be measured by the endurance of elite criminal impunity. With the exception of Ghislaine Maxwell, who went on trial for sex trafficking in late November 2021, none of the accused participants in the Epstein ring have been indicted. The flicker of accountability that emerged when Maxwell was found guilty for trafficking in December was snuffed out by the possibility of a retrial or mistrial, as Maxwell's legal team alleged juror impropriety.[56] Official details of the Epstein operation and what role members of the US and foreign governments played in it remain under wraps.

Given the successful attempts to bury the litany of crimes that the Trump administration committed in plain sight, which includes memory-holing an attack on the Capitol that transpired on live television and was plotted on social media, there is little reason to believe that revealing the truth about the Epstein plot—a shadowy and sprawling operation encompassing some of the world's most powerful men—will be a priority of the Biden administration or of any administration that follows. Suppressing information about the Epstein and Maxwell operation was, and remains, a bipartisan endeavor.

It is common for pundits and politicians to claim that there are "two Americas"—red and blue, liberal and conservative, coastal and heartland. This is not only fallacious in and of itself—there are dozens of Americas in a five-mile radius from my house, a diverse array of backgrounds and beliefs that defies the cheap categorizations of pundits and polls—but it ignores what does unite Americans, which is rage at elite criminal impunity. We may not revolt as one, but we are revolted as one, *e pluribus nauseam*.

Our revulsion has a number of overlapping targets, but there is none more universally loathed than Epstein, due to both the horrific nature of his crimes and the ease with which he had escaped consequences for so long.

At this sick, sad point in our national history, Jeffrey Epstein may be the only thing holding Americans together. That our unity rests on shared loathing of a billionaire pedophile and his network of wealthy accomplices is an indictment of the United States itself.

But it is a rare affirmation that Americans do, still, inhabit a shared political reality, even if we do not fully understand its loathsome nature. Factual clarity about the case fades in and out like the cycles of the moon—slivers and partial reveals and rare clear bursts of brightness—but moral clarity shines on. No one doubts that Epstein was evil. No one doubts that he preyed on children and that the people who could have stopped his operation instead chose to enable it. No one is on Epstein's side—except some of the most powerful political and corporate actors in America, the people responsible for the policies that shape our lives and the lives of our children. That we are expected to accept this state of affairs as normal is another shared point of disgust.

For a year after Epstein's alleged suicide, officials ignored public demands for transparency, despite the case having severe national security implications as well as moral ones. Finally, on July 2, 2020, the FBI arrested Ghislaine Maxwell on charges that she helped Epstein recruit underage girls for sexual abuse.[57] Her arrest was long overdue: Ghislaine Maxwell had been involved in Epstein's crimes since partnering with him in the early 1990s. The operation appears to have been a family affair. Ghislaine's father, Robert Maxwell, was a British publishing tycoon, alleged secret Mossad agent, and organized crime liaison who died mysteriously in November 1991 after falling off his yacht, in an incident described alternatively as suicide or murder. Maxwell spent his final years helping members of the Russian mafia set up operations outside the Soviet Union,[58] working for Israeli intelligence—he was given a state funeral in Jerusalem where Israeli officials praised his great contributions to their enterprise—

and committing an array of financial crimes that left the Maxwell family deep in debt. Exactly when Epstein and Maxwell met is uncertain, but according to Julie K. Brown, Ghislaine Maxwell discovered after her father's death that Epstein had been helping hide his remaining money in offshore accounts.[59]

Maxwell moved to New York in 1991, and spent the next three decades as Epstein's confidante and criminal partner while hobnobbing with celebrities and political officials. Beginning in 2015, Maxwell was sued by numerous victims of Epstein's child trafficking operation. Among the lawsuits' claims were that she had recruited a sixteen-year-old girl from Trump's Mar-a-Lago compound and forced her into prostitution and that she had raped several of the girls she had forced into sexual slavery. The cases dated back to 1994, and the victims were as young as eleven.[60] Questions emerged about why Maxwell had not been arrested earlier, and officials responded she was hard to locate—a claim difficult to believe when there are over one thousand photos of her at high society gatherings in the Getty photo archive alone, surrounded by celebrities, politicians, journalists, presidents . . . [61]

On August 15, 2019, a few days after Epstein's alleged suicide, right-wing tabloid *The New York Post* published a photo of a nonchalant Ghislaine Maxwell at In-N-Out Burger, smirking at the camera while holding an open copy of *The Book of Honor: The Secret Lives and Deaths of CIA Operatives*, a 2001 nonfiction bestseller about intelligence agents whose roles remained secret after their deaths. (The book brings to mind the clipping on intelligence agents Spence held at his own suicide.) The *New York Post* article sparked a debate about whether the photo was doctored, and its veracity became one of many bizarre mini-controversies that emerged in the aftermath of Epstein's death and diverted attention from the severity of their crimes.[62]

Epstein was becoming memed to the point of inscrutability. "Jeffrey Epstein Didn't Kill Himself" became a catchphrase slapped on T-shirts and mugs and Christmas tree ornaments featuring a tiny Epstein hanging from a miniature noose. Meanwhile, the victims' prospects for justice became dimmer, as witnesses and alleged participants in Epstein's operation were no longer required to testify against him.

The focus, instead, shifted to discussion of the crime as a means of political weaponization. Because Epstein and Maxwell's social circle spans the political spectrum, partisans seized on theories about their agenda that fit their preferred narratives. Epstein and Maxwell had left a public kompromat trail made possible by the openness of the internet, where old articles now served as fodder for contemporary character assassinations. These character assassinations were justified, but in the end, the one-size-fits-all Epstein conspiracy fit no one's idea of justice. Politicians and officials, including Attorney General Barr, promised to bring accountability, but none of them even tried. Epstein, it seemed, was the ultimate catch and kill.

Meanwhile, a flurry of media coverage emerged in the immediate aftermath of his alleged suicide—long, researched exposés published fast and furious, much in the manner of prewritten obituaries written for terminally ill celebrities. Many articles featured confessions by the author or interviewees that they had known of Epstein's operation for years, had censored their previous work about him, or had had their findings censored by their employer. For decades, the media did not cover Epstein—they covered *for* Epstein. Among the outlets who admitted suppressing the Epstein story were *The New York Times*, *Vanity Fair*, and ABC News.[63] One *New York Times* journalist, Landon Thomas Jr., had solicited $30,000 from Epstein while writing glowing puff piece profiles about him; Thomas was not fired until 2019.[64] The slew of articles highlighted new horrors—one of which was the willingness of so many to protect a predator—but yielded no definitive answers about for whom Epstein worked or why he was not stopped earlier. This is not surprising: to answer these questions would require not just contemplation but recrimination.

Epstein was a creature of media, of politics, of prestige and power and wealth, and to shed light on his life would be to illuminate the grotesque machinations of those who shaped global affairs in the 1990s and the twenty-first century—people who could have helped shape something fair and fine instead of degraded and depraved. To consort with Epstein after his initial arrest was a choice, and every encounter is a damnation.

People are often drawn to a conspiracy because they have been victims of the same systems on a smaller scale, and they recognize the patterns. Victims of abuse recognized the dynamics of the Epstein case: the shattered trust, the layered lies, the damage control, and the control over the damaged. Perpetrators of abuse recognized it too, and moved to protect the twenty-first century's most desirable currency: impunity. Impunity, the sadist's conception of freedom, mainstreamed and marketed as the new American dream.

The public continued to demand the truth, even as it sank in a quagmire of speculation. Widespread interest in Epstein was natural due to both the repugnant nature of his crimes and the celebrity of his consort. Some attention was prurient, some was mocking, but underneath the sordid surface was a deep longing for justice—because if crimes *this* horrific could go unpunished and unexplained for decades, anything was possible. In an era of unceasing catastrophes, we longed for less to be possible—for the extent of our imagination to be limited by law, or honor, or shame.

Instead, there was only more darkness. The more you found out, the less you wanted to know. You plumb the depths, and then you drown in them.

Before Epstein was arrested and suicided and vanished into a vortex of his own infamy, I envisioned a scorched-earth future in which some 2050 version of me—some beat-down, dead-end sucker for the truth trying to figure out *the point where it all went wrong, so they can turn it around!*—stumbles upon the name "Jeffrey Epstein" on whatever surveillance state internet is permitted by the reigning crime lord technocrats, wonders "Who is that?" and disappears down a wormhole of deleted data and casual confessions, her faith in mankind never to return. I wondered if

Epstein would be the Craig Spence of the future, a footnote to a history that was never supposed to be written. I wondered if a future version of me would reel in shock or recognition.

It was the combination, in the end—that gut-punch of temporal betrayal, like history itself was mocking you, like you were prey studying the predators and by outing them you were inviting them in. That is how it felt to read about Epstein for the first time, about Spence for the first time, and about decades of other atrocious crimes involving wealthy officials and abused minors for the first time. *How could no one know about this?* I wondered, and then, a worse realization: *How could so many know? How could so many know for so long and no one care enough to stop it?*

The old question of "Where were you when this atrocity occurred?"—the question asked about pivotal traumas the entire nation experienced, like the Kennedy assassination or 9/11—has become: "Where were you when you found out that this atrocity had been transpiring in the background for your entire life, putting everything else you believed about government or the justice system or the fundamental nature of humanity in question?" Some will refer to this sensation as being "red-pilled"—the moment of departure from acceptance of the official narrative into the realm of conspiracy theory—but that implies a conscious desire to know as well as a set boundary between the mainstream and the extreme. There is no boundary, and in the beginning, I was not seeking the information I found. I took the ride before I bought the ticket.

A subculture has grown around the concept of "red-pilling"—a metaphor taken from the 1999 movie *The Matrix*, where the protagonist was given the choice of accepting his illusory but comforting reality or knowing the dangerous truth. But at this point, "red-pilling" is a mainstream American pastime, whether people want to admit it or not. This is not necessarily a bad thing. The alternative "blue pill"—the comforting illusion of normalcy—is the hopium of the masses, a delusion knowingly swallowed and savvily marketed. Normalcy is a politician's promise forever looming on the horizon, requiring a marathon suspension of disbelief. To accept the promise of normalcy, a person has to block out an enormous number of brazen abuses and state crimes that are often, on top of it all, deeply weird, and thus ignored by people craving respectable conversation.

The stranger America gets, the more respectability in its industries of influence is required. To be weird—not diagnosably weird, not commercially weird, not cool weird, but just plain weird—is the new American sin. Weird is dangerous. Weird breaks the algorithm, weird bulldozes the career path, weird shifts expectations of what is possible. Most gallingly for purveyors of false assurances about the return to normalcy, weird recognizes weird. Weird sees the rot in the sensationalism, the menacing faces of the monsters behind the carnival masks. Weird tries to show that very human monstrosity to the world, knowing full well that the qualities that allow them to see it are the same ones that will prevent them from being believed.

It is common to hear that Americans no longer inhabit a shared reality. To a large extent this is true, especially in an era of social media manipulation, but we did not share a reality in simpler times either. We never shared equal justice under the law. What we did perhaps share was an ideal—the dreamy lure of life, liberty, and the pursuit of happiness. But that dream was deferred, then mortgaged along with our future, and the question now is less whether the dream is dead but who is most to blame for killing it. We dream now of lives not so brazenly taken; liberty not so flagrantly stolen—fantasies snuffed out by those who claim accountability is forever coming soon, like an endless preview of a movie trapped in development hell. The tactics used to dissuade people from demanding accountability are discussed in detail in the next chapter. But all of them reflect both the profound social and political transformations that have taken place in the past decade and the desire to deny them.

The first thing to acknowledge is that after four years of Donald Trump as president, the fringes have been pulled to the center, with the result that the center no longer holds. Trump created a template for elite criminal impunity that aspiring successors seek to emulate. None have done so as successfully, but expect them to try for decades to come.

Trump's main tactic was never to bury his offenses, but to flaunt them. He covered his big crimes with smaller crimes, and covered his smaller crimes with scandals, and in the process attempted to destroy the very notion of truth. His presidency exposed the weakness and complicity of institutions and proved that trusting the official line was a sucker's bet. A product of wealth and privilege who spent forty years in the rarefied world of business and entertainment when he was not repeatedly running for president, Trump peddled himself as a neophyte outsider—because it was better to be thought an all-American racist renegade than a transnational career criminal, and it was better to be thought an aberration than a culmination of unchecked corruption. Trump presented himself as locked in a battle with the very forces that enabled his rise: media, law enforcement, and government. As president, he used the power of the deep state to allege a conspiracy of the deep state against him—an extremely deep state move.

Second, American history has always been a process of extremism being mainstreamed into respectability and then reassessed by later generations who refuse to excuse past abuses. Reassessments tend to emerge in times of political instability, like the 1960s state violence that spurred the 1970s investigative journalism or the muckraking reporting of the 1930s that sought to out those responsible for the Great Depression. The Trump era ushered in similar reevaluations of US history, particularly of systemic racism and white supremacist power structures. In the most well-known example, the 1619 Project—a 2019 compendium of articles that centered the enslavement of Black Americans in the narrative of America's national identity and purpose—challenged how many Americans saw their past. For many white Americans, the work was a shock; for many Black Americans, it was further confirmation of what they already knew.

In 2021, the publicization of lesser-known American atrocities prompted a referendum not only on race but on history itself. Institutionalists promised that "history will judge" powerful perpetrators of ongoing offenses to Americans who were at that moment learning about century-old atrocities, like the 1921 Black Wall Street massacre in Tulsa, for the first time. That the judgment of history had a hundred-year time lag discomfited partisans on both sides. History was written by the winners, and the winners were assholes. Some suggested that instead of the retrospective eye of history, perhaps actual, living *judges* should judge current offenders, but the institutionalists dismissed these demands as folly. Meanwhile, the backlash to accurate history of racial oppression dominated political rhetoric in 2021, at least in between flare-ups of the plague. Antagonists of historical accuracy often framed the debate as a rebuttal of "critical race theory"—an interpretative framework taught in legal and graduate schools that right-wing pundits found they could mold into whatever meaning best lent itself to banning facts in schools.

It is notable that the term "woke" entered the popular vernacular around the same time as "red-pilled," and that its use shifted in the same pejorative way. "Woke" was coined by Black Americans to describe awareness of systemic racial injustice before the term was co-opted first by sycophantic corporations, then by sneering white pundits wary of a critical mass of Americans becoming conscious of racist oppression, and finally by right-wing officials seeking a pretext for school censorship or a scaremongering election hook.

While the gulf in who uses "woke" and "red-pilled" and why can be vast, their tandem emergence points to a broader shift in American consciousness: a refusal to trust official narratives for the simple reason that official narratives have proven unworthy of trust. Why should Americans trust official narratives after the war in Iraq launched on a lie, the 2008 collapse of a financial system built on deception, the repeated acquittals of police officers who assault or murder Black Americans on camera? Why should Americans disregard what they see with their own eyes, which is a centuries-long pattern of state crimes being "solved" by being redefined as not being crimes at all? Why should Americans trust the authority of people who excuse authoritarianism? Why should trust be given away instead of earned? When did obedience become so laudable, especially when we do not know exactly who we are being made to serve?

Over the past decade, the phrase "red-pilled" has increasingly been employed by propagandists seeking validation for lies. But its initial use was an embrace of inquisitiveness: a willingness to look at terrifying truths and open the mind to troubling questions, particularly about the government. These are *good* impulses when sincere: a sign of free thought and an engaged citizenry. That "They're just asking questions" has become a mocking dismissal of people who are often *truly just asking questions* shows how deeply questions are feared—and how the caricature of the conspiracy theorist has been weaponized by those seeking to protect a corrupt status quo at all costs.

State-sanctioned racial oppression and simmering suspicion over government crimes were not the only topics to gain traction during the tumultuous Trump years. We also entered the era of 'me too.'—a movement highlighting the ubiquity of unpunished predatory behavior. After Hollywood producer Harvey Weinstein was outed as a serial sexual abuser in the fall of 2017, a slew of powerful men in politics, media, and entertainment—Matt Lauer, Charlie Rose, Les Moonves, Brett Ratner, Mark Halperin, Kevin Spacey, Eric Schneiderman, and on and on—were also exposed as sexual abusers. Their crimes had been covered up by accomplices, many of them powerful figures in their own right. The idea that celebrities who had entertained you for decades or leaders who were supposed to protect you from harm had long been serial rapists and assaulters, and that the people around them knew it, jolted the public from the myth that conspiracies are rare. Turned out everyone could keep their mouths shut after all.

Conspiracies of the powerful are common—so common that their protection is inscribed in the language of business and politics and law. For abusers and their accomplices, conspiracy is comfortable, a blanket of privilege used to smother attempts to tell the truth. "It was *a consensus about the organization's comfort level moving forward* that bowed to lawyers and threats; that hemmed and hawed and parsed and shrugged; that sat on multiple credible allegations of sexual misconduct and disregarded a recorded admission of guilt," wrote Ronan Farrow in his 2019 bestseller *Catch and Kill*, the story of how Weinstein's abuse was covered up by everyone from NBC to the Israeli mercenary intelligence firm Black Cube. "That anodyne phrase, that language of indifference without ownership, upheld so much silence in so many places."[65]

Conspiracy is not only a matter of how many people are willing to stay silent, but what tactics can be used to keep them that way. The combination of the emergent 'me too.' movement and the corruption of the Trump administration illuminated these tactics: nondisclosure agreements, private mercenary espionage agencies, catch and kill media operations, and the old standbys of blackmail, threats, and bribes. The problem was that these tactics still worked, and continue to work now, despite wider awareness of them. The power imbalance is too severe.

Fighting corruption is not a matter of changing hearts and minds but of accumulating leverage. What leverage does the American public have when confronted with acts of extreme conspiratorial corruption—the kind employed by people like Epstein and Maxwell, the kind that seems to have swallowed all the institutions of accountability that were supposed to prevent it? The only refuge left is your own conscience, and the hopes that others share your revulsion toward abuses of power and your desire for the truth—and that your fellow travelers will not be preyed upon in the process of finding it.

Until the advent of the internet, the easiest way to keep the public from examining conspiracies was media consolidation. Prior to the twenty-first-century digital media economy, investigative journalism was both better funded and more common, but information traveled slowly and was restricted to narrower audiences, often determined by geography. The Craig Spence case could be buried, along with the questions it raised about national security, by simply dropping the topic and letting time do its work. The Epstein case was initially shaped or suppressed in a similar style, but its revelations could not survive online scrutiny. The participants were too diverse and revulsion at the central crime—child abuse, one of the last universal taboos—was too uniform.

Traditional tactics of obfuscation were also not going to work with a president like Trump, whose mafia-state tactics brought discussions of the merger of organized crime, white-collar crime, and state corruption closer to mainstream attention than ever before. (This integration was, ironically, laid out in detail in 2011 in a speech called "The Evolving Organized Crime Threat" by Robert Mueller, who later failed to hold Trump and his cohort accountable for exactly this activity.)[66] The sheer number of indicted operatives and pedophiles in Trump's orbit, as well as the endless exposures of other public figures revealed to have been predators or foreign agents all along, illuminated the criminal underground long propping up the shining city on a hill.

It became reasonable to believe that a critical mass of people in power were either criminals, pedophiles, or traitors, or that they were being blackmailed, bribed, or threatened by a criminal, pedophile, or traitor. Dismissive cries of "that's just a conspiracy theory" do not work as well when the conspirators, high on their own impunity, keep confessing their crimes and posting the evidence online.

New ways of curtailing the road to critical inquiry emerged—some organically, some intentionally. The most effective tactic for silencing journalists and political opponents was threat. But the greatest weapon of obfuscation for the general public was the exploitation of American optimism. Regardless of their political leanings, Americans were invited to buy into a mirage of accountability predicated around a future date that shifts with dashed expectations—a kind of inverse of traditional apocalyptic prophecy. For centuries, false prophets told people when the world would end and simply moved the date when life stubbornly went on. But here, the opposite occurred: a glorious era of justice was forever imminent in our mortal realm, if only people would stay quiet and obey secret state forces whose existence they could never validate.

Apocalypse, literally, means "revelation." But what Americans received from their deep-state false prophets was apocalypse-lite: all the doom without any of the insight. The new apocalypse was an evangelical embrace of bureaucracy—a true hell on earth. And here we arrive at QAnon, the pro-Trump messianic cult that buried a crucial grain of truth in a morass of lies; and its mirror image, the institutionalists committed to unquestioning faith in the American justice system regardless of how obviously it fails them.

4

THE CULT OF THE CRIMINAL ELITE

They say that those who do not learn from history are doomed to repeat it. Since Americans spent centuries failing to learn from history, we get to repeat it all at once. The year is 2021 and we are living through simultaneous revivals of the worst of the American past: the Civil War, the Spanish Flu, the white mob violence of the 1919 Red Summer, the extreme wealth disparity of the Gilded Age, the fascist movements of the 1930s and 1940s, the Jim Crow era of voter suppression, the riots of the 1960s, the corruption of Watergate, the cover-ups of Iran-Contra. In August 2021, Hurricane Ida made landfall in Louisiana on the anniversary of Hurricane Katrina. One month before the twentieth anniversary of 9/11, the Taliban retook Afghanistan dressed in US military uniforms abandoned in the hasty retreat from the quagmire war.

It's like America is on its deathbed, watching its life flash before its eyes.

Shirley Jackson wrote that "no live organism can continue to exist sanely under conditions of absolute reality." This was the line that introduced her 1959 horror novel, *The Haunting of Hill House*, but it can be repurposed for modern history, or as the opening line of a new national anthem. There is only so much reality that Americans can bear before breaking, whether in the dehumanized digital reality of the doomscroll or the crushing reality of the day-to-day, where the most mundane decisions are now life or death. There is no room to navigate this senseless space. Our new problems include catastrophic weather disasters and digital surveillance, but there is no time left to learn from them: one is a road map of a grim predetermined future and one is an evidence trail of all our regrets. These are conditions that create madness.

The reaction to madness, on a mass scale, has not been chaos but conformity. The long arc of history does not naturally bend toward justice, but works like a catapult, bending backward into the past and launching you into a freefall future. Devoid of direction, stripped of stability, people increasingly cling to cults—political personality cults, religious cults, ideological cults, cults of bureaucracy, cults of conspiracy. The turn to cultishness is worsened by the constant connectivity that enables ceaseless scrutiny. Much like ordinary people now must contend with the kind of attention once reserved for celebrities, the cultish nature of fandom now applies to civil servants and doctors and others whose credibility is weighed not by their expertise, but by the followers they accrue.

The experience of being a viral object is sometimes involuntary, sometimes required, always disorienting. In some industries, you are told to make yourself a brand to stay afloat and to cling to that brand for dear life. You board the Noah's Ark of social media with a digital doppelgänger, two by two, one of them your actual self, one of them your avatar—your brand, your mark. You ride the waves of the once-in-a-century floods that now hit us monthly and stare at the dark mirror version of yourself that people seem to recognize more than your innate humanity. You wait for a divine force to make the waters recede, but they don't. The waters are relentless— and so you are the one who relents. You relent, and you look for others in your same sinking vessel, people who will convince you that you are not drowning but waving, and your doppelgänger grins in approval.

The absence of authority in the face of obscene criminality prompts delusions, peddled by propagandists and true believers alike, that noble actors are fighting the good fight but Must Keep Silent for Reasons You Will

Understand in Time. In order for this delusion to hold, the sound of their silence must drown out the evidence heard with your own ears. *They are dotting the I's and crossing the T's*, the cult of the savior state bleats, *they are playing 3-D chess, they are reeling in the big fish, they are aiming for the king so they best not miss, they can't show their cards without ruining their hand, they're getting all their ducks in a row, the dam is breaking, the storm is here, they've got this, be patient, be quiet, relax, trust the plan.*

The wheels of justice grind slow but oh they do grind fine, the cult continues, ignoring that the wheels of justice ran down American democracy and told its mangled corpse to stop being so demanding.

You will hear these pacifying mantras if you frequent social media on any topic related to a refusal of elected officials to protect Americans, which is to say, any political topic. It does not matter if you are reading Democrats or Republicans or leftists or libertarians or QAnon acolytes or FBI sycophants: mindless adulation of the savior state is the flavor of the time. Justice delayed is no longer justice denied when time has lost all meaning.

It is impossible to say if this Greek chorus of inertia enthusiasts is composed of real people, paid operatives, or automated bots. That one cannot tell the difference between a bot and a person indicates the severity of the problem. *As Gregor Samsa awoke one morning from uneasy dreams he found himself transformed in his bed into a gigantic bot*, I would think when I found myself castigated by near-identical avatars for demanding accountability, and remind myself that this Kafkaesque army is not worth battling. Cults traffic in clichés. Their repetitive proclamations are not ideas in their own right but symbols of belonging, designators of loyalty and exclusion.

And in such a lonely era, isn't it nice to be included, even if you are sacrificing yourself at the altar of your digital doppelgänger to do so? If someone would believe so deeply in phantom forces that are overtly, objectively failing them, then maybe they will believe in you too.

When Donald Trump descended the escalator of his golden tower and proclaimed himself America's populist savior, he left a trail. The trail had two ex-wives, one of whom, Ivana, reportedly declared in a sealed divorce court deposition that he raped her, and the other, Marla, who was rumored to have tax returns revealing insight into his dirty dealings. (Trump denied Ivana's accusation; Ivana later confirmed that she used the word *rape* but did not mean it in "a literal or criminal sense" and in 2016, as Trump was running for president, she retracted the claim.) The trail also featured a large number of bankruptcies culminating in an investigation of Trump's businesses by the Department of the Treasury in 2015, an investigation that ended when he became president.

The trail was a road map of thirty years of presidential ambition—he ran in 2000, 2012, and 2016, and nearly ran in 1988 and 1996—and a lifetime of engagement with the dirtiest of GOP operatives and a slew of mobsters, pedophiles, and white-collar criminals. That trail sprawled around the world, but ran a recurring route to the Kremlin, where daughter Ivanka, whom her father said he would date if only they were not related, sat in Putin's chair during one of the Trump family's many Moscow visits with their oligarch friends and mafia-adjacent business partners. Like all roads to Mar-a-Lago, the trail was laced with land mines of NDAs, threats, and bribes. But in 2015 the trail was repaved and made smooth, like when mobsters bury their victims' bodies in the concrete of a construction project.

The trail was so smooth, the pathway so appointed, that reporters strolled right over the criminal underground beneath. They were too busy gaping at Hillary Clinton's emails, which beckoned to them like neon signs on a bureaucratic Vegas strip. They were too busy gobbling down gossip spoon-fed to them from a prearranged buffet, all you can eat, almost like the person at the center of this campaign was not some neophyte political rube but a skilled exploiter of human weakness. This was a casino campaign: no clocks, no daylight, dealer wins, mark folds and keeps on playing. The trail was groomed like a racetrack, and the media's favorite horse was Trump, because he is such an easy bet—*a rigged bet always is*—and he runs round and round and round, never getting tired, never failing to deliver. The press watched him run and they did not intervene, even when the cracks in the trail became a chasm, and the bodies began to emerge, and the ground began to shake, and the hole began to darken, and the future fell in.

But there was an obstacle on the trail that could not be eliminated, one they pretended not to see. The obstacle was child rape, a dark accusation that was also heavily documented. As I explain in great detail in my previous book *Hiding in Plain Sight*, a woman forced into childhood sexual slavery by Epstein and Maxwell claimed that Trump had raped her and threatened to murder her and her family if she told anyone. The press generally refused to report on the case, despite the severity and relevance of the allegation. In 2016, the victim sued again, and lawyers commented on the near uniform reticence of journalists and officials to explore whether the allegation was true. When a video of Trump bragging that he liked to "grab them by the pussy" emerged in October 2016, prompting additional women to accuse him of sexual assault and predatory behavior, the victim decided to hold a press conference and tell her story one week before the election. She and her attorney were threatened with murder, and they called it off.

Most media and public officials ignored the Epstein-related Trump rape case because they were still refusing to tell the truth about Epstein. Here we arrive yet again at the intersection of rape, espionage, hostile foreign states, corrupt law enforcement, compromised world leaders, and the elite lawyers, academics, financiers, and journalists who enable them. Epstein's story is one of institutional collapse, a story that bridges centuries and pulls the myth of the twentieth into the mire of the twenty-first. The American century looks different now, kind of like the sky looks different when you are trapped at the bottom of a well.

The full history of this conspiracy remains untold, because the scope is so sprawling that you need a team to tackle it. It's the kind of investigation law enforcement and intelligence agencies would do if they were not also implicated in the crimes. I've reported parts of the history, caught hell for it, and hoped that the flames in my wake might light someone else's way. I do not know how much I succeeded, but I knew that it would be wrong not to try. I wanted justice and the truth, because I did not want history to repeat. I wanted to expose the past and in doing so break the future.

I was not the only one seeking answers. As mentioned in chapter three, the Epstein case attracted attention from across the political spectrum, and spurred new interest in decades of state-sanctioned depravity. The initial response of the Trump camp, which arose largely in the form of online commentary from anonymous fans, was to highlight connections Bill Clinton had to Epstein. Their claims were not baseless: Clinton had indeed socialized with Epstein, though it was prior to Epstein's first arrest in 2006. Clinton had also been accused of sexual assault by numerous women during his political career. The tactic of projection—accusing your opponent of what you are most guilty—is an old and effective one, employed by both parties and weaponized to an art by Trump mentor Roy Cohn and fellow Cohn mentee Roger Stone. Projection works best when your opponent is actually guilty of the offense in question, which was true of Bill but not of Hillary. But Hillary was Trump's presidential opponent. And so, in late 2016, Pizzagate—the narrative forerunner to the QAnon mythology—was launched.

Pizzagate is an example of preemptive narrative inversion, one of the main methods used by elites to dodge accountability. Preemptive narrative inversion is an early propaganda intervention in which outside parties interested in an actual crime are redirected toward a fictitious crime that exonerates the actual criminals and, ideally, implicates their opponents at the same time. The Pizzagate narrative claimed that Hillary Clinton, her campaign manager John Podesta, and other Democratic officials were running a child rape trafficking ring out of a D.C. pizza parlor called Comet Ping Pong. They claimed that clues about their activity were inside the emails leaked by Wikileaks throughout 2016, and that emails about pizza and other foods were code for planned abuses.

Among those who spread the Pizzagate narrative online was Michael

Flynn, the foreign agent for Russia and Turkey who spent a few weeks as Trump's national security advisor in early 2017 before quitting and being indicted in late 2017, getting pardoned by Trump in 2020, and then abetting the January 6, 2021, attempted insurrection, for which he remains unpunished. Flynn's background in military intelligence—he was the director of the Defense Intelligence Agency during the Obama administration— helped give the Pizzagate narrative credibility among Trump's followers. Popular right-wing social media personalities also pushed the narrative, in particular Flynn's son, Michael Flynn Jr., and Mike Cernovich, who, along with Alan Dershowitz, worked to smear Epstein's accusers.[1]

On December 5, 2016, an armed man stormed Comet Ping Pong, claiming he was there to rescue the abused children. He surrendered after determining there was no sign that the pizzeria was being used as a trafficking site, but not before firing a round from his AR-15. No one was injured, but the incident became a notorious example of how lies circulating on the internet can lead to physical violence on the ground.

Pizzagate was a weaponized conspiracy theory and its damage still resonates. In 2018, I gave a talk at the D.C. bookstore Politics and Prose, in a fancy neighborhood I had never visited before. I decided to eat at the restaurant next door—only to realize with a start that it was *that* pizza place, the real-life stage for the virtual lie. I walked into Comet Ping Pong and thought workers were eyeing me warily, but perhaps I imagined it, or maybe it was the way I stared. It was impossible to enter that place and not envision yourself as one of the protagonists: the shooter, the patrons, the owner, the abused children who did not exist. The shooter was hunting ghosts, and I resented everyone who had made a ghost out of the truth and diluted actual crimes and victims while traumatizing the people who worked there.

Pizzagate was violent, but Pizzagate was also meant to be ridiculous. Its moniker was intended to designate a devolution in American political crises, a reset of criminal narratives to ludicrous speed. Americans went from watching the solemn resignation of a president over Watergate in the 1970s to the Travelgate cacophony of the 1990s (the first use of the now ubiquitous -gate ending I am old enough to remember, inaugurated with the Clintons) to Chris Christie's Bridgegate to the online mob harassment of Gamergate and then, finally, to Pizzagate, the premise of which makes everyone discussing it sound deranged. The people propagating Pizzagate knew that the desperate desire of journalists to sound "respectable" has meant that facts often remain obscured, just as they were in the 1980s with the Craig Spence case. They knew that upping the absurdity would push the press even further away from the investigation of similar but *real* crimes, like Epstein's.

It is better to be thought a lunatic than a liar. A lunatic can be vindicated by time and rebranded a prophet; a liar is a liar by choice. Sounding batshit crazy when relaying the plain facts of a twenty-first-century political crisis is often the mark of an honest broker.

Respectability politics breeds self-censorship. It creates an obsession with optics that blinds you to insight. It breeds a desire for others to consider you reputable that is so desperate, it destroys your discernment of other people's motives. Forsaking the fallacy of respectability politics—the assumption that an office or profession imbues a person with virtue, instead of the other way around—requires abandoning it not only for others but for yourself.

In 2019, a CBS reporter asked Bill Barr whether he worried his brazen deceit and malpractice would damage his reputation. Barr responded: "I don't care about my legacy—I'll be dead."[2] This was the first and only time I related intensely to Bill Barr. One of the reasons Barr and other dishonest brokers tend to win is they long ago abandoned concerns about reputation in favor of wealth and power. Those seeking to oppose criminal elites need to abandon their careerist concerns in favor of truth and justice, no matter the reputational damage they incur as a result.

As a parent of elementary-school-age children, I felt I had an advantage in telling the truth during the Trump era, because children require you to speak in straightforward terms, allowing no room for prevarication. "Who is the MyPillow Guy?" my nine-year-old asked me in 2020, after overhearing me relay the latest coup news to my husband. "The

MyPillow Guy is a guy who sells pillows, but who is also working for Donald Trump to violently overthrow the government," I said. My son turned to my husband for a more reasonable explanation, the way he did when I insisted on the existence of Santa Claus or the tooth fairy, but my husband shook his head and said, "Your mother's not messing with you, kid."

"Oh my God," my son said, laughing maniacally. "Oh my God, the government, oh my God!"

What is Pizzagate? A conspiracy theory alleging that the Democrats run a pedophile trafficking ring out of a pizza parlor. *Who is Jeffrey Epstein?* A mysterious billionaire eugenicist who ran a pedophile trafficking network meant to blackmail the world's most powerful people in between trips to his island temple shrine and liaisons with international intelligence figures. *Who is Michael Flynn?* A former head of military intelligence who secretly worked with Russia and Turkey and discussed abducting a cleric in Pennsylvania[3] and tried to sell nuclear material on the sly to the Saudis[4] and tried to sell a mind-reading machine to the KGB[5] and pledged an oath to an online entity called "Q"[6] that claimed the messiah Donald Trump was engaged in a secret plan to save the trafficked children of the world. *Who is Donald Trump?* A career mafia associate and sexual predator turned Kremlin asset turned game show host turned president of the United States who was friends with at least five high-powered pedophiles and who pardoned the indicted criminals who helped put him in office and who runs around having rallies with them and the MyPillow Guy while they try to destroy the United States from within through riots and racism and kleptocratic alliances with transnational criminal syndicates masquerading as governments . . .

Are you sure?

Yes, I'm sure!

Because you sound like one of those crazy Pizzagate people, you know. . . .

Preemptive narrative inversion does not just capitalize on the incredulity of the respectable—the dearth of political imagination they like to brand as "savviness"—and their fear of violating social mores. It exploits their faith in political norms, a faith that perversely leads to the destruction of those norms when they are not codified in law. Pizzagate fulfilled its goal of making discussion of actual elite child trafficking networks linked to powerful actors seem insane, or, at least, the kind of issue that serious people do not discuss. But the tactic was also deployed to spread doubt on the legitimacy of the 2016 election itself, and set the stage for new destructive operations. Had it not been for the susceptibility of the Democratic party to preemptive narrative inversion in 2016, the United States might not have faced the more violent contestation of the 2020 election that followed.

On January 6, 2021, shortly before his supporters stormed the Capitol, Donald Trump credited them with coming up with the catchphrase "Stop the Steal." "We will never give up, we will never concede," Trump said. "It doesn't happen, you don't concede when there's theft involved. Our country has had enough. We will not take it anymore and that's what this is all about. And to use a favorite term that all of you people really came up with, we will Stop the Steal."[7]

But Trump's fans did not come up with "Stop the Steal" in 2020. They did not, in fact, come up with it at all. The phrase "Stop the Steal" was coined by Roger Stone, Trump's political advisor since the 1980s, and was first deployed in the 2016 election, along with a broader narrative of election theft—a narrative allowed to simmer for four years before boiling over that January day.[8] The "we" who mattered to Donald Trump never extended beyond his elite immediate circle.

In August 2016, as Trump's poll numbers began to plummet, Trump proclaimed that the election would be rigged and that he might not accept the results. He proceeded to repeat this claim until November. Stone, in turn, promised a "bloodbath" should Trump not be installed as president, and militant groups around the United States echoed his call for violence. Flynn, Steve Bannon, and other elites in Trump's orbit also spread the "rigged" narrative in 2016 and vowed to "stop the steal" should Trump be proclaimed the loser. Notably, these are the same political operatives whom Trump pardoned in December 2020 for other crimes after he lost the election and who then went on to publicize and allegedly organize the January 6, 2021, Capitol attack.

Despite both the overt threat of violence and the Trump campaign being composed of an army of skilled propagandists, the Democrats still fell for their tricks. In 2016, Democratic officials responded to Trump's accusation that the Democrats were plotting to steal the election by insisting that it was impossible for an election to be rigged: this was the United States, after all, the world's most enduring democracy, respected worldwide for its reliable peaceful transfer of power. Their assurances that norms and laws would hold ignored a slew of blatant threats: not only Trump's and Stone's "bloodbath" vows, but the potential for electronic manipulation following the hacking of multiple government agencies (among them the State Department, the Department of Defense, the Treasury, the White House, the Republican National Committee, and the Democratic National Committee) during Obama's second term. They also ignored interference by hostile foreign regimes, particularly the Kremlin and its operatives such as intelligence officer Konstantin Kilimnik, with whom Trump campaign manager and Russian foreign agent Paul Manafort was sharing election data in 2016.[9]

None of this nefarious activity was spurious or subtle. Trump, who boasted thirty years of ties to organized crime networks from the former Soviet Union, had asked the Kremlin for his opponent's emails at a July 2016 press conference. In August, Senate Minority Leader Harry Reid had sent an open letter to James Comey warning of the Kremlin's ability to "falsify election results."[10] Comey ignored Reid, instead releasing deceptive information on Clinton's emails that he later admitted had no validity. In October, Reid sent another open letter to Comey demanding that Americans learn the full scope of the threat before they headed to the polls. There was every reason to be concerned and to take every measure possible to ensure the transparency of the election process and re-sults. Part of transparency is admitting when you are under attack—and admitting that you failed to stop it in time. Humility is vital to integrity, and integrity is vital to a functioning democracy.

Instead, the Democrats doubled down on the claim that elections cannot be rigged and found themselves backed into a corner when Trump was proclaimed the winner of a very close race. Trump's surprise wins were in Pennsylvania, Wisconsin, and Michigan, three states that Manafort had deemed "battleground states." Manafort had shared data about these states with operatives for the Kremlin, which had by that time penetrated voter databases in all fifty states.[11,12] The official US government line is that Russians had penetrated voting equipment and had the capacity to change votes, but decided not to do so for reasons that were never explained. Four days before the election, Manafort, who had been lying low since he fell under federal investigation for criminal activity in Ukraine that summer, emerged on Twitter to boast that his "battleground states" would flip for Trump.[13] By proclaiming that the integrity of the election was unassailable, Clinton and other Democrats made it impossible to challenge the validity of the results without seeming like hypocrites or sore losers.

Other institutional actors—intelligence agencies, the Obama administration, Congress—also would not say if the election was illegitimate, for that would require admitting that they had allowed an unparalleled national security crisis to fester. It would mean acknowledging that despite ample warnings and vast evidence of criminality in the public domain, the US government had failed to protect its people in the most essential way. It would entail conceding that US institutions were compromised, just not in the way Trump's team had claimed. Telling the truth would mean inverting Trump's narrative, and because Trump's preemptive narrative inversion was effective, they knew they would either not be believed or would be challenged, rightly, on why they failed to stop the attack.

Preemptive narrative inversion combined with an implicit threat of violence—*"The Democrats are stealing the election; we must stop the steal!"*—led to the forfeiture of vital inquiry. We do not know who actually won the very close 2016 election. Maybe it was Trump after all. But we do know that all Americans deserve irregularities to be examined, and that they were not—because they reveal the institutional weaknesses and arrogance of the establishment. The behavior of establishment actors is easy to predict, and therefore, easy to exploit. The Democrats' obsession with optics was advantageous to their enemies: they could not see the threat coming because they were afraid of how it would make them look.

But in 2017, it became harder to turn away from the truth, in part because the guilty parties kept confessing it. In May, former FBI director Robert Mueller was appointed to investigate possible Trump administration criminality after Trump fired FBI director James Comey, confessed to obstruction of justice on television to NBC anchor Lester Holt, and celebrated Comey's firing with Kremlin officials in the Oval Office.[14] By the end of 2017, Mueller had indicted two key players in the 2016 campaign operation, Manafort and Flynn. Another operative, Stone, was under investigation for a multitude of offenses. Neither Manafort nor Flynn were indicted for illicit activity in the 2016 election. Instead, Manafort was indicted in October 2017 for conspiracy against the United States, tax fraud, and money laundering that he had committed throughout the 2000s—the period when Mueller was head of the FBI and did not stop Manafort's globe-trotting crime spree.

Flynn pled guilty in December 2017 to lying to the FBI about his contacts with Russian officials and agreed, at the time, to cooperate with the Mueller probe. Manafort later made his own plea deal with Mueller and broke it, continuing to commit crimes from prison. Flynn then broke his plea deal as well. This was a pragmatic calculus on their part, the kind you would make if you were a mobster and your don became your judge and jury. The gamble paid off: Flynn, Stone, and Manafort were pardoned by Trump in 2020.

Both during the 2016 campaign and during his first six months in office, Trump's fealty to the Kremlin was treated as an absurd conspiracy theory by much of the media—something cooked up by the Democrats to justify his win. Trump insisted he had "nothing to do with Russia" even as decades of evidence in the public domain proved otherwise.[15] Trump's thirty-year relationship with oligarchs from the former USSR who rebuilt his properties after his early-1990s bankruptcies; his selection of foreign agent Manafort as his campaign chair; his decades of ties to organized crime and, in particular, to mobsters who lived in Trump Tower after fleeing the Soviet Union in the 1980s; his public praise of Putin and solicitation for Kremlin assistance during his presidential run; and countless other incriminating examples were initially played down or presented as disparate from the story unfolding in plain sight.

By the fall of 2017, even more direct evidence was in the public domain: emails between Trump's lawyer Michael Cohen and Trump's former business partner Felix Sater, childhood friends who were both longtime associates of the Russian mafia, discussing how they planned to rig the election for Trump with the help of "all of Putin's team";[16] Donald Trump Jr.'s July 2017 tweets about a June 2016 Trump Tower campaign meetup with Kremlin spies and oligarchs; the attendance of numerous Russian oligarchs at Trump's inauguration, which was in itself a swindle run by Tom Barrack, who was later indicted for being a secret operative for the United Arab Emirates;[17] the Trump team's transformation of the Republican platform to match Kremlin goals; and so on.

It had become impossible for even the most die-hard denialists to buy Trump's claims that he had "nothing to do with Russia" or that he was a political neophyte surrounded by fellow wide-eyed naïfs who had all coincidentally participated in white-collar crime schemes and illicit international activity for decades. Since 2017, over a dozen Trump campaign managers and administration officials have been indicted for offenses ranging from conspiracy to child rape to fraud and beyond. If I were to list them here, along with the offenses for which they were never charged, this book would be the length of an encyclopedia. The indictments of Manafort and Flynn were the first signs that there may finally be accountability for an obvious crisis: the Trump administration was a transnational crime syndicate masquerading as a government.

Manafort's and Flynn's indictments and plea deals, respectively, coincided with the resignation of Harvey Weinstein from his executive role at Miramax Studios and the rise of the 'me too.' movement. Investigations into Weinstein revealed that he was not only a sexual predator but an employer of the Israeli mercenary firm Black Cube, and that Black Cube was part of a broader transnational operation designed to prevent damning information about the rich and powerful from circulating.[18] One of the key players in the "catch and kill" operation was David Pecker, the CEO of A360 Media, LLC, parent company of the *National Enquirer*, the supermarket tabloid that not only paid hush money to suppress stories about powerful predators (among them Trump) but also pioneered the practice of burying serious crimes in outlandish scandal. Pecker was the inheritor of a long tradition of tabloids being prized possessions of dangerous and powerful actors—the paper that became the *Enquirer* was started by Generoso Pope Jr., a CIA-trained operative and lifelong friend of Roy Cohn who was funded by mafiosos like Frank Costello.[19]

In 2017, the exposure of not only elite crime but the mechanisms of coverup revived attention on the buried Jeffrey Epstein case in online discourse, if not yet in formal investigation. This was enormously threatening to the global elite. The world of Epstein and Maxwell, after all, is where all these stories collide.

And so, on October 28, 2017, an anonymous post appeared on the troll-magnet bulletin board 4chan stating that Hillary Clinton was about to be arrested for her role in a global child trafficking operation serving elite pedophiles, and that these traffickers were going to be stopped by the heroic Donald Trump and his anti-crime crusaders. The poster claimed to be a government insider with the highest-level security clearance. He proclaimed that a "great awakening" was coming, and that officials from past Democratic administrations, as well as their foreign funders, like billionaire George Soros, would be held accountable for horrific offenses.

The 4chan poster did not have a name. He was known as Q, and the fervent followers of his posts became known as QAnon.

The QAnon movement is the pinnacle of preemptive narrative inversion. Q's posts flipped the script on what had already been established but what politicians and pundits were reluctant to bluntly state: Trump had spent his entire life surrounded by criminal operatives, shady foreign backers, and wealthy pedophiles—categories that often overlapped. Among the wealthy pedophiles whose company Trump voluntarily sought out were Epstein and Maxwell; modeling agent John Casablancas, for whose company Trump sent Ivanka, a teenager at the time, to work; UAE lobbyist and convicted child trafficker George Nader; oligarch Tevfik Arif, who worked alongside Trump and Sater in the suspected money-laundering operation Bayrock Group and who was acquitted of child trafficking charges despite significant evidence; and allegedly Alan Dershowitz (who denies all accusations) and Roy Cohn.[20]

QAnon was a successful early propaganda intervention. It redirected anyone appalled by evidence of elite criminal impunity into a movement that promoted Trump as an arbiter of justice and a protector of the vulnerable, in particular, children. It reassured Trump fans who were concerned about Flynn's and Manafort's arrests that there was a secret plan to save them and to protect Trump. It offset Trump's role as the leader of the establishment—he was the president, after all—by presenting an alternative deep state that countered the actual military-industrial complex that the kleptocratic Trump family and their inner circle were exploiting for their own gain. And it played out online using the tactics of soap operas and spy novels, encouraging average Americans burnt by the hellfire of institutional corruption to probe into the ashes.

Institutional corruption was exactly what criminal elites did not want investigated, but they understood where curiosity would lead, and preempted it accordingly. America's first reality TV president got a brand-new storyline.

As an exemplar of the "rogue" deep state, Q was expected to remain anonymous. There have been a number of individuals since identified as the source of the posts, but for the sake of narrative appeal in 2017 and 2018, anonymity was more important than authorship. The idea that the most reliable government sources were anonymous had become ingrained in American political mythology since Deep Throat became a Watergate icon. It gained further traction in the 2010s with the rise of Wikileaks, whose method of theft and release of classified documents made even dull bureaucratic missives seem salacious. This faith in anonymity did not exist in a vacuum: the grassroots success of both Wikileaks and QAnon was a response to a media that had, for decades, refused to challenge power or expose government crimes—for example, the fraudulent war in Iraq, the use of torture, and yes, child trafficking—before the public paid the price.

It was no surprise that Americans would search for the truth and also not be able to decipher what they found. It was no surprise that the savvy architects surrounding the QAnon phenomenon—who included Trump, Flynn, and Stone—knew how to exploit this longing for clarity and cheapen the very search for meaning in the process.

As time went on, QAnon became more expansive in its mythology, more cryptic in its missives, and more diverse in its adherents. The posts that "Q" dropped were vague and enticing, encouraging scrutiny but ultimately demanding trust in Q above all. As with Pizzagate, adherents were urged to look for secret clues in public places: a misspelling in a Trump tweet, a background image in a photo, the use of numbers or symbols that seemed to imply a malevolent meaning, sometimes linked to Satanism. But when a participant in a QAnon conversation would bring up a similar reference about someone in the Trump fold—say, Jared Kushner's record-setting purchase of 666 Fifth Avenue, for example, or the fact that all of Black Cube's international phone numbers ended in 666—they would be dismissed. The QAnon slogan—"Where we go one, we go all"—was a call not only for solidarity but for submission. QAnon exploited valid fears about deep corruption in powerful institutions and attempted to cut off critical inquiry through ostracism of those who refused to trust the plan.

Early 2018 was a period where the mainstream media regularly covered the criminality of the Trump administration, in part because the initial indictments of the Mueller probe led the media to believe they would be looking at a Watergate-style collapse. That the Mueller investigation was in fact plodding and superficial given the depth of the criminality at play was largely lost on journalists and the general public, but the media saturation nonetheless prompted Q to ramp up its parallel narrative. Arrests were imminent, QAnon commentators insisted, secret saviors were working behind the scenes. QAnon, like Mueller mania, stoked a culture of complacency more than a culture of conspiracy.

The most effective propaganda has a core grain of truth, and the truth buried in the morass of QAnon was the participation of wealthy power brokers in child trafficking and the coverup of this crime by complicit parties in government and media. Here the truth becomes all the more powerful because of the refusal of many in government and media to acknowledge abuse and trauma. Citizens who were frightened and rightfully angry about elite criminality were told to have endless patience with the very bureaucracy that had carried out the crimes. That this tactic worked so effectively on both those who opposed Trump and those who admired him speaks to the depth of fear and the impulse, still, to embrace authority. The aggrieved could be appeased because so much of their grievance was rooted in a sense of abandonment—pain that was real and easily exploited. The two movements became a Janus head of aggressive passivity, their demands for compliance masked as critique. *Probe institutional rot, but only in our sanctioned way; trust no one, except for the sources we demand that you trust.*

Both Mueller acolytes and QAnon followers were accused of being conspiracy theorists, but that is an insult to anyone who tries in a serious way to solve a conspiracy. The danger of these online movements was not their examination of conspiracy, but their encouragement of conformity. What they were later asked to embrace—for QAnon, violence in the name of Trump and his causes; for Mueller acolytes, unyielding faith in a Department of Justice that protects corrupt and violent actors—set the movements far apart in terms of their tactics. But in the end, their senseless devotion benefited the same people: elite criminals and the system that protects them.

In spring 2018, the loosely assembled QAnon community began to focus increasingly on the Epstein and Maxwell case. This was months before the *Miami Herald*'s exposés prompted a revival of interest from both mainstream outlets and the courts. QAnon's narrative focus remained on the Clintons and the Democrats, but now included broad allegations of cannibalism and ritual sacrifice, both of which had been alluded to years before in the Pizzagate myth. It also incorporated specific outlandish claims, like that John F. Kennedy Jr. had not really died in a 1999 plane crash but had been living undercover for decades, helping Q divulge state secrets and rooting for Trump to avenge the death of his murdered relatives. In 2020, Vincent Fusca, a Pittsburgh financial services manager, was identified by some QAnon adherents as JFK Jr. in disguise. He was touted as a potential vice president for Trump, an act that went too far for many QAnon acolytes.[21] But the combination of Camelot nostalgia, old-school Kennedy assassination spit-balling, and abject absurdity did what leaders of QAnon needed it to do: attract confused baby boomers and spur media scorn. This is the quicksand in which one can bury a crime.

The main crime they sought to bury was, of course, the Epstein and Maxwell operation, because it implicated such a broad array of powerful players. The moment of triumph for QAnon—the moment at which this whole narrative nightmare could have maybe been turned around—came in the summer of 2019, when Epstein was arrested and allegedly committed suicide.

Because mainstream outlets and politicians had ignored the case while QAnon covered it, the wild circumstances of Epstein's demise coupled with the grim revelations that followed gave QAnon a sudden veneer of legitimacy. Here was a fringe movement with a reputation for lies and innuendo detailing a criminal conspiracy with more accuracy and depth than the professionals who were being paid to solve it. That QAnon was proven correct about Epstein—and the enabling of Epstein's crimes by elites—prompted spectators to question whether other improbable claims QAnon had made might be true after all.

That many of QAnon's claims were nonsensical or libelous led social scientists, politicians, and journalists to declare it the nexus of a "disinformation crisis." This is not entirely wrong, but putting the onus on QAnon is like scraping sediment off a rotting corpse and calling it clean. QAnon was a *reactive* movement, both in the manipulative intent of its organizers and in the organic disillusionment of its adherents. The solution to the disinformation crisis was not to merely debunk the lies of QAnon, but to debunk the lies of the government that spawned them. The best way to counter the QAnon cult is to be brutally honest about deep institutional corruption—in particular, child trafficking and blackmail by criminal elites, which is exemplified by but not limited to Epstein's operation. Regaining public trust in institutions necessitates a thorough and transparent inquiry into these operations and how they shape policy.

Such an investigation would never have been instigated by Bill Barr or by Trump, given their personal connections to the case. In 2021, the investigation into Epstein was overseen by Southern District of New York attorney Maurene Comey, the daughter of James Comey, the former FBI head who refused to indict Epstein during his tenure or move against other members of his network.[22] Epstein had also been let off the hook by Manhattan District Attorney Cyrus Vance Jr., who in 2011 ensured that Epstein's sex offender status was the lowest possible, to the horror of other legal officials.[23] The decision was not an outlier: Vance, the son of Jimmy Carter administration Secretary of State Cyrus Vance, also refused to prosecute Donald Jr. and Ivanka Trump for financial crimes in 2012 and Harvey Weinstein for his sex crimes, despite an abundance of evidence.

This is not a justice system. It is a protective ring for predators, a dark circle of nepotism in which elite criminal impunity nests and thrives.

That said, there is a difference between expecting corruption and accepting it. There was no reason that the Epstein case should not have been pursued, especially given that the methods used to suppress it are so predictable that officials should have anticipated working around them. It could have been pursued by officials working in good conscience (assuming there are some) and treated seriously as not only a moral horror, but a national security threat. The refusal of officials to pursue it for decades on end—their utter disregard for accountability, their determination to remove the possibility of justice from the American imagination—set the stage for further acts of elite brutality. The hands-off approach also was an ominous indicator of collusion. They all were in on it—the cover-up, if not the crimes. A case that should have been pursued with rigor by agents of the law was instead chased by citizens gripped by fury.

In August 2019, one week before Epstein was declared dead, the FBI labeled QAnon a domestic terrorism threat.[24] When describing the individuals in QAnon who make threats or facilitate acts of violence, this characterization is appropriate, and it became more accurate over time as many adherents embraced Trump's coup attempts. (The FBI also embraced Trump's coup attempts, but we'll get to that later.) By the fall of 2020, QAnon had become a topic of mainstream conversation, thanks in part to the willingness of its acolytes to publicly gather at the height of a pandemic that they did not believe was real. Their leap from online to on-the-ground action was irresistible to reporters seeking sensational imagery during lockdown and eager to showcase their own rationality.

There is a template to how QAnon is described in the mainstream media (excluding the more nuanced descriptions from journalists who tracked the movement from the start), and it goes like this: "QAnon followers believe that the world is run by a secret cabal of Satan-worshipping Democrats and Hollywood celebrities who are engaged in wide-scale child trafficking, pedophilia, and cannibalism. Despite there being no evidence to support any of the claims, the visibility of the movement has surged."[25] This is from a September 2020 podcast on QAnon from *The Guardian*, but it could be from any mainstream outlet due to its trademark use of absolutes. There is *no* evidence for *any* of the claims, says *The Guardian*, much as Politico writes that QAnon is *entirely* fictitious,[26] much as Buzzfeed asserts that QAnon is *baseless* and *evidence-free*.[27]

But it's not. There are decades of evidence for specific claims, and no evidence for other claims, and that is why QAnon is such an effective propaganda apparatus, and such a tragic one. We would be living in a safer world if QAnon were operating on pure invention instead of alternating between exposing real crimes and mixing the details of real crimes with fabricated stories or manipulative embellishments. Instead, we live in the world of Epstein, Maxwell, Spence, Cohn, and other documented predators who infiltrated the highest echelons of power, whose lives and deaths remain mysteries and whose victims pay the greatest price. Everything about QAnon is an indictment of a broken criminal justice system that not only refuses to indict a criminal elite but sometimes joins them in the crimes.

To an extent, the tendency of the press to make sweeping condemnations of QAnon is understandable: Who would want to seem like they are siding with a group making defamatory claims of devil-worship and human sacrifice, especially when those allegations have led to threats to innocent people? But conversely, who would want to side with the powerful actors whose undeniable acts of evil get ignored when QAnon's claims are dismissed wholesale? For that is what happens when the media is quick to apply a pejorative label of "conspiracy theory" to an actual conspiracy instead of parsing and analyzing the claims at hand.

There is a flip side to dropping a grain of truth in a morass of lies. On the one hand, people will believe all sorts of ridiculous things when you get one big thing right. On the other, that key revelation will be dismissed as fake due to the terrible reputation of those who helped expose it. As a result, crimes that were painstakingly uncovered will continue to go unpunished, and the greatest beneficiaries will be the criminals, who coast on shattered trust and ruined reputations.

What begins as preemptive narrative inversion turns into silence through social stigma. Much as those who raised the specter of Epstein in 2017 were dismissed as "crazy Pizzagate people," those who discuss criminal conspiracies and institutional cover-ups today are accused of sounding like QAnon. This is very useful to the criminal elite whom QAnon claims to despise. QAnon is a propaganda operation and QAnon is a cult.

But above all, QAnon is an alibi.

In Springfield, Illinois, there is a bookstore called Prairie Archives that I visit when I drive from St. Louis to Chicago and need a break from the farms and factories and the fervent rhyming ode to guns planted in a series of signs stretching along a soybean field next to the highway. Prairie Archives is down the street from the tomb of Abraham Lincoln, Springfield's most famous resident. In 1838, a twenty-eight-year-old Lincoln stood in Springfield's town square and proclaimed of the United States: "At what point then is the approach of danger to be expected? I answer, if it ever reach us, it must spring up amongst us. It cannot come from abroad. If destruction be our lot, we must ourselves be its author and finisher. As a nation of free men we will live forever or die by suicide."[28]

Lincoln had been inspired to make the speech after a white mob in St. Louis set a Black man on fire and cheered as they watched him die. It is heady country between St. Louis and Springfield, weighted with the worst of history, and the drive makes me want to explore and to disappear.

I like Prairie Archives because I know I will find something weird, and I don't know what it will be, but I know it will be weird in a way that is different than what I find online: spontaneous, serendipitous. There is no algorithm to guide me, no data to mine. It is only me and aisle upon aisle of used books and magazines and maps. I am of the last generation to have spent their youth in the analog age, and Prairie Archives reminds me of childhood memories when information was very hard to find. Now and then I try to explain this era to my children and they recoil with incomprehension. Not only did I lack instant gratification, I often had no gratification at all. I would wonder about things for years and never find the answers. I was a useless repository of botched song lyrics, dubious political trivia, history filled with holes. I hoped that someday I would stumble upon the information I sought, like people had done for centuries before me. I knew that if I did find what I was looking for, it would likely be through luck and not will. After all, it wasn't like I could just google it.

Then, when I was sixteen, I got the internet, and the way my memory worked changed forever. I am of the last generation to remember the memory we lost.

In July of the year of our plague 2021, I bought a 1976 copy of the magazine *UFO Report* at Prairie Archives, because why not? The Pentagon had just announced that UFOs were real and that it had long had a secret division studying them,[29] an insane development that got lost in the fires and floods and freezes and mass death that dominated the rest of the year. I wanted to know what the type of people who read *UFO Report* during a bicentennial year were thinking about during those glory days of anomalous American accountability. The Pentagon Papers, the Watergate hearings, the Pike Committee, the Church Committee. Richard Nixon's farewell helicopter fading into the sky. Those were boom times for patriotic paranoiacs, and I had been born too late. As a teenager, I fantasized about the mid-1970s like others my age did about Woodstock, before my generation got its own Woodstock in 1999 and burned it down with peace candles.

I sat on a bench down the street from Lincoln's corpse and started reading *UFO Report*. On the first page, an advertisement screamed: YOU ARE NOT BEING TOLD THE TRUTH ABOUT THE FUTURE! This was intriguing to me as a resident of the future, so I kept going. "The United States Government has been and is now involved in an unbelievable 'Cosmic Watergate'! The U.S. government, controlled by a small group in this country, certain exiles, fugitives, and foreign world manipulators, is involved in a neo-Nazism conspiracy that threatens to control the economy and the people of the world. YOUR FUTURE IS IN DANGER AND YOU SHOULD KNOW THE TRUTH!"

Well, shit, I thought, *that sounds like my books*. I comforted myself with the fact that my books did not (yet?) feature a picture of a four-headed monster with the caption REVELATION 666: BEAST . . . FROM THE SEA!

The advertisement listed the topics into which I would gain insight should I be willing to shell out $6.95 for an eight-track recording. I would learn the truth about the assassinations of the Kennedys and Martin Luther King, impending environmental disasters including "a terrible warning for New Orleans," the mafia, the Rockefellers, Charles Manson, Richard Nixon, a "crushing economic depression," the Vatican, and UFOs, which perhaps held all of this together, though it was not explained how. I was mildly unnerved that the subjects in this wild-eyed ad had either manifested as true threats or still contained incredible cultural currency. In 2019, journalist Tom O'Neill published his comprehensive exposé of the Manson murders, *Chaos*, a book that took him over twenty years to complete because as he researched what he thought was an isolated crime, he discovered ties between the Kennedy assassinations, CIA mind-control experiments, the FBI, the LAPD, and Charles Manson.

"My work had left me, at various points, broke, depressed, and terrified that I was becoming one of 'those people': an obsessive, a conspiracy theorist, a lunatic," O'Neill wrote. "I don't consider myself credulous, but I'd discovered things I thought impossible about the Manson murders and California in the 1960s—things that reek of duplicity and cover-up, implicating police departments up and down the state. Plus, the courts. Plus—though I have to take a deep breath before I let myself say it—the CIA."[30]

I knew that feeling well. O'Neill was writing a book he did not want to write, telling truths he did not want to believe, asking questions he was not sure he wanted answered. It went beyond worrying about being seen as "one of those people"—the type of person, for example, who puts an ad in a 1976 issue of *UFO Report*, or the type of person who reads it forty-five years later. It was the anguish of witnessing evil and knowing that others would not believe you, and that the people most likely to believe you were the ones responsible for the evil.

There are grifters and liars and fantasists immersed in conspiracy culture, but there are also many people who simply refuse to surrender their conscience or curiosity to a social imperative to look the other way. There are people who want to destroy institutions for sheer love of chaos, and there are people who simply want the façade of institutional integrity to end, who long for institutions to give the people the protection of law they are promised. There are people who expect officials to keep their word and are startled when others abandon that expectation to cynicism instead of translating it into demands.

Some people immersed in conspiracy culture go on to do terrible things, like target strangers with incendiary rumors or threaten passersby with violence or storm the US Capitol wearing matching T-shirts that say "January 6: Civil War." Their conviction does not cancel out their crimes. Their more benign brethren are pilloried as pawns: Everyone wants an easy villain when the big targets seem unreachable. But it is striking how many people who pride themselves on rationality are willing to exist in what seems to me an alternate universe: a regular and reasonable realm, inverse to observable reality, a world of protocol and norms and social contracts. These slippery and ephemeral forces seem tailored for fools: you cannot hold a norm, you can slither around a protocol, and you need trust to cement a social contract—and trust must be earned, not given away based on the social status of the recipient. The inhabitants of this universe are the people suffering under "normalcy bias," and I discuss them in the next chapter.

But I cannot look down on my fellow occupants of the twenty-first-century fever dream—the people who reject the false façade of law and order, no matter how inane their other beliefs. I obviously cannot look up to them either. I do not feel that I am better than anyone else, or beneath anyone else, but that I am simply myself, existing in my own haunted vortex. I believe in responsibility, but I also believe in redemption, and it's hard for me to condemn people who got lost in the same funhouse mirror I got dropped into and came out with different memories of distorted reflections. Like Shirley Jackson said, no live organism can continue to exist sanely under conditions of absolute reality, and absolute reality has never been so abundant or abhorrent. They got it right in the 1970s: it's one big Cosmic Watergate, man.

5

SAVIOR SYNDROME AND NORMALCY BIAS

There's not much left in the way of life and love and possibilities for these shortchanged children of the '80s.
—Hunter S. Thompson, "The Trickle Down Theory," 1987

There are times I think I imagined it: the magazine covers, the TV news reports, the everyday talk about the end of the world and how to stop it. They are memories of late-1980s crises—crises that were either overstated in their time or handled better in later decades. These elementary school memories, like my D.A.R.E. guide to using drugs or the dirge-like recitation of my teachers that sex equals AIDS equals death, are faded. Sometimes I wonder if I made them up. Maybe my nostalgia for the future is so all-encompassing that I have retconned my childhood to include a country of competent and concerned adults.

But little things come back to me. My babysitter abandoning the aerosol hairspray she used to propel her bangs to the sky because the sky now had a hole in the ozone layer. The discontinuation of the greatest sandwich to grace the menu at McDonald's, the McDLT, due to its polystyrene container. The supermarket installing a recycling machine where I would deposit my dad's empty Coors Light cans in exchange for precious nickels. President George H. W. Bush proclaiming that "Every day is Earth Day" and Americans believing he meant it. Doing projects from the bestselling book *50 Simple Things Kids Can Do to Save the Earth* in a run-down public school filled with people who were not particularly environmentally conscious, but that did not matter, because the concern was mainstream. Everyone was in favor of saving the earth: scientists, teachers, gang members, Republicans. What kind of self-destructive sadist would oppose it? It was obvious that the earth was in trouble: acid rain scorched the landscape, rainforests were vanishing, cities were smothered in smog, *Exxon Valdez* oil filled the seas. The crisis was so basic a child could understand it, and so they taught children to care.

The crisis had a timeline, and the timeline was my life. The timeline was laid out like the "Choose Your Own Adventure" books I had devoured as a child, where stories ended in varying levels of triumph or doom depending on what decisions were made, and I was told we were well on the road to triumph. In the late 1980s, children were not only told that society had to act now, but assured that adults *were* acting now. This was not entirely false. In 1988, according to a Gallup poll, the environment was the number one concern of the voting public. Membership in environmental organizations was skyrocketing, and Gallup predicted that the 1992 presidential candidates' stances on climate could determine the winner of the 1992 election.[1] They did not—the Gulf War and a recession intervened—but they were a factor, with vice presidential candidate Al Gore hailed for his embrace of environmentalism. Solar-powered homes, electric cars, clean air—these were the promised inevitabilities of my future, a future sealed as neatly as the ozone layer, which closed up at a point that I do not remember, because by then people had stopped caring. Not all people, not scientists, but people deemed important enough to be put on television to claim there were "two sides" to climate change.

The two sides were still triumph and doom, but the media did not present them that way. An existential threat was framed as an existential argument. *Was global warming real?* pundits implored. *After all, it's cold today. Let's hear both sides!* Scientists frantically tried to inject a new term—climate change—only to get the same reaction. *Is climate change really real? After all, it's the same temperature today as it was yesterday. Let's hear both sides!* The conversation was a suicidal fever dream, a post-9/11 embrace of death masked as defiance. If the so-called unimaginable had happened—America attacked on its own soil—then the rules of logic had to be obliterated in favor of rejecting more bad news. Reality TV, bubble economies, truthiness: the twenty-first century operated on illusion, and the greatest illusion was that we still had time.

"It is a human tendency to cling to the belief that the natural environment or climate to which we have become accustomed will remain more or less the same from year to year and from decade to decade," began a February 1978 *Bulletin of Atomic Scientists* report detailing what was in store for earth unless humanity changed course: rising temperatures from carbon dioxide, melting ice caps, devastating effects on agriculture.[2] My mother was pregnant with me when this article was published. Twenty-eight years later, I was pregnant with my own daughter when I watched Al Gore's 2006 climate documentary *An Inconvenient Truth*, which addressed many of the same problems as well as new crises that had risen in the interim due to the refusal of politicians and corporations to stave off the problems documented in 1978.

Sometimes I imagine what unheeded alarms will be ringing if my own daughter has a baby at age twenty-eight, like my mother and I both did, but then I remember there will be no hypotheticals by 2035. There will be fires and floods and loss and grief, but no hypotheticals. That disaster looms is certain. To what extent is, literally and figuratively, a matter of degrees.

In 1816, a volcano erupted in Indonesia, creating what would become known as "The Year Without a Summer." The global temperature dropped half a degree Celsius, causing a global food shortage, the indirect deaths of millions, and, in Europe, unprecedented summer precipitation and cold.[3] This abrupt, mysterious climate transformation also birthed the modern horror genre. In Switzerland, English writers Mary

Godwin, Percy Bysshe Shelley (Godwin's fiancé), Lord Byron, and John William Polidori took refuge from the relentless rain in a friend's villa. They staved off boredom by challenging each other to write the scariest story they could. Mary Godwin—later Mary Shelley—invented Frankenstein. Byron wrote "Fragment of a Novel," one of the first English-language vampire stories, which in turn prompted Polidori to write "The Vampyre," a direct inspiration for Bram Stoker's *Dracula*.

All of their stories revolved around the untrustworthiness of human beings—our ability to hide horrific acts under a veneer of respectability and trick society into believing situations are more stable than they seem. "I saw the pale student of unhallowed arts kneeling beside the thing he had put together," wrote Mary Shelley, explaining the visions that plagued her that summer. "I saw the hideous phantasm of a man stretched out, and then, on the working of some powerful engine, show signs of life, and stir with an uneasy, half vital motion. Frightful must it be; for supremely frightful would be the effect of any human endeavor to mock the stupendous mechanism of the Creator of the world."[4]

In 1981, ExxonMobil, the largest oil company in the world, composed some fiction of its own. The story was that the toxins it released into the world were harmless and that anyone claiming otherwise was a liar. Its story, like that of Mary Shelley and the other horror writers, was inspired by climate events in Indonesia. "Exxon first got interested in climate change in 1981 because it was seeking to develop the Natuna gas field off Indonesia,"[5] wrote Exxon in-house scientist Lenny Bernstein in a 2014 email leaked to the public in 2015. Exxon knew that developing the Natuna site would cause and accelerate permanent damage to the earth.

"Whatever their public stance, internally they make very careful assessments of the potential for regulation, including the scientific basis for those regulations," wrote Bernstein. "Exxon NEVER denied the potential for humans to impact the climate system. It did question—legitimately, in my opinion—the validity of some of the science."

Perversely, Bernstein's email confessional, which stood in stark contrast to Exxon's public stance of climate change denial that it used to justify its role in environmental devastation, was intended to *defend* Exxon. He saw those who helped Exxon spin its narrative of lies as pitiable victims, arguing that the billionaire hard right-wing ideologues the Koch brothers were mere scapegoats of the press and that Saudi Arabia lobbyist Donald Pearlman may have helped destroy the planet, but should be remembered first and foremost for helping fund a Holocaust memorial museum. Bernstein was one of many unrepentant flacks employed by Exxon to keep the confirmation of climate catastrophe a secret. Over four decades, Exxon paid millions of dollars to over one hundred prominent lobbying groups and think tanks that promoted climate change denial.[6]

Climate change denial is a weaponized conspiracy theory. Like most propaganda narratives concerning corruption, it exploits "normalcy bias"—the idea that if a situation is truly dangerous, if massive misdeeds are being committed in plain sight, somebody would intervene and stop them. The absence of accountability and alarm lends credence to the conspirators' claims that no serious crisis is occurring and that those claiming so are doomsayers or conspiracy theorists. This deadly delusion is also a comforting one. Rejecting "normalcy bias" forces you to envision not only a dangerous present, but a stolen future. The natural instinct of human beings to envision the environment as unchanging, as described by the *Bulletin of Atomic Scientists* in 1978, is tied to hopes for younger generations and the idea that we exist in a continuum, that someday people will look back in time and analyze us like we have our forebearers. To accept the conclusions of climate scientists means to not only contemplate the loss of the future, but the annihilation of the past through the extinction of memory.

There is a kinship, nowadays, between the climate scientists and the epidemiologists and the scholars of authoritarian states. The people who research worst-case scenarios are stuck breaking bad news while protectors of profit margins and purveyors of institutionalist mythologies market false assurances. The latter remain successful not in spite of the evidence, but *to* spite the evidence. They'll throw down an alternate route to a dead end and call it freedom, and people will follow.

For this is no longer a crisis of evidence: the evidence is in our blood and in our air and in our government. The crisis is the lure of a road that disregards where the evidence leads. It is the belief that somehow everything will work out on its own, because we could not have possibly gotten to a place where so many severe cataclysms intersect and feed off each other at once. It is belief in the ultimate conspiracy theory: that an invisible beneficent force operates behind the scenes, but it's not God, it's *man*, it's suddenly efficient bureaucracy, suddenly benevolent corporations, a reverse Frankenstein, a vampire staking itself. It's believing you can end a horror story by closing the book.

There is no satisfaction in saying "I told you so" during a crisis. All that means is that people who could have mitigated disaster chose not to do so and people got hurt. It means the old warning has expired and been replaced with another, one even more grim due to the avoidance of the initial prediction. The unheeded warning now acts as a clarion call, but to the person issuing it, it still feels like screaming into an abyss: echo and distortion and an urge to jump inside, to lose yourself in the nothingness, in the not-knowing.

One devastating impact of climate change is the seeming futility of a leap of faith, because a leap of faith depends on a guarantee of time. The consolation to not having an immediate impact in one's work used to be the promise of posterity—but what is posterity when the future is stolen? You cannot leap into a void. But that is what is required to survive the present. There is reprieve in the void, there is relief in that which cannot be quantified: love, imagination, integrity, and, especially, mystery.

Mysteries are different from secrets. A secret is man-made. When connected to government and corporations, a secret is a weapon that can be wielded in the pursuit of power, hoarded and hidden for nefarious aims. A mystery is open territory that can be explored by anyone, with unpredictable results. This distinction is similar to the difference between conspiracy and conspiracy theories. A conspiracy is a secret plot whose existence is denied by the conspirators. A conspiracy theory is, at best, the open exploration of a mystery, without necessarily expecting resolution but insisting on the pursuit of truth. At worst it is its own opposite: a method to undermine science and facts. To value mystery is not to deny science or facts, but to free your mind from the confinement of institutionalism and authority.

Conspiracies succeed in part because many of the conspirators' potential opponents are easily corralled by societal pressures. Opponents are anyone with enough expertise to parse the conspiracy, but we live in a society where status and power more than actual knowledge determine who is considered an "expert" worthy of promotion.

Experts gain status and power through their willingness to conform to rigid and rarefied social rules, even in supposedly intellectual fields like academia and media. The stigma of "conspiracy theorist" is so strong that it prompts experts to operate on the defensive instead of examining a conspirator's motives—because that examination could be seen as "conspiracy theorizing" in itself. Therefore, the potential opponent becomes bogged down in refuting the conspirators' lies. The time wasted on basic refutation—seen in recent years as epidemiologists, scientists, and scholars of autocracy battle not only propaganda of the conspirators but the toxic positivity of "reasonable" people who dismiss expertise as doomsaying—stifles the creativity that could lead to a real way out of these crises.

In 1944, the philosopher Carl Jung wrote a series of essays drawing a distinction between mystery and secrets. Like the nineteenth-century horror writers from the Year Without a Summer, he worked from inside a home in Switzerland, barricading himself from the outside world. "Mystification can be pure bluff for the obvious purpose of exploiting the credulous," he wrote in *Psychology and Alchemy*, describing a process of manipulation similar to the weaponized conspiracy theories employed by propagandists today. "There are a great many fraudulent publications written by charlatans. But mystification can also arise from another source. The real mystery does not behave mysteriously or secretively; it speaks a secret language, it adumbrates itself by a variety of images which all indicate its true nature. I am not speaking of a secret personally guarded by someone, with a content known to its possessor, but of a mystery, a matter of circumstance which is 'secret,' i.e. known only through vague hints but essentially unknown."[7]

Jung lived, like we do, in a momentous time. He wrote *Psychology and Alchemy* at the height of World War II, when there was no indication of victory on the horizon, and the war had fulfilled premonitions of destruction he had made decades before, the confirmation of which only caused him agony. The word "momentous" suggests a moment so meaningful that it encompasses an era, in contrast to the fleetingness of "momentary." Today, the reliable catastrophe of climate change has altered the concept of time and the momentous.

We are in store for both permanent chaos and the erosion of what a momentous event means. "Once in a century" weather events now happen regularly. Disasters and death tolls that once would have lingered in the public consciousness are quickly replaced by new atrocities, blurring together much like mass shootings now do in the United States. This is dangerous, not only for its inherent tragedy but also for the dehumanization it inspires. Constant momentous, devastating climate events can lead to the normalization of mass death. The normalization of mass death is a stepping stone to the normalization of mass murder. The climate crisis is a gift to fascism, and it is already being exploited by authoritarian kleptocrats worldwide.

What is predictable is preventable: that is why corporations like Exxon and their political backers worked so hard to tar the experts who saw it coming. We are now at the point of no return, there is no going back. But there are still choices to make about how to move forward and mitigate the damage, and one of those is to be honest about the crisis—to be honest about everything. It means feeling around the edges of the void, grasping at loose ends, and following them back to where they lead, even if it's a place appalling in its familiarity.

It is as important to understand why people believe a lie as it is to find out why the lie was told. In a momentous era, it can take a dark imagination to see the light.

As previously noted, normalcy bias is the belief that if something terrible were to happen, a responsible party would intervene and stop it, and that if no one is intervening, the terrible thing must either not really be happening or must not be as bad as it seems. The framework of "normalcy bias" relies on tacit agreement about who is considered "somebody" and who decides that this "somebody" matters. The status of "somebody" stands in inverse relation to "nobody"—people viewed as so worthless that they need not be identified. But "nobody" is out there, rolling their eyes and clenching their fists as the stratified somebodies declare that all is well.

As I wrote in *Hiding in Plain Sight*, the oft-recited claim that "nobody saw it coming" is an admission of whom the speaker considers to be nobody. In the United States, "nobody" historically included women, immigrants, poor people, and anyone who is not white. People dismissed as nobody are those most likely to be affected by a terrible situation and therefore the most likely to warn about it in advance. "Somebody" is a similarly convoluted category. For centuries, to be somebody in the United States meant to be a wealthy white man or to be treated like one. This idea of "somebody" is baked into the founding of the country, in which only white male landowners were granted the right to vote. White, landowning men who deviated from the establishment were often punished for their efforts: castigated as troublemakers or conspiracy theorists. The goal was to reduce them, at least in their ability to gain institutional support, to the status of "nobody."

"Nobody" is rendered invisible until they become unavoidable, at which point they are deemed a threat to power unless they echo mainstream assertions or are amenable to being used as a prop. If they refuse, the powerful may still designate them as important, but only in the worst of ways: as a threat to society or an enemy of the state. The unrepentant "nobody" turned "somebody" has committed the sin of altering the expectations of the public.

This dynamic continues today. Normalcy bias rests on a narrow view of what is considered normal, one that taps into nostalgia for a free and fair America that never fully existed. Normalcy bias is a self-inflicted wound, one that preemptively silences people who not only can predict catastrophe but have insights on how to prevent it.

In 1856, scientist Eunice Foote attempted to publicize her research showing the link between carbon dioxide emissions and global warming in one of the earliest documentations of the deleterious effect of burning fossil fuels. But because she was a woman, she was unable to present her work at scientific conferences or in journals. As a result, her research was selectively copied by men, misinterpreted, and ignored for a century and a half. The excuse men used at the time to dismiss her work was that she lacked institutional affiliation, which she lacked because of her gender.[8]

In addition to being a scientist, Foote was an activist. She was one of the five female political activists to sign the 1848 Seneca Falls Declaration on women's rights, which they were only able to print because famed Black abolitionist Frederick Douglass offered them the use of his printing press.[9,10] Douglass was born enslaved, defined by United States law as three-fifths of a person. His writing was condemned by bigots but also shunned by some liberal intellectuals of his era because his horrific and accurate portrayal of a country founded on the enslavement of Black people—a country founded on a conspiracy against Black people, with the plotting and propaganda that entails—made white people who fed off the fruits of that conspiracy feel uncomfortable. Douglass started his own paper, *The North Star*, because it was the only way for him to disseminate the truth without compromise.

The battle to be recognized as "somebody" in the United States is rooted in a refusal to let those who deem you "nobody" define you—and then, in some cases, to force them to codify recognition of your humanity in law. Douglass and the Seneca Falls feminists collaborated not in order to get the approval of white, wealthy men, but to no longer need it.

But every gain is tenuous. It is one thing to acquire the means to tell the truth, it is another to get people to believe you, and still another to get people to act. Douglass became renowned as a philosopher and abolitionist yet is now one of many Black intellectuals considered too controversial for some US public schools.[11,12] Foote was reduced to a footnote for over a century, with her work revived in the last decade as victims of the fossil fuel industry began realizing, to their horror, that the first works documenting climate change were published before the Civil War. *Why did nobody warn us?!* the people shriek as they shield their eyes from the fires and the floods and the terror and the blood as the ghostly voice of Nobody whispers: *But we did.*

Everyone has something to gain at the end of the world if they are the ones left standing. Kleptocrats, theocrats, autocrats, plutocrats, technocrats, aristocrats—any kind of *crat* except the unfortunate small-d democrats, the people who value "the power of the people" over pure power itself. Maintaining a democracy requires sacrifice, the Founding Fathers declared. "A republic, if you can keep it," Benjamin Franklin famously said. Destroying democracy also requires sacrifice—the sacrifice of others in the name of greed dressed up as a divine mandate, the slaughter of human beings to protect the wealth and safety of a few, rationalized by denying their humanity. When Native Americans were massacred by settler colonizers or died through diseases caused by European contact, the global temperature dropped by 0.15 degrees Celsius.[13,14] Between 1492 and 1600, 90 percent of North American indigenous people died, about 10 percent of earth's population at the time. The aftermath of this period is known as the Little Ice Age.

There is a hierarchy to depopulation. In 2020, when a pandemic was allowed to rage unchecked by inept or vicious leadership, when corporate profits reached unparalleled heights for the world's wealthiest people,[15] life expectancy plunged in 93 percent of countries, the largest decrease since World War II. The number of people who died of covid in 2021 has exceeded the number in 2020, meaning that life expectancy will further fall worldwide. It would have been possible to vaccinate everyone on earth using the profits earned by the world's ten wealthiest men during the first nine months of the pandemic alone,[16] but these billionaires had no interest in doing that and neither did the politicians who placate them. The victims of the pandemic in the United States have disproportionately been ethnic minorities: Black, Native American, Latino.[17] The victims of the pandemic in the United Kingdom are disproportionately Black or South Asian.[18] The people least likely to have access to vaccines in 2021 live disproportionately in impoverished countries in Africa.[19] As public health journalist Dr. Steven W. Thrasher observes, powerful actors who could have slowed the pandemic's spread chose instead to "manufacture a viral underclass."[20]

We have been here before: not only in the distant past, but in the eternal rerun decade of the 1980s whose players keep returning to infest the political scene. The United States is a gerontocracy devoid of accountability and ridden with selective amnesia, where younger generations discover past offenses only when the same perpetrator strikes again. "Anthony Fauci, you are a murderer. . . . Your refusal to hear the screams of AIDS activists early in the crisis resulted in the deaths of thousands of Queers," wrote gay rights activist Larry Kramer in a scathing 1988 letter, one of many sent to Fauci, then and now the director of the National Institute of Allergy and Infectious Diseases.[21] Kramer forgave Fauci when Fauci eventually admitted the severity of a plague killing gay men and in particular Black gay men,[22] but the key word is *eventually.* The first plague of my lifetime, the AIDS epidemic, raged for years until officials like Fauci were forced to care about the mass death of marginalized people. The second plague, COVID-19, emerged at a time of unparalleled loss of faith in institutions, and the same man was put in charge of curtailing it.

Is there no one *else to oversee this?* I wondered about Fauci, the same way I wondered when Robert Mueller—the FBI head who declined to investigate criminal operatives within Trump's circle—became the special counsel investigating Trump. Mueller was valorized by the media as the consummate lawful G-man, but he went on to let Trump slide too. The institutionalist fallacy—that because someone spends a long time in a powerful bureaucratic position, they become an exemplar of competence instead of an enabler of corruption—appealed to Americans because it offered relief from the frenetic Trump, who had deceptively typecast himself as a political outsider instead of syncretic swamp spawn. In 2019 and 2020, frightened Americans bought prayer candles adorned with pictures of Mueller and Fauci, candles that burned down facts with the smoke of delusion. This is savior syndrome, the accomplice of normalcy bias: the belief that the "somebody" who is supposed to stop the crisis has arrived, when all too often, they are complicit in the crisis or apathetic to its victims.

Just as the pseudo-saviors of the 2020s are throwbacks to the 1980s, so are the villains. The continuity is startling, the commitment impressive in a perverse sort of way: such steadfast devotion to a white supremacist klepto-cratic one-party state. *They were around my age when they launched this plot*, I think when I see 1980s pictures of Donald Trump and Rupert Murdoch reinventing reality in the tabloids, Roger Stone and Paul Manafort at their oligarch consulting firm nicknamed "the torturers' lobby," and other opera-tives rewriting the rules so that the consequences Nixon faced for Watergate could never happen to another Republican. They were abetted by libertar-ian plutocrats like the Koch brothers and hard-right organizations like the Federalist Society and the Council for National Policy—what investigative journalist Anne Nelson calls "the shadow network"[23]—who chipped away at every avenue of accountability for forty years. Imagine living long enough to see your worst ideas fulfilled on a global scale—ambitions deemed im-plausible by the self-professed rational actors of your time, crimes deemed impossible even after the perpetrators confessed to them.

I spent my academic career studying the former Soviet Union, whose ideologues were trained to think in terms of decades instead of years—and still do, as former KGB agent turned attempted destroyer of the West-ern alliance Vladimir Putin makes plain. Climate scientists also think in decades. Most American politicians do not think in decades: they live for the day-to-day of the election cycle and the polls. But the Reagan acolytes did. They thought in terms of decades and left those of us born into a plot masquerading as prophecy to wonder how much time we had left.

In 1984, three years after Exxon circulated its internal research proving that climate change was real and accelerating at a deadly pace, over one hundred mainstream religious leaders signed a statement expressing their concern that President Ronald Reagan not only believed that Armageddon was imminent but also did not seem to mind. "Never, in the time between the prophesies up until now, has there been a time in which so many of the prophecies are coming together," Reagan told *People* magazine in December 1983. "There have been times in the past when people thought the end of the world was coming, and so forth, but never anything like this."[24] Among the signs Reagan saw were the creation of Israel in 1948 and the reunification of Jerusalem in 1967.

People magazine was not the first venue where Reagan rhapsodized about the apocalypse. He had raised the topic, unprompted, to televangelist Jim Bakker in 1979[25] and to Alabama senator Howell Heflin in 1981, telling Heflin that Russia was going to be involved in delivering the end times.[26] In October 1983, he told the executive director of the American Israel Public Affairs Committee, Thomas Dine: "I turn back to your prophets in the Old Testament and the signs foretelling Armageddon, and I find myself wondering if we are the generation that is going to see that come about. I don't know if you have noted any of those prophecies lately, but, believe me, they describe the times we are going through."

In 1981, Reagan selected as his secretary of the interior James G. Watt, a Dispensationalist Christian fanatic who believed that it made no difference how much of earth was destroyed in the near future because the apocalypse was going to annihilate it all in the end. "I do not know how many future generations we can count on before the Lord returns," Watt said at his confirmation hearing to a senator who asked him about preserving the earth for future generations.[27] "It's been two thousand years since the last coming of Christ and it might be another two thousand before the second coming." The Senate confirmed him 83–12 anyway.

In October 1983, Watt announced his resignation from the home of his undersecretary, Thomas Barrack.[28] Barrack is another Reagan-era relic who returned in 2016 to get Trump into power while working on behalf of a foreign country. It was allegedly Barrack who recruited Kremlin agent Paul Manafort to run Trump's campaign.[29] (The two GOP operatives turned foreign agents had originally met in Beirut in the 1980s.[30]) A decades-long partner of Trump and the chairman of his inaugural committee, Barrack was indicted in 2021 for being a foreign agent of the United Arab Emirates and lying to the government about it.[31]

While Barrack and Manafort were old-school foreign operatives, they were joined in the Trump circle by newer individuals who also had suspicious ties to the former Soviet Union and the Middle East. There was indicted foreign agent Michael Flynn, who worked for Russia and Turkey and was indicted for lying to the FBI about illicitly trying to broker a settlement deal for Israel.[32] There was son-in-law Jared Kushner, whose ties to indicted Israeli prime minister Benjamin Netanyahu date to his childhood and who has been described by biographers as having such all-encompassing devotion to Netanyahu that, in 2016, "it was as if Kushner viewed Netanyahu as his boss and Obama as his enemy."[33] And there was Exxon CEO turned secretary of state Rex Tillerson, who received the Order of Friendship Medal from Vladimir Putin in 2013, the same year Trump hosted his Miss Universe competition in Moscow.

I could go on for a while, listing all the foreign agents and hostile actors within the Trump team, but it is like walking in the woods through a series of spider webs. Eventually all you feel is dread at the sight of the next one and an overwhelming urge to shower. There are so many overlapping offenses in the Trump crime cult that it is difficult to keep them straight even if you have chosen the regrettable path of cataloguing them for a living. A friend of mine remarked while trying to distinguish between Barrack and Flynn: "It's like those logic puzzles: 'This convicted felon sat next to Putin at the 2015 dinner in Moscow, discussed kidnapping a Turkish cleric, and tried to sell nuclear material to Saudi Arabia, but was NOT a head of the inaugural committee.'"[34]

In the interest of brevity, let's get back to the apocalypse—after all, as James G. Watt reminds us, we may have little time left to discuss it. The inner sanctum of the Reagan administration included not only plutocrats and corrupt Nixon leftovers but also officials who either believed that Armageddon was imminent or who used other people's belief that Armageddon was imminent to justify their kleptocratic ambitions. Included in this agenda was allowing climate change to reach a catastrophic point, a development that, in our era of plagues and fires and floods, can then be marketed to the masses as the fulfillment of biblical prophecy.

They were never climate change deniers. They were climate change exploiters. One can question whether the motive behind environmental collapse is theocratic or kleptocratic, but there is no denying it is man-made. It is also continuous: a government that once justified slaughter through Puritan Calvinism and Manifest Destiny became one that operates on the pretense that a divine power has made all but the biggest corporate donors and their preferred politicians disposable.

The end times talk was tempered in official government channels during the 1990s under the Bush and Clinton administrations, in part because the collapse of the USSR and its nuclear threat reduced public expectation of annihilation. But it returned after 9/11 under George W. Bush, who, like Reagan, marketed corrupt policy as divine mandate. In 2002, Bush tried to convince foreign leaders to back the Iraq War by claiming it fulfilled the biblical prophecy of "Gog vs Magog,"[35] an argument his audience responded to with fear and disdain. But the fatalist fanaticism of the Reagan era did not return full-force in government until 2017. The Trump administration was composed of zealots of varied faiths, none of whom respected the separation of church and state and wallets. They were not shy about their doomsday ambitions. In 2015, evangelical Christian and former CIA head Mike Pompeo, who replaced Tillerson as secretary of state in 2018 after reportedly meeting illicitly with a band of Russian spies,[36] proclaimed, "We will continue to fight these battles. It is a never-ending struggle . . . until the Rapture."[37]

It is, of course, a very bad idea to structure foreign policy around the Rapture. But for kleptocrats, the end times provide a useful framework in which to gather a religiously diverse array of operators for mutual enrichment. Pompeo spent his final months as secretary of state having mysterious meetings throughout the Middle East, most notably with Yossi Cohen, the head of Israel's Mossad. Pompeo, like other Trump officials, including former National Security Advisor John Bolton, is an Iran warmonger who became extremely rich through the support of the Israel lobby.[38]

In 2020, in violation of US law, Pompeo began giving speeches to the Republican Party while in Israel, posing in front of holy sites and vouching for Trump as a savior.[39] In a move that alarmed many Israeli officials, Pompeo continued meeting with Cohen after Trump had left office.[40] After meeting with Pompeo, Cohen retired from the Mossad and, in possible violation of Israeli law,[41] considered forming a financial partnership with Trump's former secretary of the treasury, Steve Mnuchin, and David Friedman, who was Trump's bankruptcy lawyer and a coinvestor in West Bank settlements with Kushner before Trump made him ambassador to Israel in 2017.[42]

In May 2018, Friedman was photographed in Israel grinning in front of a poster showing the Temple Mount, a holy site for Judaism, Christianity, and Islam. In the poster, the Al-Aqsa mosque, the third-holiest site in Islam, had been eliminated from the Temple Mount, with a Third Temple constructed in its place.[43] In some factions of Judaism and Christianity, the building of the Third Temple is believed to herald the Messianic age. Fervent followers of Trump embraced this sign, along with Trump's pronouncement that Jerusalem was "the capital of Israel,"[44] as yet another indicator that his presidency was divinely mandated. Trump encouraged their belief both in words—he proclaimed that Israeli Jews view him as the "second coming of God" and "the King of Israel"—and actions.

In 2018, Trump moved the US embassy from Tel Aviv to Jerusalem after Republican megadonor Sheldon Adelson demanded it and agreed to bankroll it. Adelson was a fellow casino magnate who had expressed regret for serving in the US military instead of the Israeli one.[45] His final act, before he died in December 2020, was lending convicted American spy for Israel Jonathan Pollard his private plane after Trump had pardoned him.[46]

This blunt proclamation of loyalty to Israel over the United States is not unique to Republicans. In December 2018, Nancy Pelosi told Democratic megadonor Haim Saban—who, like Adelson, defines himself as a one-issue donor, with that issue being Israel[47]—"If the Capitol crumbled to the ground, the one thing that would remain would be our commitment to our aid, I don't even call it our aid, our cooperation with Israel."[48] Pelosi has never explained why she was discussing the Capitol crumbling at all, much less why, if it were attacked, her loyalty would be to a foreign government instead of to the United States of America. But she kept her word: following the January 6, 2021, attacks on the Capitol, the only bills that passed with bipartisan ease were billion-dollar increases of military aid to Israel.

All of the people I have mentioned in the section above are millionaires several times over, and some of them are billionaires. They are all making more money, and accumulating more power, through the exploitation of religion and destructive acts that they justify with biblical prophecy. Their wealth is the most important thing to know about them, because whether their agenda is based on a perverse interpretation of piety or wanton greed, they have the capacity to fulfill it. What faith they profess to follow is irrelevant. They are transactional actors, and you—all of you—are the transaction. Ordinary people are incidental to them; the United States nothing more than a land mass to be stripped and sold for parts. They are not working for the benefit of the American public, and several have stated or implied their fealty to a foreign power. But their deepest loyalty is to their money. Money buys power and impunity, and perhaps they believe it buys protection from the fallout of climate change, which promises apocalyptic events whether one is a religious believer or not.

I do not judge those who, when facing cruelty and chaos, would prefer to see it as God's plan. I do judge the powerful people who inflict pain upon the world and wrap it in the mantle of piety.

In 2018, Lev Parnas and Igor Fruman, the two criminal operatives who, with Rudy Giuliani, abetted Trump in his attempted shakedown of the president of Ukraine, informed Donald Trump that he was the messiah. Their conversation was taped without Trump's knowledge, and while Trump's threat to "take out" the US ambassador to Ukraine attracted the most attention and led to his first impeachment, the religious rhetoric is also notable. In the cell phone recording, Parnas is heard presenting Trump with a gift, unnamed in the conversation, from "the head rabbi of Ukraine" and from rabbis in Israel. He informs Trump that "in the Hebrew religion, they're waiting for the Messiah to come. So the Messiah Moshiach will be revealed." He tells Trump that according to Jewish numerology, the letters in Trump's name add up to 424, which is the same total as the Messiah.[49]

"What does that mean?" asks Trump.

"It's like you have the same numbers as the Messiah."

"Is that good?" asks Trump.

"It's not good, it's the best. It's like a miracle!" says Fruman.

"Why 424? What other numbers you got?" asks Trump.

"It's your name . . . The messiah is the person that has come to save the whole world," explains Parnas. "It's like you're the savior of the Ukraine . . . Go to Jared, he'll explain it to you."

At first Trump says nothing. Then: "You know, we were going to spend a million dollars on that building, but I got it for one hundred and fifty thousand."

Trump's lack of interest in being the Jewish messiah would seem at odds with his notorious narcissism, but it is not. The messiah is an unpaid position. There is a difference between being worshipped and being God, much like there is a difference between governing and being the president.

Trump understands which is the better end of the bargain, just as he understood that playing a successful businessman on *The Apprentice* was easier than being one in real life. There is no reality for Trump: the entire objective is to avoid reality and the responsibility and connection to humanity that it entails. Trump needs to be a brand because he is terrified of being a person. Any pretense of piety is an illusion he markets to his followers, some of whom believe he is God, and some of whom believe he is the antichrist, but they see that as a positive sign, because they believe that the presence of such a blatant sinner in a position of power heralds the messianic age.

Trump's conversation with Parnas and Fruman was recorded during a period when pundits often suggested that Trump was losing his mind or suffering from dementia, and was therefore not fully cognizant of his words and actions. Feigning mental infirmity is a common strategy of career criminals, both as a legal defense and a way to get the public to underestimate you. The tapes reveal a lucid and focused Trump, obsessed with money and power and eliminating anyone who threatened his pursuit of them, like US ambassador to Ukraine Marie Yovanovitch, whom he implied he wanted killed. The clip is a rare glimpse of the true priorities of an unscripted Trump, whose army of lawyers have controlled his image for decades—even his *Apprentice* outtakes are suppressed. They are insular, self-protective, calculating. The adulation he craves is the cult of celebrity, the most sacred American creed.

There is a photo of Trump's mentor, Roy Cohn, in the White House in January 1983, introducing Rupert Murdoch to Ronald Reagan.[50] Looking at it, if you did not know who was president, you would assume that Cohn is in charge. Cohn's primary goal at this meeting was enabling a right-wing takeover of American media, led by the Australian publishing magnate Murdoch, that would ensure Reagan was always protected in the press.[51] Cohn's relationship with Murdoch had developed around their mutual commitment to Israel, which they also shared with Reagan. That May, Cohn, an attorney for organized crime, was feted by the B'nai B'rith Banking and Finance Lodge and the Banking and Finance Division of State of Israel Bonds.[52] Murdoch helped chair the "testimonial dinner"; New York senator Al D'Amato was the guest speaker. Reagan sent Cohn a personal note of congratulations after the affair.

Three years later, Cohn died disbarred and in debt after ripping off wealthy fellow mafia associate Lewis Rosenstiel,[53,54] but not before setting his protégé, Donald Trump, on the path to the presidency using the same right-wing media, political, and financial apparatus he had built for Reagan, down to the "Make America Great Again" slogan.[55] The only difference was in their stance toward Russia: Reagan initially profited off its enmity; Trump operated as its asset.

In between Reagan's January 1983 meeting with Murdoch and Cohn and his *People* magazine interview on Armageddon in December, the world was almost obliterated by nuclear war. In September, a Soviet air defense force official, Stanislav Petrov, got a computer alert that an intercontinental ballistic missile was heading from the United States to the USSR. He chalked it up to error, doubting that the US would initiate what would be full-scale annihilation, and he was correct. Petrov's caution is, in retrospect, miraculous: it could have easily gone another way. Two months later, the world came closer to annihilation yet again, when aggressive NATO exercises were interpreted by already wary Soviet officials as a run-up to actual nuclear war, and they began preparing to retaliate.[56] The truth of this near-miss was not revealed until 2015, when documents about the incident were declassified.[57]

But Reagan knew. He knew the world had almost ended when he was cheerleading the apocalypse later that year. And there are people in government now who know of how close Trump—who had expressed a fatalistic belief that the world would end in nuclear annihilation since the 1980s, and espoused a desire to use nuclear weapons during his term— came to nuclear war while in office.

They stay quiet, because this is the terrain of conspiracy theory, or the terrain of national security: the two are treated interchangeably these days as terrain on which the humble citizen is not supposed to tread. We are supposed to pretend that the government would not be so cruel or maniacal or incompetent as to let masses of people die as we ride out a global plague in which the government was cruel and maniacal and incompetent enough to let masses of people die. We are supposed to accept, somehow, a preordained scorched earth future, and think it is normal that there is no urgency within the US government to mitigate it, and accept, somehow, that other governments—in particular, Russia—see the melting of the Arctic as an economic opportunity. We are supposed to ignore that the only condition in which the actions of elites make sense is one where they need to cull the herd before climate catastrophe rearranges the global order.

We are supposed to treat the worst people in the world as good faith actors, in defiance of logic or compassion or history, and deny the obvious grim conclusions. For oligarchs and plutocrats and dictators, a depopulated earth is easier to control. For accelerationalists and religious fanatics, the end of the world is desirable in its own right. These are mainstream objectives, held by people in positions of enormous power. If the reaction to covid is a test for how the powerful deal with climate change—let the plague spread, deny people resources, and hold no one accountable for the damage—we are in tremendous trouble. Everyone is assured that a savior is coming: an agent of the Lord or the law. I cannot attest to the former and I am pretty sure the latter broke down long ago, but I understand the rationalizations. It is a horrible feeling to be a pawn in someone else's plot masquerading as prophecy.

Wouldn't somebody do something, if it's really that bad? Yes, they would: they would stand back and let you die and profit off the pain and other people would stand back and let them. Inertia is action; complacency is complicity. Normalcy bias is more destructive than paranoia. It encourages people to rationalize abhorrent behavior, to ignore open evidence of sadistic plots, and to dismiss the emotional resonance of an end times narrative as something intriguing only to fools. The most logical conclusion of why this is happening—powerful corporate and political actors have aligned to profit off predictable catastrophe, in what writer Naomi Klein has called "disaster capitalism"—is also the most horrifying. There is no way out but through, and that's the crux of the fear. The apocalypse takes longer than you thought.

In the summer of 2021, I attempted to travel back in time. This was a coping mechanism in response to Missouri spawning a plague variant after a year of mass death and intermittent lockdowns and heartbreak so encompassing, it left me feeling removed from reality, or like reality had been removed from me. That this grief was not at all unique, that it was shared by almost everyone, provided little comfort, because grief was being weaponized in endless ways for baseless reasons.

There is a pool down the street from me that was built nearly a century ago, when St. Louis was a guiding light of America instead of a harbinger of its demise. It looks like a Spanish fortress and costs five dollars and is surrounded by a park across from a row of abandoned lots and storefronts rendered vacant by the pandemic. Every day I would walk to the pool with no cell phone, just a towel, a book, and a Walkman. The Walkman was a source of amusement to everyone at the pool who was older than forty, and of intrigue to everyone younger than twenty, but I clung to it like a security blanket. I bought it to play cassettes I had found in my basement, unlabeled tapes from middle school in the early 1990s. I wanted to know what was on them. But most of all I wanted to escape. I wanted something no one could take from me. I wanted my memories back.

At the pool I would lie back on a plastic chair and let the sun shine down on me and disappear into political songs that in the early 1990s were considered mainstream. George Michael on materialism and the death of God, Sinead O'Connor on state brutality in Thatcher's England, Guns N' Roses on the military-industrial complex, En Vogue on racial profiling, Poison on homeless veterans, Living Colour on political personality cults, Tracy Chapman on generational poverty, Don Henley on the end of America. These were songs I had taped off top 40 radio or that friends had put on a mix. They were songs that you watched on MTV or heard at the dentist's office. They were not esoteric, because it was normal to have serious political concerns and express them. They were relics from the anomalous era of American accountability: the late 1980s and early 1990s, when white-collar criminals went bankrupt or were sent to prison, global warming was considered an urgent crisis, and the Cold War had ended and no one, except possibly Leonard Cohen, understood that the mafia had won.

I would stare at the clear blue sky and soak in the cynicism and passion of this bygone age, one that seemed to be commenting on 2021 more than twenty-first-century pop culture was willing to do. And I would notice, a little each day, how the blueness of the sky was fading, and a bitter scent had arrived, not the familiar aroma of Missouri summer barbecue but something acrid and dying. The sky had turned white but there were no clouds and I began swimming laps just to be underwater, away from everything but a narrow lane and its constricted vision, my breath held with purpose instead of in reaction to a contaminant. The smoke from the wildfires burning down the West had reached St. Louis. My little oasis had fallen.

I had wanted oblivion from the oblivion, and this was my mistake. There was no escape except in my own mind and whatever reprieve I could find there, and so I gave in to the void. I let the past intertwine with the present, I forgot the future, I surrendered to mystery. I do not find it strange or sad that people wonder if we are living in the end times. I find it strange that people consider this an untouchable subject unless you are drenched in money, in which case it becomes a political platform or a woeful eccentricity.

But we are living among accelerationalists and I want to outrun them. We are ruled by people who abet mass death and I want to record my refusal. They knew this was coming: they, the corrupt and powerful, made it happen. But we knew, too, decades ago—maybe in the most lowbrow of ways, but we knew. Children knew, adults knew, and for a brief period of time, knowledge seemed to function as leverage. How we lost that, and how to get it back, is addressed in the next chapter.

On the day the pool closed for the season, the sky came back into view. It was a sliver at first, an opening of blue so vague as to be almost imperceptible. But the blue circle widened, and a white cloud appeared inside, like a rebuttal of the invasive blankness, a reminder that nothing lasts forever. "Nothing lasts forever" is one of those phrases, like "it could be worse," that function these days as both a threat and a promise. But I view it as the latter. I welcomed that cloud, it let me see the sun.

6

MEMORY-HOLING A COUP

On January 8, 2021, Donald Trump's Twitter account was obliterated. "After close review of recent Tweets from the @realDonaldTrump account and the context around them we have permanently suspended the account due to the risk of further incitement of violence," Twitter's official Safety account confirmed.[1] The "context around the tweets" was the violent coup that Trump's backers had attempted with his encouragement two days before. But Twitter did not simply suspend the president, who in the past had used Twitter to instigate violence, amplify death threats, and threaten nuclear war with no penalty. They did not merely prohibit him from writing new tweets. They deleted everything he had ever written or shared, and in doing so, erased evidence and altered collective memory.

As of late 2021, Trump's removal from Twitter is the most lasting repercussion he faced for helping launch the worst attack on the United States Capitol since 1812. Both Congress and the FBI refuse to impose meaningful consequences or carry out a thorough investigation into people who sought to kill them. Trump is still holding rallies, which television networks air live and without criticism, and is still collecting donations. Twitter is where his absence is most notable; Twitter is where the balance of power shifted. But the erasure of his account was not a punishment. It was a gift. "Who controls the past, controls the future," George Orwell wrote in his dystopian novel *1984*. "Who controls the present, controls the past. Past events, it is argued, have no objective existence, but survive only in written records and human memories. The past is whatever the records and the memories agree upon."[2]

Trump's 57,000 tweets are still out there. They are housed, in a scattershot style, on data storage sites and will allegedly be preserved by the National Archives, though as of late 2021, Trump is suing the National Archives in an attempt to suppress information.[3,4,5] Trump's fans still bask in his social media legacy; former CNN president Jeffrey Zucker had a framed Trump tweet hanging in his office.[6] But Trump's tweets are no longer on Twitter, where prior to January 8, 2021, his critics would revive them daily. Instantly accessible on the network from which they derived, they were held up as examples of hypocrisy, paragons of irony, or proof of a plot. They were time-stamped reminders used to name and shame, and they were scrutinized—both by investigative journalists and by acolytes of his personality cult—in an attempt to make sense of a tumultuous present and an uncertain future. They showed who knew what and when, and gave some insight into why.

Trump, who cannot exist in unscripted reality, rarely held press conferences and refused to appear at hearings during his time as president. Twitter was his primary medium because it was ideal: one-way communication providing ceaseless attention over which he alone retained full command. But it was also the most likely venue for his downfall. It is not enough for Trump to commit an illicit act: He needs to know that you know that he got away with it. He needs to flout the law and flaunt his impunity. This predilection is his weakness, particularly when, like in the immediate aftermath of January 6, enough powerful people are jolted by an attack on their own domain that accountability seems possible. But how do you remind people of what is no longer there? Twitter corporate officials claimed they deleted Trump's account in order to protect the public. But when they cut Trump off, they also set him free.

Had there been a rigorous investigation of the Trump administration's federal crime spree, the obliteration of Trump's social media accounts, along with those of his accomplices, would not be so important. But instead, their erasure—combined with the understandable desire of citizens in a pandemic to forget a traumatic period—has caused people to doubt their own memories. Trump's strategy in office was to make a crime a "not-crime" by having his lackeys rewrite the law to position himself above it. Now evidence was "not-evidence" because no one was using it.

One year after the Capitol attack, the only people punished were the low-level foot soldiers, not elite coordinators like Michael Flynn, L. Lin Wood, Steve Bannon, Roger Stone, and not Trump himself. For the entirely of 2021, the public became witnesses not only to crime but to institutional complicity in the refusal to prosecute it. A video of a person placing bombs around the Capitol building went viral, but the subject was not apprehended. Violent seditionists bragged about their victories online[7] as the FBI claimed they could not find evidence of coordinated involvement and a citizens' group called "Sedition Hunters" cropped up to force them to confront the evidence.[8,9] The task of Sedition Hunters became more difficult when, in December, Twitter had a shift in management thanks to a purchase of stock shares by hard-right billionaire Paul Singer.[10] A new policy that Twitter claimed was devised to protect people from having their photos circulated was used to ban people who posted photos of right-wing extremists,[11] even if they had done so before the policy was implemented—like on January 6, 2021.

A congressional committee to investigate the January 6 attack was not formed until July. After founding it, they had one hearing and went on vacation. The lack of urgency from the Biden administration and law enforcement bolstered belief that it was the viewer, and not what they had viewed, that was in the wrong. *If the violence I witnessed on live television and social media were serious, if our country were truly under attack from the inside, surely our officials would put it at the forefront of their agenda,* Americans thought. *Surely they would not just let it go!*

When agencies of accountability refused to act, Americans began to second-guess their own recollections. It's more comforting to think you made it all up than to contend with elite criminal impunity—and even

more assuring, for some, to decide that the attack must have been justified. And when you decide the attack is justified, you decide that the lie
behind it must not really be a lie at all.

On November 10, 2020, 80 percent of Americans believed Joe Biden
won the election, while only 3 percent believed Trump won.[12] By January
11, 2021, after three months of Trump and his backers contesting the election results vigorously while Democrats and the media pretended all was
normal and that Trump's slow-rolling coup was merely a grift, 20 percent
of American voters came to believe the storming of the Capitol was justified.[13] By May 25, after seven months of right-wing media talking about
stolen elections and dark-money Republican operatives running bogus
audits while Biden officials delivered boilerplate rhetoric about infrastructure budgets and the sanctity of bipartisanship, 30 percent of adults and
61 percent of Republicans came to believe that Trump was the rightful
winner of the 2020 election.[14] By December, after a yearlong tepid response from the Department of Justice and the January 6 Committee and
a continued propaganda blitz from right-wing media, only 58 percent of
Americans—and only 21 percent of Republicans—still believed that Biden
was the legitimate president.[15]

It is easier to rewrite a criminal narrative when the villain's confessions are missing, and Trump was not the only coup plotter whose sedition diary got deleted. After January 6, Twitter suspended over seventy
thousand accounts linked to the attack after releasing a statement that
said, "Given the renewed potential for violence surrounding this type of
behavior in the coming days, we will permanently suspend accounts that
are solely dedicated to sharing QAnon content."[16] These accounts were
sharing disinformation—but they also revealed high-level networks and
agendas. Michael Flynn lost his account along with his son, Pizzagate
purveyor Michael Flynn Jr. So did L. Lin Wood, a lawyer best known
for his involvement in the JonBenet Ramsey murder case who joined
Trump's legal team in 2020 after becoming heavily involved with QAnon.
Wood is best known today as a conspiracy theorist, but like the rest of
the high-level operatives surrounding Trump, he is a conspirator whose

"conspiracy theorist" designation made political and media elites take his threats less seriously.

After losing the 2020 election, Trump followed the predictable pattern of any aspiring autocrat: contest the results in the press, then in court, and then, should the court proceedings fail, with violence. But one needed no specialized insight into the history of autocracy to anticipate the coup: Trump's accomplices promoted their plan on the internet and recruited participants in public. The radicalization played out in real time, on view for all to see. In the weeks before the Capitol attack, I watched Wood lay out the January 6 agenda and encourage hesitant QAnon followers toward violence. What struck me most was the prosaic nature of the prospective militants' concerns. They worried about who would watch their kids while they were overthrowing the government, how to afford a hotel near the Capitol that they intended to storm, what excuse to give their boss for time off if "sedition" wouldn't fly. Some asked Wood whether an insurrection was taking it too far—was all of this really necessary?

Yes, Wood insisted, it was. He told his Twitter followers that a vast network of elite pedophiles and sadistic criminals had infiltrated the United States government and needed to be taken out, and pointed to the Jeffrey Epstein case as evidence. This is a paradigmatic example of the weaponization of an unresolved real conspiracy that I described in previous chapters. Wood's claim that the US government was enmeshed with transnational actors involved in child rape and trafficking was not wrong. The problem is that Wood was acting to protect the very individuals who were abetting this monstrousness. It was Barr and Trump who refused to investigate Epstein's alleged suicide in prison or the broad transnational criminal operation he had led for decades, because such an investigation would get linked to them and a multitude of their associates. Wood's confident insistence that the opposite was true functioned as both a lie and a lure.

The other problem, of course, is that Wood was stoking violent insurrection. Wood told his Twitter followers that there was no choice but to attack the certification proceedings in the Capitol and promised that their patriotic sacrifice would be rewarded. He said the insurrectionists would help preserve documentation of state crimes, make the guilty parties pay, and, most importantly, save the children. He interspersed his commentary with biblical verses and allusions to the apocalypse. Among those who retweeted Wood's demands was Ashli Babbitt, the Trump supporter who was killed by Capitol police after she and other attackers broke into the building.[17]

On January 5, my podcast, *Gaslit Nation*, ran a Capitol Attack Preview Special. We were able to do this because the plans for the attack were so open and obvious that our only question was whether the seditionists would succeed in preventing Joe Biden from becoming president. On January 6, I clicked through the Twitter doomscroll as the attack played out, taking notes for a follow-up episode, watching a preplanned plot manifest into livestreamed reality. I was so busy working that I did not hear my children's footsteps down the stairs, or the television set being turned on, or my husband leaving his makeshift home office to join them. I walked into the kitchen and heard the sounds of smashed glass and screaming mobs coming from the living room.

"You guys are watching the Capitol attack too?" I asked, pouring myself a cup of coffee, and then noticed their expressions. They were in shock, and the enormity of the moment hit me—that most Americans, including my own family, had truly believed this could not happen, that in the end, it would not go this far. My youngest child turned to me, his voice shaking, and said, "I don't like this, Mommy, I know it's a big deal but I don't want to see it, can we turn it off? Please, Mommy, I want to turn it off."

"Of course we can turn it off," I said, remembering when I was three years younger than him and saw the Challenger explode, recalling that my mother was three years older than him when she watched Lee Harvey Oswald get murdered on air. I sat on the couch and hugged my son, who was ten years old and living through a global plague and an economic collapse and an attempted coup and had now watched a barricaded Capitol get breached by frenzied supporters of a cruel and lawless president.

I realized that if my children ever went to Washington, D.C., and saw the Capitol building in real life, this day would be their primary reference. An imprint was being formed on a new generation: not only that the Capitol was attacked, but that people tasked with protecting the country let it happen. They knew it was coming, and they did not stop it.

I knew it was coming too, and I did not look out for my son that day in the way I should have, because I had forgotten what it was like to have faith in adults to do the right thing and the feeling of shock when they do not. I wanted my son to retain at least a semblance of expectation, to not plummet into total cynicism before he hit fifth grade, so I told him I thought everything would be OK in the end, that we just had to get through this day. I lied to him because he was a little boy who deserved a comforting story. Later on, many US officials, including Joe Biden, told the public variations of that lie—*don't worry, we're going to be OK*—and I reeled at their condescension and wondered how they thought they would get away with it, all of them: the perpetrators, the enablers, the revisionists, the deniers. The whole country had watched the attack on television. There was evidence so blatant and ubiquitous that there had to be consequences. There had to be something different this time around.

And then the cold grip of history pulled me down, and I realized that I did in fact understand the longing my son was feeling, because I was lying to myself. I was ignoring the American present so I could have hope for the American future. In an emerging autocracy, hope is dangerous, because hope is inextricable from time, and an enduring strategy of autocrats is to run out the clock. That was the botched institutionalist strategy that had led to the events of January 6—a strategy of inertia masquerading as patience, of smugness sold as savoir-faire. You cannot govern on hope and you cannot be governed by hope. Hope is a drug that gets you high on too many tomorrows; hope is a flight of fancy on a hijacked plane. Hope leaves you lost in a fantasy future, sidestepping the embers of the present while they smolder. Hope leaves you placid and malleable like a child—and we all know how the American government treats its children. I cast off my delusions that night and retreated into my documents and demands.

In March 2016, shortly before Trump became the Republican presidential nominee, CBS president Les Moonves gloated about how profitable his run was for cable news. "Bring it on, Donald. Keep going. It may not be good for America, but it's damn good for CBS."[18]

There is a common misconception that the reason the media covered Trump relentlessly in 2015 and 2016, letting his rallies air unimpeded and saturating the airwaves with his every utterance, was to make money. While news networks certainly found him profitable, this does not tell the full story. A Trump crime sells as well as Trump sycophancy or Trump scandal, but the most serious allegations about Trump—his decades-long involvement with organized crime figures, in particular the Russian mafia; his illicit ties to the Kremlin; the multiple felons and foreign operatives in his campaign and inner circle; and the rape allegation from a Jeffrey Epstein trafficking victim—were rarely discussed before the election. Some of these topics still remain largely absent from public discourse, though still preserved in books—hiding in plain sight, one might say.

The mainstream media caters to power, and power rests on networks of criminal elites. This is a synergistic relationship, but one side wields more influence than the other. To interrupt Trump's rise was not only to threaten media profit margins, but to incur threats of blackmail and violence from Trump's lawyer goon squad. It was to challenge organized crime rather than streamline it into obsolescence.

Because Trump had been a public figure for over forty years by 2016, many of his criminal connections were documented in the public domain. For a brief period in the late 1980s and early 1990s—the aforementioned anomalous age of American accountability—his offenses and his finances were covered in a straightforward way by the press. All it took to understand the mafia and oligarch network backing Trump were back issues of

SPY, Vanity Fair, or any of the New York–based publications from that era. Trump's propensity for confession also provided a wealth of insight.

The surfeit of documentation made it very suspicious when law enforcement and intelligence failed to stop an established transnational criminal operative from leading the military and overseeing the national security of the United States of America. There was no way they did not know, since this was information one could put together with Google and a library card. The only question remains why they knew and refused to act: complacency or complicity, careerism or corruption.

As the kleptocratic goals of the Trump administration became harder to deny, and as his circle increasingly fell under criminal investigation, the media, which was also fully aware of Trump's backstory, resorted to a tactic I came to call "déjà news." Déjà news is the repeated reporting on a well-documented phenomenon as if it were brand-new information. It is the presentation of a well-established yet damning fact as a shocking revelation, which thereby relieves the reporter of the blame they would otherwise receive for not investigating it before. The "shocking revelations" often arrived through coverage of plodding investigations, like the Mueller probe, that confirmed obvious threats and prior illegal acts while doing nothing meaningful in practice to hold the perpetrators accountable. Officials also embraced the déjà news tactic of treating old news as fresh information, because doing otherwise—admitting that they knew the danger the whole time—would mean admitting they had failed to protect the public. Instead, they feigned shock to avoid accountability.

I have a reputation for bringing hidden truths to light, but the most damning truth about the Trump crime world is that very little of its illicit activity was hidden. It was out there, decontextualized and obscured, but reported in real time for decades on end. I stood out as an anomaly not for what I claimed but that I thought it was important, particularly when it came to predicting how he would act as president. From 2015 until 2021, my response to inquiries about how I was able to predict Trump's behavior was: "It was in the public domain." I lost track of the number of times I told a dubious reporter deeming my allegations of Trump and his associates' past behavior "a conspiracy theory" to simply consult their old archives for proof.

But it was the availability of archival materials that allowed me, and other journalists and social scientists, to put the pieces together. For nearly the entirety of Trump's campaign and tenure in office, most media outlets remained free. Many offered archives that provided a window into decades of dirty deeds. But in the beginning of 2021, after democracy had been defenestrated, that window abruptly closed. He who controls the past controls the future, said Orwell, and now they who control the past decided people needed to pony up to see what had happened. By spring 2021, nearly every major news outlet had erected a paywall, often prohibitively expensive, that blocked content from general view. Journalists, both frustrated with the paywalls or facing layoffs after financial restructuring, quit and started their own newsletters or podcasts—many of which also required a subscription to access.

What remained free of charge? Misinformation, propaganda, and lies. Memes, fact-deprived political websites, and social media gossip continued to circulate as the hard news hid away. Isolated bits of articles—headlines, quotations, paragraphs—floated around the internet, decontextualized and stripped of authorship or date of publication. People relied on each other to find out what a paywalled article was about, including articles about public health crises like covid, and the summaries traveled like a bad game of telephone, with the result that a lot of people spent late 2021 scarfing down horse paste. Local newspapers, severely downsized since the 2008 recession, paywalled their websites to stay afloat, leaving panicked citizens relying on NextDoor posts to navigate a dystopia. It is hard to imagine more fertile terrain for a propaganda war, one that the paywalled side is destined to lose. There is no longer a public sphere, but there is a public flat earth.

Even television, the last gasp of the American monoculture, became fragmented. The pandemic boosted streaming services and made network heads realize they could reap profits by slicing and dicing the networks that had long united American viewers. Within two decades, Americans went from watching the same shows at the same time, to watching the same shows at different times thanks to DVRs, to not even knowing what shows existed and when they found out, not being able to afford to watch them. The partitioning of television mirrored the earlier dissolution of the music industry and foreshadowed the film industry's direct-to-streaming downfall. Cheap entertainment, one of the last unifying American pastimes, was now a labyrinth of toll roads to gated communities.

Prior to 2020, Americans had voluntarily sequestered themselves in information silos: consuming different news outlets and therefore different facts, urged by algorithms to limit their horizons. This was considered dangerous, a reason for our bitter debates over facts and factions. Now the silos contained not only political information but the distractions and relief from it, the shared entertainment we had taken for granted. Now we could not choose to leave the silos even if we wanted to: they are being constructed around us, demanding ever-steeper admission fees to ever-shrinking cultural conversations.

This restructuring of mass media in 2021 was not a conspiracy against democracy, but it was exploited by those who sought to create one. The end of the Trump administration led to dramatically decreased consumption of mainstream news outlets and massive profit loss. People who hated the news had come to rely on it in order to manage the inescapable peril that had entered their lives—the autocracy, the plague—and now that both seemed on the wane, they turned away in relief.

But the restructuring arrived at the absolute worst possible time for a country struggling for a sense of shared reality. Investigative reporting on the demise of democracy continued, paywalled from a public who instead gossiped about the latest "Karen" gone viral. Comprehensive analyses of policy plans hid behind prohibitive fees while short memes lying about what was in the plans circulated freely. We shared fantasy, we shared enmity, we shared fantasies about enemies who were in reality just figments and fragments, blips on a malfunctioning radar, human trading cards.

There is no longer a public domain. Journalism has come to resemble the insular world of academia, where research had long been sequestered from the masses. Unless you have an institutional affiliation, individual academic articles can cost twenty or thirty dollars, sometimes more—a price no one pays, but that was constructed to keep the general public away and maintain an elite grip on publicly funded knowledge. The article fee is a symbolic amount: the price of entry, the cost of exclusion.

I left academia a decade ago in part because of my frustration with this system, which not only does not serve the public but considers doing so to be a distasteful enterprise. I wanted my research to be read, and in order for it to be read, it needed to be accessible. The free, open internet was a welcoming alternative. Though some journalistic publications had always been paywalled, it had never been the majority of sites. In 2021, this no longer was the case. While researching my previous books, my biggest problem was managing the incredible amount of information I found. My new problem is getting the facts without going broke. If it's a problem for me as a full-time journalist obsessed with hunting down information, imagine what it's like for the average American without time, resources, or professional obligation.

The end result of all of this—the déjà news, the paywalled facts, the free-floating lies, the absence of official accountability—is the erosion of history. It is the loss of collective memory, including the digital collective memory that had come to augment and even supplant citizen consensus since the advent of the internet. In 2021, the United States of America became the first country in world history to memory-hole a coup. It is unprecedented for a democracy to face a physical attack organized by wealthy seditionists and foreign operatives intended to nullify a legitimate election and then decide to do nothing to prevent it from happening again.

A failed coup is a dress rehearsal. Government officials know that. The public should know that too, but if they do not, there are obvious culprits to blame for their lack of awareness. This is a perfect storm of forced forgetting, and American democracy is drowning inside.

When the pandemic began, my husband and children and I began gathering together each night to watch old sci-fi shows. We did this to establish a family routine, because time had lost all meaning, but also because we found comfort in fictional dystopias. Outrageous plots had become relatable. We started with *Lost*, the story of confused people trapped in a place they cannot leave while being bombarded with surreal crises fomented by a variety of conspiratorial madmen. We continued with *Fringe*, *The Twilight Zone*, and the short-lived 1991 children's series *Eerie, Indiana*.

One night we watched an *Eerie, Indiana* episode about a man called "The Donald" who comes to town posing as a successful businessman, turns people into zombies through subliminal advertising, and tries to steal their souls, because he doesn't have one of his own. "The Donald," revealed to be the devil in disguise, is defeated by his most feared nemesis: the IRS.

In the early 1990s, Donald Trump being a consummate tax cheat was so well known that children were expected to understand it as an in-joke. My own children got the reference instantly in 2021, just as I had as a child when it originally aired. Meanwhile, on cable, reality took a holiday, with déjà news continuing unabated even as administrations changed. Trump's tax dodging was reported as a shocking breaking story while his actual tax returns remained hidden—first by Trump's secretary of the treasury, Steve Mnuchin, and then by Biden's secretary of the treasury, Janet Yellen. We were watching old fiction while living real-life reruns.

While *Lost* proved relatable and *Eerie, Indiana* educational, my ultimate plague comfort TV show was *The X-Files* because of its wild conceit that competent people work at the FBI. "Time for civics class!" I would yell to the kids, and we would gather together to watch the opening credits mantras: "The Truth Is Out There," "Trust No One," "Deny Everything,"

"Fight the Future." These were the baseline beliefs of the 1990s, when distrusting authority was common and then commodified.

I had just turned fifteen when *The X-Files* debuted, putting me at the tail end of its Gen X target audience. I have wondered if Gen Xers are more attracted to conspiracy theories, and possibly more adept at deciphering them, because they grew up in an era of information scarcity, and enjoyed the process of search and discovery. The last generation to have an analog childhood, we spent our youth hunting down obscure movies, music, and magazines, developing selective expertise and curated collections. Building up that knowledge was beyond a hobby for many: it was a journey. We were raised in an era of ubiquitous corruption and lies—Watergate and Vietnam in the 1970s, Iran-Contra and white-collar crime in the 1980s and early 1990s. When you combine political cynicism with an obsessive urge to track things down, you wind up with a bootleg culture of information exchange.

Now that there is minimal effort required to get even the most obscure pop culture, Gen Xers have become hipsters of conspiracy, losing themselves in state secrets and creating communities of like-minded individuals stymied in their quests for the truth. This undertaking can, of course, go awry. Obsessive information analysis is what QAnon does as well, and members of Gen X flood its ranks. MAGA and QAnon rallies may well be filling in for the cheap concerts and high-octane events that Gen Xers—and Boomers, for that matter—grew up thinking would last forever.

For many Americans, *The X-Files* horrified not because of its fictions but because of its facts. The story of beleaguered FBI agents Fox Mulder and Dana Scully's quest to understand paranormal activity and state corruption was how I first learned about many actual horrific conspiracies carried out by my government. Operation Paperclip, in which Nazi scientists were brought to work for the United States after World War II; Unit 731, in which the Imperial Japanese government conducted biological warfare experiments on Chinese captives; the existence of Area 51; and other historical events they did not teach us in school. *The X-Files*, debuting after the fall of the Soviet Union but before the rise of Al Qaeda, tapped into paranoia at a time when it seemed safe to ask questions. "We actually test marketed the show and what I was really surprised to learn was that everyone in the test audience believed that the government was not working in their best interests," executive creator Chris Carter told *Rolling Stone* magazine in 1995.[19]

In January 2016, shortly after Donald Trump landed his first Republican primary win, *The X-Files* returned after a fourteen-year absence. The first season of the revival found an unemployed Mulder and a still skeptical Scully investigating, among other things, a global plague designed by a transnational cabal of sadistic elites to depopulate the earth with the complicity of rogue actors in the US government, but that's neither here nor there. The revival was a moderate success, and in March 2018, *The X-Files* returned for its first season in the Trump era and its final season ever. But with Trump and his propagandists ensconced in office, abetted by institutions that wore their corruption on their sleeve instead of hiding it in the shadows, Mulder had a new perspective.

"The world was so dangerous and complex then," he says, referring to the 1990s. "Who would have thought we'd look back with nostalgia and say *that* was a simpler time, Scully? Everything we feared came to pass. How the hell did that happen?"

Mulder bemoans that the truth he struggled to find is now openly out there, but it makes no difference. No one in power will do anything beneficial to humanity, and the public is too saturated with both facts and disinformation to care. In a satirical episode mocking both the show and its audience, Mulder meets a mysterious man who informs him that his quest is over: "Your time is past. We're living in a post-cover-up, post-conspiracy age." The man's name, of course, is Dr. They, because They are behind everything, and They get away with it.

"Our current president once said something truly profound," Dr. They says. "He said, 'Nobody knows for sure.'"

"What was he referring to?" Mulder asks.

"What does it matter?" Dr. They responds with a shrug and a grin.

Debuting on September 10, 1993, *The X-Files* was one of the first shows to spur an online fandom, and people within that community discussed the actual government conspiracies that inspired the series as much as they did its fictional plots. As a teenager, I would lurk in *X-Files* fan forums, and now I wonder if any of my virtual pals ended up storming the Capitol. Like *Twin Peaks* before it, which alerted mainstream audiences to Project Blue Book—the secret government study of UFOs between 1947 and 1969—*The X-Files* thrust a number of shady topics into public light, and the nascent internet provided the space for once isolated people to discuss them together.

In the 1990s, this seemed like a good idea—maybe even a sign of healthy civic discourse. Yes, the people having these discussions were weird nerds, but that went with the territory of *X-Files* fans who were also internet early adopters. It was not yet cool to be a weird nerd (though the seeds of commodification were being sown) and the series provided a sense of community for outsiders searching for the inside story. The 1990s were the last decade when theorizing about conspiracies was viewed as a relatively harmless endeavor, one undertaken by citizens of a country whose problems—*The president is a philanderer! The government surplus is too big! Y2K is confusing!*—seemed slight in comparison to past crises. The time seemed right for the truth to be revealed, for old crimes and conspiracies to be solved. That spirit of free-flowing inquiry came to an abrupt halt on September 11, 2001.

America was under attack. Suddenly the amorphous sense of dread that had powered *The X-Files* for eight years seemed less like the backdrop to a patriotic tale of rogue FBI agents battling internal enemies and more like the vilification of institutions that Americans were supposed to trust without hesitation. The Bush administration gave Americans dubious villains, the "axis of evil"; and infallible heroes, the US government and military. Citizens were discouraged from looking too closely at the terrors of the recent past or the fact that recurring political personalities powered each crisis.

Sure, the military-industrial complex had done some things. Watergate things, Iran-Contra things. Things involving the mafia, things involving mind-control experiments and illegal arms trading and rehabilitated Nazis and empowered autocrats. To quote Reagan and Clinton and Bush— all of whom eventually embraced this infamous phrase—"Mistakes were made."[20] But never mind all that: a new blood-dimmed tide had wiped out the sins of the past, because *the unthinkable had happened.* America had been attacked on its own soil by planes that struck the World Trade Center in a terrorist plot that spurred the United States to war.

For years, politicians and pundits insisted that nobody could have foreseen the 9/11 attacks. At a September 16, 2001, press conference, President George W. Bush declared: "No one could have conceivably imagined suicide bombers burrowing into our society and then emerging all in the same day to fly US aircraft into buildings full of innocent people. . . . This is a new kind of evil."[21] National Security Advisor Condoleezza Rice echoed this claim, telling CBS in May 2002: "I don't think anybody could have predicted that they would try to use a hijacked airplane as a missile."[22] When asked on a September 30, 2001, *Meet the Press* if he had ever imagined that a building could be attacked with an airplane, Secretary of Defense Donald Rumsfeld replied, "Oh, goodness no. Never would have crossed anyone's mind that a commercial airline [would do that]."[23]

The idea that the 9/11 attacks were unfathomable was always absurd: both the target and the perpetrator were old news. Terrorists first bombed the World Trade Center in 1993. In the late 1990s, Al Qaeda launched a series of attacks on US embassies and military infrastructure abroad and Osama bin Laden went on to threaten more. In the months before 9/11, researchers at both the CIA and the FBI had, separately, come to believe Al Qaeda would launch an attack on US soil. They made their findings known to the Bush administration, even including it in Bush's daily briefing, but it was to no avail.[24] In September 2001, there was, *at the least*, a massive failure of intelligence, law enforcement, and the federal government to protect the United States and its people.

But there was not failure of the imagination—and one did not need classified information to envision the September 11 scenario. An extremely similar attack had, in fact, been depicted on TV six months before on *The*

Lone Gunmen, an *X-Files* spin-off series. The Lone Gunmen were three technologically savvy nerds whom Agent Mulder had befriended as they shared his interest in government conspiracies and desire to expose them. Fan favorites, they were given their own show in 2001, run by Vince Gilligan, an *X-Files* writer who would later go on to create *Breaking Bad*.

The plot of the first episode, which aired on March 4, 2001, is as follows: the Lone Gunmen discover that a commercial flight headed to Boston had been hijacked. Initially fearing there was a bomb on board, they learn that the plane itself is the weapon, and that it had been commandeered to fly into the World Trade Center and cause the buildings to collapse. "They intend to bring this down in the middle of New York City?!" John Fitzgerald Byers, one of the Lone Gunmen, says in disbelief. The series depicts the plane, hijacked via computer, heading to the same sections of the Twin Towers that were hit on 9/11, until the Lone Gunmen override the system and prevent disaster.

The episode concludes with a horrifying reveal: rogue forces from within the US government had staged the World Trade Center attack themselves. Byers's father, a retired government consultant, explains their plot to his son: "The Cold War is over, John. But with no clear enemy to stockpile against, the arms market is flat. Bring down a fully loaded 727 into the middle of New York City and you'll find a dozen tin-pot dictators all over the world just clamoring to take responsibility, and begging to be smart-bombed." Byers implores his father to tell the world the truth. His father replies that doing so would be both pointless and dangerous: "My silence will keep me alive. And you. I know you and your friends are fighting for the American dream. Just don't expect to win."

The point of this anecdote is not to imply that the US government carried out the 9/11 attacks, or that *The Lone Gunmen* production staff had advance knowledge of them. It is to note that, once again, a terrible threat that "nobody saw coming" was so foreseeable that it played out on a high-rated television show six months before it played out in reality. (*The Lone Gunmen* was not alone either; similar plots, though less precisely on the nose, are also found in the 1998 movie *The Siege* and Tom Clancy's 1994 novel *Debt of Honor*.) "What's disturbing about it to me is, you think as a fiction writer that if you can imagine this scenario, then the people in power in the government who are there to imagine disaster scenarios can imagine it, too," said executive producer Frank Spotnitz, who was so startled by the similarity of the storyline to 9/11 that his first reaction was worry that *The Lone Gunmen* had inspired the terrorists.[25] In 2002, *TV Guide* wrote the first article on the overlap, and called the article "The Sept. 11 Parallel Nobody Noticed." Once again, the sagacious "nobody" saw it coming.

The Lone Gunmen, which was canceled in June 2001 after thirteen episodes, has largely disappeared from American consciousness. (*The X-Files* was canceled in 2002, in part because of post-9/11 disdain.) But clips of the pilot float around the internet, dissected by Americans obsessed with learning the full story of the 9/11 attacks. The World Trade Center episode both validated preexisting conspiracy theories—for example, that 9/11 was an inside job—and bolstered newer ones, like the idea of "predictive programming," in which mass media foreshadows real life events in order to get the public to accept them. Conversely, that *The Lone Gunmen* is somewhat difficult to access—it is available only on DVDs released in 2006—has inspired some to believe it has been intentionally suppressed, as the very existence of the episode contradicts official government claims that the attacks were unfathomable.

Twenty years after 9/11, there are conspiracy theories about conspiracy theories, propaganda about propaganda, obfuscation about obfuscation. But what we do not have is truth or a reliable avenue through which to find it. The belief that the public does not know the full story of the 9/11 attacks is not fringe or unfounded. It has been expressed by multiple elected officials, intelligence experts, investigative journalists, and members of the 9/11 Commission, some of whom, like former Florida senator Bob Graham, wrote about their anguish that the full facts have not been made available to the public.

"September 11 was an avoidable tragedy," Graham wrote in his 2004 book *Intelligence Matters*. He described "a cover-up orchestrated by the

White House to protect not only the agencies that had failed but also America's relationship with the Kingdom of Saudi Arabia."[26] He called out FBI head Robert Mueller, in particular, as a key player in the cover-up—a chilling echo in light of Mueller's later refusal to fully investigate Trump's criminal ties—as well as Bush, who he said should be impeached. In September 2021, Graham was vindicated when the Biden administration released declassified FBI documents that ran counter to the 9/11 Commission's prior report and showed that Al Qaeda had in fact operated in the United States with the active, knowing support of members of the Saudi government.[27,28] But vindication seventeen years later, after two catastrophic wars justified by the "war on terror" that followed the attacks, is cold comfort.

9/11 was by any definition a conspiracy: an organized secret plan by nefarious actors working together to carry out an illegal act. But in an era where "just asking questions" has been demonized as the purview of people who falsify answers, it has become harder to dissect the nuances of a plot in public. Declaring "We do not have all the facts, but we deserve to know them" is different from professing faith in an alternative narrative or regurgitating rumors, but deriders often label them as one and the same. The identities of the conspirators, the enablers, the abettors, the obscurers, and the beneficiaries are all still up for debate—at least, when people feel brave enough to weigh in.

In the first decade after 9/11, expressing uncertainty about the Bush administration's narrative of 9/11 was taboo. While this stigma is lifting as more facts come out, the subject remains fraught not only due to the vortex of propaganda, lies, and cover-ups that emerged in its aftermath but because of a protracted effort to inhibit investigation. Those who sought the truth about 9/11 were not labeled concerned citizens, but "Truthers"—paranoid lunatics, unpatriotic evildoers. The use of "Truther" as a pejorative term was a precursor to the Trump administration's creation of "alternative facts" as a governing principle. Truth was irrelevant, they implied. The search for it was futile, the people who sought it no match for the machinations of power.

In 2002, around the time the Bush administration was lying about weapons of mass destruction in Iraq, Bush advisor Karl Rove gave a startling confession to *New York Times* reporter Ron Suskind. "We're an empire now, and when we act, we create our own reality," Rove said. "And while you're studying that reality—judiciously, as you will—we'll act again, creating other new realities, which you can study too, and that's how things will sort out. We're history's actors and you, all of you, will be left to just study what we do."[29]

This self-proclaimed fantasist, this unrepentant manipulator, is the type of authority whose narrative the American people were not supposed to challenge. "If you're not with us, you're against us," Bush told the world shortly after the 9/11 attacks, but this phrase applied to inquisitive Americans as well. Truth became the enemy of the people who sought to create reality.

In 2012, I was driving around St. Louis when I spotted a sign near the headquarters of biotechnology company Monsanto. For the next half mile, the sign proclaimed, this stretch of highway would be cleaned by the St. Louis 9/11 Questions Meetup Group. "Adopt-a-Highway gone awry," I texted my husband, bemused by the sight. At the time I didn't think too much about my casual dismissal of the group. If I had, even for a moment, I would have perhaps wondered why I rejected the idea of asking questions about 9/11, when asking difficult questions is what I had always done for a living, both as a journalist and then as an anthropologist studying corrupt and brutal regimes.

My offhand rejection of the St. Louis 9/11 Questions Meetup Group's premise was not, in fact, instinctive: I had been taught to disregard it. I had spent years hearing from the media—including when I worked for the media—that 9/11 "Truthers" were anti-American lunatics who delighted in baseless innuendo. Hateful propagandist Alex Jones, who rose to prominence as a right-wing radio host in the late 1990s, had become the face of the 9/11 Truth movement, amplifying and hijacking texts and films others concerned with 9/11 had put out in good faith. Jones's cruel dismissals of real tragedies as false flags—in particular, the mass shooting of kindergarteners at Sandy Hook Elementary School—tarnished the cause's credibility by proxy.

Jones served the same purpose for citizens investigating 9/11 as QAnon's ludicrous lies later served for those investigating elite traffickers and government corruption. His name became shorthand for delusional rhetoric with which no decent person wanted to be associated. *Tinfoil hat much? You sound like Alex Jones!* respectable pundits bleated in 2015 at those speculating that this Trump fellow may not have his finances on the up and up. Alex Jones functions as a living, breathing straw man for anyone seeking to dismiss critical inquiry of the powerful.

One canard that pundits and politicians use to dismiss conspiracy theorists is to claim that they seek a simple, unified explanation for everything bad happening in the world. While this is certainly true of some conspiracy theorists—antisemitic bigots, for example—it is not an accurate description of the conversations about actual conspiracies. This is particularly true when an inquiry is not limited to who carried out a terrible act, but who enabled it or covered it up. The JFK assassination, for example, has spawned a number of theories that dispute the "lone gunman" narrative. Depending who you read, it was the CIA, the mafia, the Soviets, the Cubans, Richard Nixon, Lyndon Johnson, and a variety of other suspects. The JFK cover-up crew includes the Warren Commission, the media, Lyndon Johnson (again), and so on. But you'll be hard-pressed to find a JFK assassination theorist who believes it was everyone, all at once, or that the conspiracy is at all simple.

What they will agree on is that the story is *traumatic*. The obfuscation adds layers to the trauma, deepening it. The documentation conducted by many of the JFK theorists is thorough and upsetting, and the more years that pass without oft-promised transparency—the JFK records were originally supposed to be released, according to federal law, on October 25, 2017; they were most recently delayed in October 2021[30]—the more suspicious the situation seems. When government authorities keep secrets for decades on end, it leaves people only able to assume. It gives license to bad faith interpretations, creating a blank canvas on which to project any idea, no matter how poorly conceived, and then they are blamed for not painting a perfect picture, or not accepting the paint-by-numbers version they were sold.

What the JFK assassination was to the Boomers, I suspect, 9/11 will be to my generation—the generation that was sent to war in its aftermath. I lived in New York City in 2001 and covered the attacks while working at the *New York Daily News* for two years after. The trauma of that time is visceral: I can still smell death in the air, I cannot walk down certain streets when I visit because I remember them covered in signs for the missing who were really the dead. But I have questions, and I am not alone. Twenty years after the attacks—twenty years of lies by multiple administrations, four years of a career criminal in the White House, countless horrific revelations brought to light about people who were in positions of power during the attacks, and a world that has been rearranged to benefit them—it has become more acceptable to have questions about 9/11. My questions are less about the mechanics of the attack—the topic most associated with pilloried "Truthers"—than about accountability. They are about how a government failed to protect its people and then exploited their fears and silenced their dissent.

It has become more acceptable to have questions, but still difficult to ask them in a public forum, in part because the evidence of America's first major tragedy in the digital era has become so corrupted. Every year it has become harder to find articles and broadcasts about 9/11 from 2001 and the years leading up to the Iraq War—not the famous outlets, but the smaller ones. The breaking news and local reports from New York or Washington, D.C., the ones that raised questions in real time that remain unanswered. Part of the reason for these omissions is technological: a number of online publications switched from manually coding in HTML to using automated software to post breaking news, and in the process, wiped portions of their early archives from the internet.

But there are also a number of articles and videos about 9/11 taken offline over the last few years, pages I bookmarked and was surprised to see deleted soon after. Real-time information is vital for anyone trying to make sense of an event without the biased vision of hindsight. I have lost track of the number of times I've found copies of primary sources—news articles from mainstream papers and outlets—housed solely on conspiracy sites, often surrounded with inflammatory rhetoric, thus making them impossible to share without a disclaimer. The side with the least public credibility is holding the information that the side with the most public credibility, professional media outlets, let slip from public view.

There are things I want to tell you, speculation I want to share, but I do not, because the evidence is not yet enough and I don't want my words weaponized. I do not want to deal with lawyers and liars and scammers and creeps. I do not want to ride a third rail in a country with so many fifth columns we could build a new White House out of them. I am trying to be a responsible citizen, an upstanding conspiracy theorist if you will, but it's a fine line. I carry the burden of knowing too much and not enough at the same time. It's not a burden I am carrying alone: this is the modern American condition. We carry the collective weight of a collective mystery about a collective tragedy, one in which we find the officials who ran New York City in 2001—like federal investigation target Rudy Giuliani and Trump-pardoned felon Bernard Kerik—aiding an anti-American coup in 2021; one that a foreign power, Saudi Arabia, was never confronted for having abetted; one that leaders of other foreign powers like Israel remarked was a boon;[31] one whose aftermath reoriented the world to ruin. We drown under that weight while they float above us, buoyed by money and impunity.

Like 1/6, 9/11 was both memory-holed and buried in bullshit. The endless competing narratives of 9/11 combined with the utter refusal of the US government to answer rudimentary questions about foreknowledge created an environment of institutional distrust that the architects of the 1/6 coup attempt exploited. In 2021, you can plot your government overthrow in painstaking detail months in advance on the internet, and officials will still say nobody saw it coming. The category of "nobody" expanded in the twenty-first century along with the consolidation of wealth and power to a very narrow few "somebodies." "Nobody" is the 99 percent. "Nobody" is nearly everybody, and nearly everybody is deemed disposable.

One of the most common responses to any insinuation that the US government either abetted the 9/11 attacks or looked the other way and let them happen was that the American government would never kill three thousand of its own people in one day. I remember believing that, until covid came around and we hit the 9/11 death toll on a daily basis while the government lied and denied and profited off our pain. All conspiracy theories are debatable, except one: the American government will absolutely leave its citizens to die.

7

AMERICA IS PURPLE, LIKE A BRUISE

n February 2021, I walked across a bridge from Missouri to Illinois, and then walked back from Illinois to Missouri again. The bridge is called Chain of Rocks and it sits at the edge of Route 66, America's mother road, and straddles the Mississippi River. Two Romanesque water intake towers, built over a century ago, sit in the river like frozen castles, their turrets pointing at the sky like a rebuke. On the railings are Route 66 signs and political graffiti and memorial plaques for murder victims who died near the bridge. Like everything in St. Louis, this place had seen darker days.

In 1980, John Carpenter filmed his postapocalyptic movie *Escape from New York* in St. Louis because the city was so run-down, he didn't need to build a set. Chain of Rocks stood in for the 69th Street Bridge over which Snake Plissken—the reluctant hero tasked with rescuing a president he did not respect to win his freedom in a country he no longer recognized—raced to get out of Manhattan, which had been transformed into an island prison.

Escape From New York was so humiliating for St. Louis that the city cleaned and restored all of the crumbling Gilded Age and Roaring Twenties relics that Carpenter had selected to represent his dystopian wasteland. No longer primarily known for fictional and real-life murders, the renovated Chain of Rocks became one of America's longest pedestrian bridges, a place where families stroll and play, at least during daylight hours. Every January, global plague notwithstanding, my family goes to the Eagle Days Festival, an annual event held to celebrate the return of the bald eagle to the mighty Mississippi. Local volunteers bring telescopes so onlookers can watch the eagles fly back and forth across the river, between the former slave state of Missouri and the former free state of Illinois, between what I have been told with great authority are "two distinct Americas" by coastal pundits who ignore the mottled middle and the people who live here.

The two Americas, I have been informed, are red and blue, Republican and Democrat, with no room for gradation. No room for mostly liberal cities in mostly conservative rural states, no room for the gerrymandering and voter suppression that make a state legislature neither resemble nor respect the people it governs. No room for political opinions that span a spectrum instead of checking a box, no room for the distinctive hardships and joys residents of a state share regardless of their differences. No room for the truth, which is that America is purple—purple like a bruise. No room for acknowledgment that "red" and "blue" are not fixed identities but terms that politicians have spent over twenty years molding like clay that they hope will harden. No room for paradox or surprise or defiance; no room for people to change.

In winter 2021, there was no Eagle Days Festival, but we decided to walk over Chain of Rocks anyway. The television told us that this would be an exciting adventure, akin to the one Huck and Jim made 150 years ago, because we were walking from a "deep red state" into a "blue trifecta." Everything was so *different* in the blue trifectas, liberal pundits crowed, where civic responsibility reigned and the plague honored county lines. Missouri yokels like us, living in a metro region of three million people, simply could not grasp the magic of living in a state that had boasted an indicted Democratic governor instead of an indicted Republican one. We crossed the bridge from St. Louis County, Missouri, represented by Ferguson protester turned Congresswoman Cori Bush, to Madison County, Illinois, a heavily Republican area that Donald Trump had just won for the second time.

Madison County is in a part of Illinois we call Metro East because it, too, is part of the St. Louis region, state lines be damned.

And truly, state lines be damned, because I live on the line, and the line feels like a ledge when operatives are trying to divide and conquer in order to destroy your country from within.

The Civil War and the Cold War never ended, and oligarchs and plutocrats won both. These are not conspiracy theories. These are conspiracy facts.

In 2015, I warned that Trump would win the presidential election, and that when he won, he would rule like a Central Asian kleptocrat, employing autocratic tactics to consolidate his power. I warned that white supremacists, organized crime operatives, theocrats, technocrats, and other nefarious actors from around the world had aligned and sought to strip the United States down and sell it for parts, and that the Republican Party, which had refashioned itself into an apocalyptic death cult, was amenable to this prospect. I warned everyone so much, I was accused of beating a dead horse while everyone ignored the pale rider on top.

After Trump took office and proceeded to purge agencies, pack courts, and swindle his way into impunity, I warned that his administration was a transnational crime syndicate masquerading as a government. I said this on television and it was not appreciated. In 2017, I warned that he would never leave the White House of his own volition, but would instead employ violence to attempt to hold power, even if he lost the election, and that this destructive crusade would continue until the criminal elites surrounding him were held accountable. All of these statements were treated as lunacy when I first made them but are now regarded as conventional wisdom. That's the way it goes in America, where it is a sin to be right too early.

I called Trump an autocrat, a kleptocrat, a criminal, and a racist, but what I have not called him is a fascist. It is here where I depart from other scholars of autocracy. Fascism requires loyalty to the state. A traditional

fascist dictator seeks to embody and expand the state. They see themselves as the exemplars of the state, and the state's preservation and triumph over rival states empowers their personal brand. That is not the case
with Trump and much of his cohort, who appear to *want* the country
to collapse. A depopulated, partitioned United States is easier to exploit
and control, particularly in a chaotic era of climate change, which they
anticipated decades ago. To them, the state is just something to sell. They
do not care if the buyers are foreign or domestic. The United States of
America is merely a landmass to split into oligarch fiefdoms. It inspires no
sentimentality and requires no veneration. Its laws are irrelevant, its rights
ephemeral, its population disposable. Its history can be rewritten.

I do not object to others calling Trump a fascist, however, because he
uses the tactics of fascists, and people should note the parallels. Trump
employed the dictator's playbook through American infotainment, an
arena he long ago mastered, and let his bureaucratic backers rewrite
the laws and his bagmen handle the money. He is currently emulating
the path of Hitler, whose personality cult flourished after his attempted
putsch because no one took the prospect of a political comeback seriously. Trump, a career criminal Kremlin asset with no qualms about
destroying the country he once ruled, is not a fascist, but it is far more
realistic to call Trump a fascist than to call him a patriot or "a president
about to pivot." The delusion that the office of the presidency would reshape Trump rather than Trump reshape the office marred mainstream
predictions about what direction the United States would turn.

Trump and his backers have been straightforward about their plans.
They relied not solely on subversion but on American unwillingness to
believe that their dark ambitions could be realized. They exploited flaws
of America long disguised as assets: exceptionalism, institutionalism, optimism. The less likely you were to have benefited from any of these systems, the more likely you were to see the danger of the Trump crime cult
coming. But as a person on the periphery, your warnings were unlikely
to be heeded by those who control the center. Trump's backers exploited
that paradox too.

On February 14, 2014, four months after meeting with Vladimir Putin at the Miss Universe pageant he hosted in Moscow, Trump went on Fox News to announce that Americans should never criticize Russia because "we will go on and win something important later on, because [Russia is] not going to be opposed to what we're doing." Trump also declared his vision for the American future, claiming that economic crashes, riots, and everything going to "total hell" were what would make America great again.[1]

Trump's ideological backer, Breitbart editor-in-chief turned national security advisor turned pardoned indicted grifter turned coup abettor Steve Bannon, shares a similar worldview. In 2016, a reporter from *The Daily Beast* recalled a conversation in which Bannon announced that he was "a Leninist." When the reporter asked what he meant, Bannon explained: "Lenin," he answered, "wanted to destroy the state, and that's my goal too. I want to bring everything crashing down, and destroy all of today's establishment."[2]

Bannon's vision is shared by Russian far-right ideologue Alexander Dugin, who is popular in both Trump's and Putin's circles.[3] "It is generally important," Dugin wrote in his 1997 book *Foundations of Geopolitics*, "to introduce geopolitical chaos within the American daily experience by encouraging all manner of separatism, ethnic diversity, social and racial conflict, actively supporting every extremist dissident movement, racist sectarian groups, and destabilizing the political processes within America."[4]

Any student of American history knows that it is not particularly hard to introduce geopolitical chaos within the American daily experience given that the country was founded on it. The ideal that the American experience is calm and meritorious is upheld only by excluding the bulk of Americans from the American experience: Native Americans, Black Americans, immigrants, labor activists, impoverished people, anyone bearing a marginalized identity—and even then, you are left with a band of feuding elites who, until recently, would not overlook their differences to work together toward a broader destructive purpose. This has changed: elites who once fought for control over the country are now negotiating over the scraps born of its dissolution.

But America has always been chaotic, as is any country: that we were exceptional in this regard was always a pernicious myth. What the United States did have, which other countries lacked, was a reliable and mostly peaceful transfer of power between elected officials and increased demographic inclusivity over time in those who got to elect them. It was laws, not goodwill, that contained the violence lurking under the surface. It was tradition and expectation, not knowledge of civics, that prompted Americans to accept the loss of their candidate or changes in policy. Democracy is a force of habit, and habits can be broken.

In 1997, when Alexander Dugin was publishing his post-Soviet revenge plan and Trump was getting bailed out by oligarchs from the former USSR and Bannon was reading the new book *The Fourth Turning*, which posits that massive world crises run in eighty-year cycles, with the next due in 2020,[5] the developing world was being encouraged to embrace democracy by the last remaining superpower, the United States of America. Russia was now considered part of the developing world, to the humiliation of former KGB agent Vladimir Putin, who deemed the collapse of the Soviet Union the most tragic event of his lifetime.

A hypercapitalist, ultraviolent Russia had emerged, one that dispensed with communist ideology but kept the brutal state surveillance apparatus of the Soviet Union. To many in Russia and other former Soviet republics, "democracy" came to be synonymous with constant chaos, lost income, and flagrant violence. To oligarchs and mafiosos, "democracy" was a sneering euphemism for an unparalleled opportunity to rape the land and rob its people and ultimately capture the government itself.

Though they relied on state apparatuses and sometimes cloaked themselves in nationalism, these oligarchs and mafiosos are transnational operators. Their plots were only successful because of deals made with foreign backers and the increasing fluidity of foreign markets and digital media. When Putin and a corrupt oligarch network came to rule Russia, they did it with the support of the United States' most powerful security operatives. Even two former heads of the FBI, Louis Freeh and William Sessions, worked as lawyers for the Russian mafia after leaving office, while a number of prominent Republican and Democratic campaign operatives—including Paul Manafort and former presidential candidate Bob Dole—worked as liaisons for the Kremlin.[6]

There was a coup in America, and no one noticed. It was a slow-moving coup, decades in the making, forged by redefining laws and loyalty until the contours of betrayal blurred. Sovereignty became negotiable, and over time, US officials abandoned even the pretense of obligation to Constitution or country. Lincoln predicted that the United States could only die by its own hand, instigated by Americans instead of foreign powers, but what happened is more like assisted suicide.

The Kremlin was not the sole player in the hijacking of America: operatives and officials from Saudi Arabia, Israel, the United Arab Emirates, the United Kingdom, and other countries all played roles. As Hillary Clinton said, decades before losing the 2016 election to a Kremlin asset with forty years of ties to organized crime, "It takes a village." There was a conspiracy, and complicit US officials either participated or pretended it was not happening. There was a crime, and we were all its victims, even if we see the crime from different angles. There is too much continuity in this corruption, too much retread in the cast of characters at its center. People in power do not want to discuss it, because that would mean admitting they knew it all along.

Trump is not a fascist, and the mafiosos and oligarchs and plutocrats backing him are usually not either. They are something worse: catalysts for the destruction of the United States of America and its partitioning into smaller entities, none free, all profitable for those who rule them. The model for this dismantling is the breakdown of the Soviet Union, but the United States' position differs considerably in that the USSR was already carved into fifteen republics, which became independent states in 1991. There is no neat demarcation of territory corresponding to ethnicity or ideology in the United States, which is why political operatives have been pushing rigid conceptions of "red" and "blue" states—terms devised during George W. Bush's contested election win in 2000 when television news anchors used them to designate state voting results on maps.

This is why secessionist movements that have always lurked on the fringe in states like Texas and California are now being pushed into the mainstream by operatives in Russia, through monetary investments in separatist rallies and social media propaganda.[7] There is no neat or natural way to delineate the United States into separate countries, but they will try to convince you that there is and always was.

Autocracy is a stepping-stone on the path to the forced dissolution of the United States into multiple mafia states, which will possibly war with each other for profit. The motivation behind the collapse is as old as time: money, power, and territory. This outcome is not inevitable, but it is their aspiration, and it is certainly the worst-case scenario: worse than chaos, and worse even than autocracy, because the United States is too big to manage, which is why they want to tear it apart and control each piece separately. The old leverage of the nation-state is gone, as is the lure of the superpower.

We have a class of megamillionaires who no longer need this country to exist. Should it collapse, they can carry on with their lives as before, with wealth that they pass down to their offspring, and possibly with digital currency that exists beyond the dollar. They do not need to worry about civil rights, public schools, voting rights, or health care. They do need to worry about climate change, but the goal is to insulate themselves from its most deadly effects. They are not worried about the United States of America, for they are citizens of the world—citizens of a world that is ending, and they welcome death's embrace.

In 1941, the poet T. S. Eliot, hiding in his home from World War II Axis Power bombs raining down on the United Kingdom, wrote "The Dry Salvages." The poem opens with a description of his native St. Louis:

> *I do not know much about gods; but I think that the river*
> *Is a strong brown god—sullen, untamed and intractable,*

Patient to some degree, at first recognised as a frontier;
Useful, untrustworthy, as a conveyor of commerce;
Then only a problem confronting the builder of bridges.
The problem once solved, the brown god is almost forgotten
By the dwellers in cities—ever, however, implacable.
Keeping his seasons and rages, destroyer, reminder
Of what men choose to forget.

Born in 1888, Eliot grew up in St. Louis during its golden age, when it was the fourth-biggest city in the United States and its 1904 World's Fair was the most popular destination on earth. Like many St. Louisans, Eliot is known for leaving the city and never coming back, embracing a new identity as a British writer. But he could not get the Mississippi River out of his mind. Eliot's home was blocks from the river; it is now an abandoned lot with weeds growing out of the plaque bearing his name. He was six when the castle towers at Chain of Rocks Bridge were constructed and a teenager when the grand buildings that John Carpenter would film in ruin a century later were built. He saw paradise around him and sensed it would be lost. For the Mississippi River was relentless and taken for granted, overused and underestimated. It was the heart of America, the Missouri and the Ohio and the Arkansas Rivers clinging to it like inferior arteries, none able to hold the country together and split it apart at once like the Mississippi.

"Time the destroyer is time the preserver, like the river with its cargo of dead negroes, cows and chicken coops," Eliot wrote, and it is impossible to see the Mississippi and not think of the banality of evil, the ships with human cargo in their holds that made their way up and down the river, the rank white indifference to whether people were bought and sold like animals. You stand at the banks of a river that has seen too much: across from St. Louis on the Illinois side is Cahokia, a Native American metropolis that was once the largest city in the world, bigger at its height than London, that vanished without explanation in the fourteenth century, leaving mounds of mystery behind. You drive your children up the river to Keokuk, Iowa, where you know a guy who will let you search for geodes on his land if you give him twenty bucks, and you break plain brown rocks with a pickax until you find one, wondering how many millennia it lingered here with crystals hidden inside.

You follow the river down to Cape Girardeau, where three days before the 2016 election your children play on the banks, small and oblivious to the flood wall mural bearing Rush Limbaugh's face. Your children skip rocks on the water and shriek with joy like children have always done on the Mississippi, like the children of Cahokia did a millennium before. You cross the river back into Illinois to a rock tower forest called the Garden of the Gods and climb prehistoric formations to see the sun shine on the treetop colors of fall, and when you are done you keep heading south, where the Mississippi and Ohio Rivers collide, to an old bandit hideout called Cave-in-Rock, and you climb inside and watch ships sail to Kentucky. Your children find other children, strangers turned fast friends, and they find sticks and write their names in the mud and watch them vanish in the gentle waves, and you know this is the last good day.

During the pandemic and after the attack on the Capitol, when your children are older and not naïve, you follow the Mississippi downtown to Cliff Cave in St. Louis. The three of you climb the river-wet rocks until you reach a cavern covered in graffiti and moss and blockaded with iron bars. Cliff Cave began as a sacred site of the Osage tribe, then became a tavern for eighteenth-century French fur trappers, then a Confederate hideout, then a saloon for Civil War veterans, then a cave winery, then an Anheuser-Busch beer storage area, then a Prohibition-era body dumping ground for the St. Louis mafia, then a cave tavern called "Girlies," then a body dumping site for other criminals. Now it is the home to an endangered species of bats, because human contact did not work out well. This is a sleazy river in a lowdown town, where the worst people keep passing through and finding places to plot and bury bodies and secrets. This is your hometown, you tell the children, but they already know.

You love this river so much it consumes you, you love this country so much it destroys you, because it's the kind of love you have for your children: there is nothing it can do to make you stop loving it and wanting to protect it. You love it and it loves you back; this is no unrequited romance. What you feel is outside of logic or law and it sure as hell is outside government. It is the bedrock, the water: what they cannot take away. You go to the river when you feel like you are drowning inside, searching for safety as if you can find it in the soil, but the soil of the Mississippi is mud.

There is no other home for you, there is nowhere for you to go, because you are too American. You live in the dead center—the dead, rotting center—of America, of every battle and every misdeed, every hideous thing that was said and done, every cemetery split to accommodate the dead of both the Union and the Confederacy. If they try to carve up the country, you do not know what will happen to your city or your state or your family or your friends. You do not know if you are north or south or east or west. You are a Gateway and a Memorial, you are the Lewis and Clark landing and the Mother Road, you are the Louisiana Purchase and you are one bad bargain. You stare at the implacable Mississippi and remember another line of Eliot's poem—*"When the past is all deception, the future futureless"*—and you know you are not leaving, no matter how bad it gets. In Missouri, everything compromises except for that river and you.

In the summer of 2021, millionaire celebrities and partisan pundits began talking about a "national divorce." Americans could no longer live with each other and dividing into multiple countries was the best move, proclaimed liberal comedian Sarah Silverman[9] and right-wing pundits Ben Shapiro and Glenn Beck.[10,11] They parroted the points of Steve Bannon—and before him, hard-right Republican operative Pat Buchanan[12]—to their respective partisan audiences. Later that year, politicians, including Ted Cruz and Marjorie Taylor Greene, announced they were contemplating the idea.[13] They were among many mouthpieces testing the waters by sputtering the sentiments of backstage brokers, marketing treason in a more palatable package.

It is easy, when you do not care about your country, when you do not see people as fellow human beings but as kindling on which to pour your rhetorical kerosene, to have such conversations. You win no matter what, because your color is not blue or red but the green of money. The pay rolls in, the bloodshed rolls on, and you play court jester in the color war, while the rest of the country tries to survive—individually, and together.

The Civil War was an open conspiracy of slaveholders against the United States of America. Like most political conspiracies, its architects used weaponized conspiracy theories, rooted in projection, to terrify locals into supporting their cause. They spun tales of northerners out to steal their land and harm their women, invented tales of treachery about Abraham Lincoln that would befit Confederate leaders like Robert E. Lee or Judah Benjamin, and portrayed Black enslaved Americans as innate brutes who, if freed, would carry out horrific acts similar to what they, as slaveholders, had been practicing.[14] Today, secessionist rhetoric is cloaked in this same cloth—aggression masked as protection—but who is protecting whom from what, and why, is more ambiguous.

The current push toward secession and "national divorce" is a conspiracy by kleptocrats exploiting both the bitter entitlement of the Lost Cause and the stereotype-fueled snobbery of liberal Americans in Democratic-majority states against regular people who live in states run by GOP legislatures.

There have always been secessionist groups on the fringes of American political life—particularly in large states like Texas, which briefly existed as a sovereign nation; and in California, where Silicon Valley technocrats have sought to secede[15]—but the streamlining of sedition is a post-Trump phenomenon. The new secessionism is as contrived as the "red" and "blue" designations. Following the heated 2000 election, pundits and political operatives began using these colors as shorthand for entrenched Democratic and Republican identities that never reflected the reality on the ground. "Red" and "blue" states were manufactured to create monocultures out of a multifaceted nation, narrowing the parameters of political possibility in a country where most people are not even registered members of either party.

In 2004, Barack Obama, then state senator in Illinois, condemned this false dichotomy at the Democratic National Convention. "The pundits like to slice-and-dice our country into red states and blue states—red states for Republicans, and blue states for Democrats," he said. "But I've got news for them, too. We worship an awesome God in the blue states, and we don't like federal agents poking around our libraries in the red states. . . . We are one people, all of us pledging allegiance to the Stars and Stripes, all of us defending the United States of America."[16]

When Obama made that speech, I was living in Bloomington, Indiana. Bloomington, the proverbial small town that resident John Mellencamp immortalized in song, stood out as liberal compared to the rural region surrounding it, but not in a way that felt jarring—why would, or should, *any* state be a monolith? This bizarre assumption is one easy for locals to debunk, but national propagandists were building a monopoly over the residue of gutted local media. Portrayals of the Midwest increasingly came not from the region itself but from corporations in New York City, the proverbial metropolis where Wall Street and Fox News and Donald Trump and Rudy Giuliani sold fatuous fantasies of their own city as a liberal hellhole in contrast to "the real America" of the heartland. I had lived in New York City before moving to Indiana, and what unites most Hoosiers with most New Yorkers is that wealthy elites do not care about *any* of them. Elites are banking—literally—that the rest of the country is too incurious to know the truth about other states or too powerless for their corrections to be heard.

In 2004, Obama's debunking of the red and blue state fallacy left me relieved. A future presidential contender had seen through a pernicious lie, and preemptively sought to stomp it out. This relief was undone four years later by Obama's sneering campaign declaration that small-town Midwesterners are "bitter people" who "cling to their guns and religion."[17] I knew I would be hearing this quote for decades to come, and I was angered by his recklessness. In 2008, the Great Recession hit, local newspapers crumbled, Facebook rose, Obama won, and his quote was immortalized as a meme, words stripped of all context but their callousness, like everyone's words came to be, digital daggers for the information war. I had moved to St. Louis by then, the breeding ground for everything from the Tea Party to the Ferguson protest movement, and I watched as wealthy political operatives traveled to the region to exploit its prejudice and pain.

The Great Recession birthed an unequal recovery. Big coastal cities like New York and San Francisco thrived and became unaffordable, driving out native residents through gentrification. Meanwhile, small towns, lower-class suburbs, and run-down Midwestern cities like Detroit and St. Louis—which had enjoyed a brief comeback in the late 1990s and 2000s—nearly collapsed. The Midwest's assets were bought up by American plutocrats as well as foreign oligarchs—like Ihor Kolomoyskyy, a dual citizen of Ukraine and Israel who became the largest real estate holder in Cleveland in the recession's aftermath. Officials either ignored or encouraged the takeover.[18] In Obama's first two years in office, both the Democrats and the Republicans bailed out Wall Street while doing little to remedy the hardship of Americans outside their donor base. In 2010, the Supreme Court upheld *Citizens United*, deeming corporations to be people and removing constraints on campaign financing. That ruling was a decisive moment in the movement to end America, and it was followed three years later by the Supreme Court's partial repeal of the Voting Rights Act.

Those two Supreme Court decisions stripped away what was left of American representative democracy, allowing the puppet masters to emerge from behind the curtain and flaunt their strings. Laws are both more formidable and more fragile than propaganda. Laws overrule the best intentions and codify the worst. Ordinary people can combat bigotry and stereotypes, and reject the contrived animosity that prejudice breeds. But once legal rights are lost, they are very difficult to recover, particularly when a key mechanism to protect them—voting—is harmed. The judiciary acts as the cage bars of autocracies. How it wields its power sets the stage for the future, overriding other avenues of liberation. In the United States, the new state voter suppression laws made possible by the partial repeal of the VRA codify the tyranny of the minority into the law of the land.

Republican legislatures can lock down a "red state" identity by preventing people from voting while flooding the state with dark-money propaganda as local news sources disappear. They can redraw its districts through gerrymandering so that their permanent rule is all but guaranteed. When confronted with citizen dissent, they can simply decide that certain people's votes do not count, as Missouri did after residents statewide—including most Republicans—voted in progressive ballot initiatives that included the protection of labor unions, an increased minimum wage, and the Clean Missouri Act, which would ban dark money in politics. The will of the majority was clear, but the Missouri GOP representatives ignored it and disregarded the measures. As Missourians struggled to defend their fading democracy, coastal pundits crowed that Missouri—once known as the bellwether state for its propensity to fluctuate between parties and reliably back the winner of the presidential election—was a "deep red state" that got the terrible policies it deserved. They went on to say the same about Texas, Georgia, and other states whose legislatures ignored the stated will of the people or created new laws to prevent or disregard their votes.

The idea of a "deep red state" was a lie, part of a litany of lies. But repetition is necessary for the political elite to attain its goal. Hostile operatives want their prophecies of monolithic political cultures to prove self-fulfilling, because that will make the partitioning easier. If you keep telling people that their states—states with fluctuating populations and complex histories and vacillating political preferences—have been immutable entities since time immemorial, perhaps they will come to believe it.

Perhaps they will look to the distant past—in particular, the Civil War—to justify the crises of the present, like the crisis of a government apathetic to their despair. Perhaps, in desperation, they will seek to revive what they have been told is their "true" political culture: the "good old days" that were only good for a select population. When that fails, perhaps they will see differences as irreconcilable, and back secession plans peddled by elitist plotters who would never leave their gated citadels to live in the regions they seek to dominate and destroy. These tactics are not limited to conservatives; they work on anyone. Maybe liberals will view themselves as above countrymen they have now reduced to clichés, envisioning themselves as residents of a future "blue paradise" removed from the backwards "red states"—even though the "blue states" are just further fodder for an oligarch takeover.

Wherever you live, you must remember you are no longer a human being in this scenario. You are a pawn to push, an asset to mine, and an imposition should you grasp the plan. At every step of the way, you are seen as disposable.

In the 1990s, journalist Robert Kaplan wrote a series of superficial, inflammatory, and popular books about the post–Cold War states of the former Yugoslavia and the Soviet Union. In Kaplan's view, conflicts between Serbs and Croats and Bosnians were an inevitable result of tensions held for nearly a millennium, intervening periods of peace and intermarriages be damned. The post-Soviet countries of Central Asia were, in his view, similarly bound for regional warfare due to the bloodlust of their distant ancestor Genghis Khan. (No such wars took place.) Today Kaplan's work is used by anthropologists to teach their students what *not* to do. His ethnic essentialism was not only lazy and inaccurate but dangerous. It ignored modern structural crises in favor of a vision of primordial destiny, the same way dictators and warlords do to justify their brutality and greed.

There is no easier way to get people to enact the unimaginable than to convince them this is the way it always was, and therefore the way it will inevitably be. Kaplan's narrative tactics are the same ones being used by hostile operatives now to harden partisan labels onto geographic territory. Should the red state–blue state divide reveal itself as a fallacy, operatives will reach deeper into the darkest moments of the American past for inspiration. They rewrite losers as winners, sinners as saints, and treason as triumph.

This is why the GOP is working to redefine accurate history as "critical race theory"—an academic term right-wing conspirator Christopher Rufo admitted they chose to repurpose and weaponize into whatever they need it to mean at a given time. "We have successfully frozen their brand—'critical race theory'—into the public conversation and are steadily driving up negative perceptions. We will eventually turn it toxic, as we put all of the various cultural insanities under that brand category," Rufo wrote in March 2021. "The goal is to have the public read something crazy in the newspaper and immediately think 'critical race theory.' We have decodified the term and will recodify it to annex the entire range of cultural constructions that are unpopular with Americans."[19]

They need the culture war to distract from the war on national security—a war that *all* Americans are losing, because the government has decided to forfeit its sovereignty. In November 2021, the Federal Election Commission ruled that it would become legal for foreigners to fund US referendum campaigns—subversion that was until recently not only reviled but illegal.[20] Another loophole has been created to function as a noose around the neck of American democracy.

If you want to know who owns the United States of America, follow the money—it is in offshore accounts—and monitor who pays the people rewriting the laws and marketing these policies as normal. These donors give to both parties, often in record amounts. Billionaire Len Blavatnik, for example, a USSR-born partner of sanctioned Russian oligarchs, gave millions to the Republicans until House Democrats announced in 2019 that they were investigating Trump, at which point he gave the Democratic Congressional Campaign Committee the largest donation in its history.[21] Under pressure, the DCCC returned part of the funds, but as of 2021, he is again lavishing the Democrats with money, including $50,000 for House Speaker Nancy Pelosi alone. In 2019, Blavatnik was a useful vehicle for foreign interests because his American citizenship meant that his donations were legal; now, the FEC is eliminating the need for such go-betweens.

This crisis is not a matter of Democrats versus Republicans, or "red" versus "blue." The crisis is a matter of people who seek to protect the United States versus elite operatives who want to destroy it. The latter are stripping down the country and selling it for parts and trying to convince ordinary Americans that it was their own idea.

The crisis is also not a matter of North versus South. When people discuss a Second American Civil War, they often hearken back to the battles fought around the Mason-Dixon Line. Over the summer of 2021, as the delta strain of COVID-19 spread from southwest Missouri into neighboring states and eventually into the southeast, partisans attempted to attribute the virus's spread to the Civil War's legacy, instead of the more obvious conclusion that it spread from a southern origin point to hot southern states where people were staying inside in air-conditioned spaces. (Now, in late 2021, as the delta strain dominates the cold north and is scarce in the balmy south, coastal pundits and propagandists have suddenly put their maps and their generalizations away.)

The dividing line of America is not between North and South. It is not, in fact, regional at all, nor are there "two Americas." There are a multitude of Americas, as one would expect in a country this large and diverse, but we are no longer unified by ideals—instead we are left with a common heartache of ideals betrayed. We share that pain and take it out on each other while disregarding each other's humanity and being acclimatized by algorithms to do so.

The new Civil War is fought on the internet, where lies and memes spur exhausted people to hate each other; where troll farms can make astroturf rallies; where threats have been normalized and kindness is labeled "virtue signaling." The new Civil War is fought with truncated speech in character-limited forums and in sound bites by politicians scraping at the dregs of the attention economy. The new Civil War was fought largely indoors in 2020, by people who dreamed up nightmare visions of the other states they could no longer visit, the people they could no longer meet, because regular life had been stolen from them.

"As a General, we have an army of digital soldiers," Michael Flynn told his supporters in November 2016. "This was run like an insurgency, irregular warfare at its finest."[22] Three years later, Flynn filed an application to trademark the phrase "digital soldiers" so he could profit off the virtual war.[23] This is how the new Civil War is run: as entertainment, and then as autocracy, and then as an insurrection viewed with such apathy by the institutions it is trying to destroy that it can be trademarked by a foreign agent coup plotter and used for marketing purposes. This is General Patent, absorbing the neo-Nazis into a profitability model rather than fighting them in the field. This is how a mafia state does battle against the people forced to live in its manufactured reality.

The Lost Cause of the New Civil War is a reality TV president. The weapons of the New Civil War are viral videos of ordinary people being judged in the court of public opinion, because the actual courts are not concerned with justice. The New Civil War is being fought so that you will forget that the Old Cold War ended as a corporate merger. Kleptocrats and oligarchs, pedophiles and criminals, technocrats and white supremacists: that is who runs what is indeed a New World Order, a phrase that merited the apprehension it provoked. Men of multiple passports, men of copious currencies, criminal elites who tell you their plots outright to test not only the limits of their own might but whether civic obligation still exists. No one powerful intervenes, no matter how blunt and blatant they get.

You see this threat unfold and you trust your instincts. You trust the pain instead of trusting the plan. Looking at it makes you feel insane, but seeing it makes you know you are not.

If the oligarchs partition the United States, what will happen to St. Louis? This is the kind of question you ask yourself nowadays, not as an abstract intellectual exercise, but to help plan the future. You envision a scenario in which your homeland is butchered into red and blue oligarch fiefdoms, and St. Louis—politically blue, demographically Black—is declared an enemy of whatever contrived conservative bloc takes over Missouri. You picture St. Louis asking to join Illinois, but being rebuffed due to its poverty and crime and long-standing reputation as a regional reject. Scorned by all, it resigns itself to becoming the first Midwest city-state since Cahokia: St. Louis, the Monaco of the Mississippi, the Vatican of Route 66, built on reliquaries of the American Dream. What do you do with a city like this, a city that is so American that there is no place for it when America is destroyed? What do you do with a place that is, as T. S. Eliot said, "a reminder of what men choose to forget"?

When I talk about the threat of partition in public, I often do it in a semijoking way, because the reality of the threat scares me in a way that feels too personal, too portentous, to convey outright. I know too many people from the Balkans and from the USSR who have endured the horror of dissolution. It is not only the bloodshed, not only the sudden enmity of people you thought were neighbors and friends, but the loss of your place in the world, the theft of a rootedness so reliable you treated it like air until the day you woke up gasping for breath.

The reality of secession and dissolution is that your countrymen—your friends and family members—are suddenly living in other countries that you may not be able to visit. The reality is a military transformed into mercenaries trading weapons and operating with brutal impunity on what used to be fellow citizens. It is the loss of basic infrastructure and it is privatization by the most corrupt actors in your region: a process already underway in the United States by operatives who know that the privatization of public goods can be accelerated by the shock tactics of partition.

It means the most vulnerable people in the country—people who are not white or wealthy—will suffer even more under right-wing extremist regimes whom they did not elect and cannot control, while wealthy liberals in "blue enclaves" blame them for their fate. It means the "blue enclaves" will be invaded by the "red territories," because no oligarch is going to let resources go unexploited. The idea that a liberal paradise will be tolerated in the Partitioned States of America is absurd; the right-wingers who treat small liberal arts colleges as major threats are not going to let actual nations rest in peace. They will raid you and then you will be one of us, only with more stigma and less recourse. There is no paradise in partition: all that will happen is that the things you hate most about America will multiply. This is true no matter who you are or what your political predilections may be.

A stable economy, civic institutions, public and private education, foreign relations, reliable transportation—all of this will be up for grabs to the highest bidders. Necessities will become luxuries even more than they are already. You will feel this loss, navigating daily life in a new nation of constantly contested borders. But the greatest loss will be your sense of self in a place that was never clear-cut in the first place, a country born of ideals contradicting its own laws, principles that were never fully honored in practice.

America was never the idealized melting pot it claimed to be, but it was never the bifurcated playing field it is portrayed as by pundits and politicians. It was an ineffable amalgamation, and to be American is to be shaped by ceaseless contrary influences, to not make sense and find a certain freedom in that. At times, this freedom exists only in your mind, it exists as possibilities and futures, and every confrontation with the opportunity hoarders and cannibalizing cataloguers of imagination is an attempt to drive it out. There were American dreams deferred, and then there were American ghosts.

But you still have those dreams, because no one can shake off a homeland. You still have those ghosts, those memories of the future. It is not a matter of your own life—you were done for a while ago—but of the next generation and what they deserve. When a country collapses under the weight of its own corruption, as the USSR and Yugoslavia did and as the United States seems set to do, it is common for people to say that the people of that country got what they deserved. What they usually mean is that bad actions have consequences, but we, the people, do not deserve what we have now or what may be coming. There is a great difference between what citizens bear due to the cruelty of the powerful and what they deserve as regular people who dream of more.

In the fall of 2021, my husband and kids and I drove south down the Great River Road, crossing through Illinois and Missouri and back again, until we were standing in front of a hulking formation in the water, visible from both states and straddling their dividing line.[24]

In the middle of the Mississippi River, a four-hundred-million-year-old, sixty-foot rock rises from the mud, a mound of black strata topped with wild green brush. Today it is called Tower Rock, but centuries of voyagers called it by different names. French priests in the seventeenth century reported that local Native American tribes warned them that a demonic manitou lived there and devoured travelers, so they stuck a crucifix on top, called it La Roche de la Croix, and fled the scene.[25] In the early 1800s, explorer Meriwether Lewis spent a trepidatious night by its shores, saying the area had a natural violence "no boat dare approach."[26] English settlers named it Devil's Rock, and believed the surrounding area to be haunted, leading to a number of nearby sites named after the Devil: Devil's Backbone, Devil's Elbow, Devil's Bake Oven, Devil's Honeycomb. I have an old book called *Geologic Wonders and Curiosities of Missouri*, and a solid eight pages of the index are devoted to the devil. I used that book to prop up my laptop for Zoom sessions about coup plots during the global plague.

In 1839, local legend has it, a wedding reception was held on Tower Rock. The boat of the wedding party was caught in a whirlpool after they attempted to depart, with the only survivor an enslaved man who had been forced to accompany the celebrants. On the same day of the drowning, the niece of the bride was born. In 1859, the niece held a party on Tower Rock to commemorate the tragedy, inviting the enslaved man as a special guest. During the party, the deceased wedding guests arose from the Mississippi to issue a warning. The wedding priest handed the niece a scroll of parchment that said a Great War was coming. It would pit father against son, brother against brother. The bride's own family met this fate, with one side fighting for the Union and one for the Confederacy, slaughtering each other in the process. There have been many attempts to track down the origins of this legend, and while the family has been verified as real and their deaths as true, no one has been able to identify the enslaved man who witnessed it all.[27]

But the story lives on: a legend in which the Civil War was foretold, or retroactively justified, in a tale of Tower Rock, its white decadence and its portents of doom. At the end of the Civil War, local engineers wanted to blow up Tower Rock, but Ulysses Grant issued an executive order in 1871 insisting it be preserved. It was one of many executive orders issued by Grant, the post–Civil War president who saw the demise of the United States as inevitable unless its worst instincts were restrained by law. Stories of Tower Rock—haunted, cursed, the domain of the devil—endure because legends convey more truth about the feel of a place than facts do. Legends preserve the fear, the rage, and the guilt.

Mark Twain, the Missouri writer whose most famous works took place on the Mississippi River, understood this well. In 1883, he published *Life on the Mississippi*, an essay collection in which he reflected on how the Mississippi shaped him as a writer and a man. "The face of the water, in time, became a wonderful book—a book that was a dead language to the uneducated passenger, but which told its mind to me without reserve, delivering its most cherished secrets as clearly as if it uttered them with a voice," he wrote, reminiscing on his childhood in Hannibal, the river town that inspired *The Adventures of Tom Sawyer* and *The Adventures of Huckleberry Finn*, and his teenage years hitching rides on steamboats. "Throughout the long twelve hundred miles there was never a page that was void of interest, never one that you could leave unread without loss, never one that you would want to skip, thinking you could find higher enjoyment in some other thing."

But when Twain became a riverboat pilot, the Mississippi changed. Knowing how the river worked drained it of its majesty and mystery, and stripped away its true meaning. "A day came when I began to cease from noting the glories and the charms which the moon and the sun and the twilight wrought upon the river's face; another day came when I ceased altogether to note them," Twain wrote. "Then, if that sunset scene had been repeated, I should have looked upon it without rapture, and should have commented upon it, inwardly, after this fashion: This sun means that we are going to have wind to-morrow; that floating log means that the river is rising. . . . All the value any feature of it had for me now was the amount of usefulness it could furnish toward compassing the safe piloting of a steamboat."[28]

Twain ends the essay by pitying anyone whose job it is to parse the ineffable, to strip away truth in the service of explanation. He finds reprieve in the Mississippi's unyielding ferocity: reprieve, not comfort, for those are two different things.

In November 2021, orange and red leaves fell on the Mississippi River shore, beautiful little deaths, and drifted into the water. They floated past a state border rendered invisible by a river, past a monument belonging to no man, into the whirlpools that spin uninterrupted alongside it. Tower Rock is a mystery without a secret, indifferent to understanding, motionless over millennia even as the river changed course. The water seems low enough to walk there, but you don't want to cross over now. You are saving that for later, one last adventure for when you are stateless in your own country, one more trip to no man's land to see what else the devil has in store.

8

THE OCTOPUS

On August 10, 1991, forty-four-year-old journalist Danny Casolaro was found dead in a bathtub in the Sheraton Hotel in Martinsburg, West Virginia. His wrists had been slashed ten to twelve times. A medical examiner ruled it suicide. His friends and family believed it was murder.

Casolaro had been investigating what he called "The Octopus": a vast transnational network of corruption stretching from the DOJ to the CIA to the FBI to numerous private law and technology firms around the world. He was particularly interested in PROMIS: compromised computer software produced by the American technology firm Inslaw and sold to the US government by, among others, Robert Maxwell.[1] The software was said to enable espionage once installed, allowing easy access to US government secrets. After Robert Maxwell died mysteriously in November 1991, software successors to PROMIS were handled by his twin daughters, Christine and Isabel Maxwell, whose Chiliad database technology is now used by the FBI.[2] The sisters of Ghislaine Maxwell, whose criminal partner Jeffrey Epstein forged deep ties to big tech, remained involved in the software trade for decades.[3,4]

By the late 1980s, Casolaro had identified an international network of "thugs and thieves who roam the earth with their weapons and their murders, trading dope and dirty money for the secrets of the temple," as he wrote in July 1991 in the proposal for his book, which he titled *Behold, a Pale Horse* in early drafts, but later changed to *The Octopus*.[5] Casolaro believed that this network was tied to the Iran-Contra and the Bank of Credit and Commerce International (BCCI) scandals, and that its players posed a grave threat to US national security and to the peace and prosperity of the world. "This story is about a handful of people who have been able to successfully exploit the secret empires of espionage networks, big oil, and organized crime. This octopus spans the globe . . . to control governmental institutions in the United States and abroad," he wrote.[6]

In August, Casolaro headed to West Virginia to meet a source who promised him information on the mystery he had spent a decade trying to unravel. He did not tell anyone who this source was, and did not live to reveal them. He had spent the years before cultivating a series of shadowy sources while contending with the attention of the people he sought to expose.[7]

"The Inslaw case alone is enough to drive a sane man to madness, if not suicide," *Vanity Fair* journalist Ron Rosenbaum wrote in a December 1991 article about Casolaro's investigation and its mysterious, premature end.[8] In 1993, Richard Fricker, a journalist at *WIRED* magazine, attempted to summarize the Inslaw case, which he had spent two years investigating:

> What for the past decade has been known as the Inslaw affair began to unravel in the final, shredder-happy days of the Bush administration. According to Federal court documents, PROMIS was stolen from Inslaw by the Department of Justice directly after Etian's [sic, Rafael Eitan, chief of the Israel Defense Forces' anti-terrorism intelligence unit] 1983 visit to Inslaw (a later congressional investigation preferred to use the word "misappropriated"). According to sworn affidavits, PROMIS was then given or sold at a profit to Israel and as many as 80 other countries by Dr. Earl W. Brian, a man with close personal and business ties to then-President Ronald Reagan and then-Presidential counsel Edwin Meese.

"A House Judiciary Committee report released last September found evidence raising 'serious concerns' that high officials at the Department of Justice executed a pre-meditated plan to destroy Inslaw and co-opt the rights to its PROMIS software," the article continued. "The committee's call for an independent counsel have fallen on deaf ears. One journalist, Danny Casolaro, died as he attempted to tell the story . . . and boxes of documents relating to the case have been destroyed, stolen, or conveniently 'lost' by the Department of Justice. But so far, not a single person has been held accountable."[9]

Over thirty years have passed since the death of Danny Casolaro, and there remain no answers, even as the world contends with rising autocracy enabled by billionaire technocratic overlords who have entered into alliances with corrupt states, corporations, and extremist groups. While Casolaro's main obsession was Inslaw and Reagan-era state crime, he also was examining the history of transnational mafia networks, particularly that of National Crime Syndicate head Meyer Lansky, and their infiltration into global financial systems.

In an unpublished manuscript, written around 1990, he wrote of Lansky's goal to "transform the North American crime syndicate into the most powerful business and financial combine in the world, making big time crime so insulated and so 'respectable' that it would be untouchable by any government prosecutors."[10] Casolaro was concerned that Lansky's mafia network had launched a plan to "buy up" Israel and use it as the base for a "legitimized" crime empire, operating with impunity.[11] He then speculated that after corrupting Israel, the syndicate planned to do the same to the United States. As mentioned in chapter three, Lansky's protégés included Trump mentor and attorney Roy Cohn, and his key blackmail targets included FBI head J. Edgar Hoover.

While not all of Casolaro's suppositions have been verified—a task he was struggling to accomplish in the months before he died—his vision of a global autocratic technocracy bolstered by unpunished white-collar crime has been borne out. But despite his extensive body of research, at the time of his passing, even somewhat sympathetic journalists stamped him with the mark of the shunned: *conspiracy theorist*. "What destabilized Danny was an extremely virulent strain of the information virus we're suffering from collectively as a nation: Conspiracy Theory Fever," posited Rosenbaum, while acknowledging that actual government conspiracies, like Iran-Contra and Watergate, were common. "A slow-acting virus that has infected our ability to know the truth about the secret history of our age."[12]

Rosenbaum wrote these words in 1991, during the Anomalous Era of American Accountability, when flickers of the truth were coming to light and illuminating figures in the shadows. Thirty years later, many individuals connected to the cases Casolaro investigated—the Maxwell family, Bill Barr, Rudy Giuliani, the Khashoggi family—remain in the news due to their connections to Trump campaign operatives and their corrupt associates. Casolaro wrote in the tradition of other 1980s and early-1990s independent investigative journalists seeking to expose the dark underbelly of globalized crime and government: Wayne Barrett on Trump and Giuliani's transnational criminal ties, Robert Friedman on the Russian mafia's global reach, Robert Parry on Iran-Contra and the October Surprise, Gary Webb on the CIA and the drug trade, the countless reporters who fought the system and followed the money—only to watch their own fortunes fade as the media industry shrank and funds for investigative journalism dwindled.

Thousands of books detail different tentacles of the Octopus. Yet the continuity of the corruption—the recurring names, countries, corporations, and goals—is rarely spelled out in plain terms. Part of the reason is that to elucidate it would take far more than the effort of one individual: it would take a group as committed to accountability as the criminal elite are to maintaining their impunity. Following the money of the criminal elite is both a massive endeavor and a discouraged one. Even recent large-scale investigative journalism projects, like the Panama Papers and the Pandora Papers, in which hundreds of international journalists tracked offshore money laundering by the wealthy and powerful, omit many of the most notorious US operatives, and include no US politicians at all.[13] Their rationale for this—that money laundering is so easy in the United States, criminal elites do not need offshore accounts and can simply drop their ill-gotten gains in states like South Dakota—is chillingly accurate, yet it does not help decipher what corrupt American power brokers are actually doing.

Attempts to pull back and analyze global corruption as an interconnected whole—to see the forest for the treason—are deemed "conspiratorial" by their very nature. The propensity of some to seek a simplified explanation has tarnished the efforts of others to break down the Octopus, piece by piece, and thereby regain our freedom from its grip. Horrific stories told in isolation are easier to dismiss than a connected narrative of interlocking parts, in part because of a sincere desire to believe that the situation cannot be as bad as that. It is far easier, when confronted with appalling evidence, to blame the messenger.

"Conspiracy theorist" is a way to call an investigative reporter a liar and a liar an investigative reporter. The goal of criminal elites and autocrats is to make the pursuit of truth and justice seem worthless, or a matter pursued by the unhinged. This tendency has only gotten worse in the thirty years since Danny Casolaro died.

I do not know what happened to Casolaro, though I have examined what is left of his notebooks and files, and saw no indication of suicidal thoughts. I am not going to attempt to break down the Inslaw/PROMIS epic in this book. But I do know the Octopus is real. The Octopus is global kleptocracy: the nexus where organized crime, state corruption, and corporate corruption meet, enabled by digital technology that allows the world's most vicious elites to operate across state lines and alter the global public's conception of reality. To deny that this is happening is to deny something obvious and insidious: insidious because it is obvious, and therefore enabled by the complicity and cowardice of those tasked with enforcing accountability.

The Octopus is a twenty-first-century white whale and we are all trapped on the same ship. The Octopus is no longer submerged in the swamp, and everyone is crazed from the sightings and the search and the futility and the fear. Everyone has gone a little Captain Ahab these days. Witnessing the theft of the future will do that to you.

"Encountering this odyssey, meeting it with your whole life, is to grapple with something personal," Casolaro wrote in his notes for the book he was never able to complete.[14]

It would be easier to believe that this dark orchestration was not happening, or that someone was working to stop it: someone who is not you or me. It would be easier to believe that people in power simply do not have the information, instead of acknowledging that they are refusing to act on it—or worse, that they *are* acting on it, in a way that enables all they are supposed to oppose, and opposes everything for which they are supposed to stand. All I am is a writer, but my work has become a transgression. A modern writer on politics is supposed to wait to tell the public what they know until it no longer matters. You are supposed to save information on national security for a book deal and participate in a pantomime of feigned shock and delayed realization. Your job is to help the powerful run out the clock, to serve as a stenographer while elite crimes go unpunished, until so much time passes that they are no longer categorized as crimes at all.

You are not supposed to want to slay the Octopus. You are not supposed to recoil at its touch. You are supposed to crave access to it, and with that access, you become part of it, another tentacle squeezing the life out of moral inquiry and the pursuit of truth. The worst thing about the Octopus is how many volunteered to serve it, and the greatest service is to pretend that it does not exist. There is no space for realization in this feted and fetid journalistic abyss: your reaction is a redaction.

Casolaro was not alone in following overlapping threads and getting accused of weaving together loose ends. In 1994, Mark Lombardi, a Texas-based conceptual artist who specialized in collage, decided to create visual representations of recent government conspiracies. His focus, like Casolaro's, was on Iran-Contra, BCCI, and global mafia and espionage networks. In 1999, Lombardi created an intricate piece detailing the webs between the Bush family and the oil industry, in particular operatives working with the Saudi government. His drawing "George W. Bush, Harken Energy and Jackson Stephens, c. 1979–1990 (5th Version)" detailed the ties between the Bush and Bin Laden families. It debuted two years before the September 11 attacks.

Lombardi's work was displayed at the Museum of Modern Art, the Whitney Museum of Art, and galleries across the United States. His elaborate depictions of the networks behind conspiracies were rigorously fact-checked, a process his curator, Robert Hobbs, found intimidating. "Certain things that are listed in the drawing are in red," Hobbs told NPR. "These represent court judgments, actual dollar amounts. That is verifiable information. And I think that Lombardi himself realized that not everything could be verified. So I think what you have instead is names. We know about connections of names. Exactly what is that connection is hard to characterize. So that is a line with an arrow in one direction, or an arrow in two directions. It's really the abstract component of the work of art. It's what can be represented, and—really—what cannot be represented."[15]

Lombardi was a meticulous researcher who catalogued his work in tens of thousands of notecards before drawing them in sprawling, web-like formations. He knew what happened when a person dared discuss these topics in public, and embraced a highbrow tabloid persona, handing out business cards that read DEATH DEFYING ACTS OF ART AND CONSPIRACY.[16] Lombardi relied initially on publicly available documents, but in time, witnesses of the government conspiracies he investigated came to him with information.[17] As his fame grew, he became a challenge to government claims of plausible deniability.

"John Kerry's Senate Investigating Committee on BCCI was winding down at about the same time that Mark was turning out his work," Lombardi's biographer, Patricia Goldstone, recalled in a 2015 interview. "[Lombardi] answered questions that if you read the Kerry committee report, they said they didn't have the time or the resources to pursue. And he was this artist sitting on the floor of a tiny studio in Houston pursuing them."[18]

Lombardi's art attracted the attention of the FBI, the CIA, and some of the operatives whose ties he documented.[19] But no one knows the full nature of their interest, because on March 22, 2000, Lombardi was found dead in his Brooklyn home. He was forty-eight years old. Days before his sudden death, ties between Bush, the Republican front-runner for the presidential nomination, and Khalid bin Mahfouz, a banker for the Saudi royal family, had been documented in the small business press. These ties were the same ones highlighted by Lombardi in his artwork. Bin Mahfouz, a billionaire BCCI director who was indicted for fraud and settled the case for $225 million, was later investigated for funding Al Qaeda and giving hundreds of thousands of dollars to Osama bin Laden.[20] After 9/11, FBI agents tried, and failed, to get Lombardi's art removed from the Whitney Museum.[21]

Lombardi had begun a new project in his final months: an in-depth look at how the Russian mafia had infiltrated US banking.[22] He was particularly interested in Semion Mogilevich, the head of a transnational crime syndicate that had penetrated the United States after taking root in Israel, Hungary, and other European states. Born in the USSR, Mogilevich left in 1988 after Robert Maxwell got him an Israeli passport. He then used that passport to set up a global criminal network, and landed on the FBI's Top Ten Most Wanted List in 2009.[23] James Comey removed him from the list in December 2015 and replaced him with a bank robber, despite Robert Mueller describing Mogilevich, a financial genius with ties to arms trading and drug trafficking, as one of the greatest threats to Western democracy, and vowing in 2011 that Mogilevich would stay on the list until he was caught.[24]

Between his focus on Mogilevich and on transnational operatives linked to 9/11 and global financial corruption, Lombardi anticipated the key events of a catastrophic century he did not live to see. He traced a shadow network with ruthless curiosity but without partisan bias, preferring to highlight corruption that extends beyond parties and borders. The greatest threat of Lombardi was not only that he wanted to know it all, but that he wanted the public to know it too. He saw secrets and presented them as mysteries, understanding that art would grab the average observer in a way the dry recitation of facts never could.

As in the Casolaro case, the medical examiner deemed Lombardi's death a suicide, while his friends and family suspected murder.[25] As with Casolaro, it is impossible to narrow down the list of suspects who would want Lombardi eliminated, because the point of his work was to document the intricacy of criminal elite networks, the relentlessness of the machinations of power, and the legal barriers it annihilates in its quest for impunity. If you examine the art Lombardi created in the 1990s, you will spot leads that, had they been followed by US officials in the twentieth century, could have saved American lives in the twenty-first. But officials did not follow those leads, because the trail led right back to their own institutions.

It did not have to be this way. And for short-lived periods of American history, it seemed like it wouldn't. There were other anomalous eras of American accountability, glimmers of hope that light the way to a better future, and as always, they require confronting the nightmare head-on.

In 1972, Victor Marchetti, a CIA officer who had joined the agency in 1955, and John Marks, a State Department official, wrote the first book ever to be censored by the United States government.[26,27] *The CIA and the Cult of Intelligence* was written in response to internal corruption they had witnessed in the years prior to and during the Vietnam War. They documented brutal paramilitary operations and vile dirty tricks, and warned that the CIA had transformed into an agency that endangered the American people far more than it protected them.

Upon hearing that Marchetti was writing a book, CIA officials attempted to block its publication on the grounds that his critique posed a national security risk and violated contractual secrecy agreements he had signed as a condition of his employment. When that argument failed in court, the CIA, which had retained the right to read any work Marchetti published, turned to censorship, attempting to eliminate a fifth of the manuscript. "The result was a dramatic demonstration of how censorship works," wrote journalist Anthony Lewis in an introduction to the 1980 edition. "The arbitrariness, the design very often to prevent official embarrassment rather than protect real secrets."[28]

When it was finally published in June 1974, *The CIA and the Cult of Intelligence* was an instant bestseller, due to both its taboo topic and to a series of leaked documents and public hearings that had left the nation attuned to government corruption. Though Marchetti and Marks regained the ability to print much of their original manuscript, it was still published in a redacted form, with the CIA's excised and restored passages in boldface and firm deletions marked by lines of blank space and the word DELETED. The CIA made 168 deletions in the original version. The reader is left constantly aware of what the government does not want them to know.

Marchetti and Marks were not out to destroy the Central Intelligence Agency. They did not think most of its employees intended to harm the United States. They wanted to reform the agency—and more broadly, to end the corrosive influence of excessive secrecy, which they viewed as a detriment to both democracy and public safety. They claimed that reform would never come from within, for the CIA employed a fatuous claim of "national security" whenever it needed to justify continuation of its abhorrent actions. Change could potentially come from Congress, they argued, but only if the public put pressure on their representatives. The only way the public would do that was if they knew the truth, which is why they wrote their book.

"The time has come to demysticize the intelligence profession, to disabuse Americans of the ideas that clandestine agents somehow make the world a safer place to live in, that excessive secrecy is necessary to protect national security," Marchetti and Marks wrote. "These notions are simply not true; the CIA and the other intelligence agencies have merely used them to build their own covert empire. The US intelligence community performs a vital service in keeping track of and analyzing the military capability and strengths of the Soviet Union and China, but its other functions—the CIA's dirty tricks and classical espionage—are, on the whole, a liability for the country, on both practical and moral grounds."[29]

The CIA and the Cult of Intelligence was published three years after the

American public was made aware of COINTELPRO, the FBI's decades-long surveillance, infiltration, and discreditation vendetta against American citizens, particularly civil rights activists. It included assassination plots and psyops targeting civil rights leaders, including Martin Luther King Jr., whom they tried to goad to suicide.[30] In March 1971, the Citizens' Commission to Investigate the FBI, an activist group, burgled a Media, Pennsylvania, office and emerged with over one thousand documents confirming the worst fears about J. Edgar Hoover's operation.

The revelations about COINTELPRO were followed months later by the release of the Pentagon Papers, a series of documents leaked in June by US military analyst Daniel Ellsberg that revealed the duplicitous ways multiple administrations manipulated the public about the Vietnam War. In May 1972, J. Edgar Hoover died of a heart attack, ending his forty-eight-year grip on the FBI and spurring debate about the future direction of the bureau. In June, operatives working for the Republican Party were arrested after breaking into Democratic National Headquarters in the Watergate building to steal documents, inaugurating the series of cover-ups and revelations that would lead to Richard Nixon's resignation, including televised hearings held throughout 1973 and 1974. The Watergate hearings prompted renewed attention on Ellsberg—Nixon's henchmen had burglarized Ellsberg's psychiatrist's office in an effort to discredit him[31]—and educated the American people about connected networks of corruption and the lengths to which the government would go to conceal them.

The cumulative effect of these revelations led to a shift in public consciousness: increasing cynicism and betrayal among skeptics, and disbelief and defensiveness among those still clinging to the vestiges of institutional integrity. Above all, they created a broad demand for transparency among both those suspicious of the state and those who sought to support it. The idea that the American public *deserved* a transparent government, that accountability was an inalienable right along with life, liberty, and the pursuit of happiness, gained ground after decades of covert actions being justified by the threat of the Cold War.

The atmosphere of the early 1970s was very similar to that in the United States in 2021, with the key difference that, in the 1970s, elected officials felt compelled to do something about it. They felt an obligation to tell the public the truth.

By September 1974, one month after Nixon resigned, elected officials had begun to express their frustration with the CIA and with cabinet officials like Henry Kissinger and their ceaseless conspiracies and cover-ups. Mainstream publications like *TIME*—at that point the most popular magazine in the United States[32]—ran cover stories with titles like "The CIA—Has It Gone Too Far?" They answered their own question in stark terms: "The affair served to confirm all the worst suspicions about the CIA and its exaggerated image as a vast conspiracy," *TIME* wrote in a long exposé on the CIA's illicit operations abroad and its deleterious effect on America's reputation.[33] It was time for a gutting: of Nixon, of corrupt intelligence agencies, of media cover-ups, of warmongers and mercenaries. It was time for Americans to reclaim America, and in order for that to happen, they needed to know how it all went wrong.

The realm of conspiracy theory had become the realm of mainstream politics. No topic was off-limits now: plots and lies and revelations permeated the most milquetoast venues as well as publications targeting the counterculture, like *Rolling Stone*, where Hunter S. Thompson dissected the Nixon administration with ferocity. The year 1974 ended with Seymour Hersh's devastating investigative series on the CIA's massive domestic intelligence operations, featuring interviews with Marchetti, landing on the December 22 front page of *The New York Times*.[34]

The shocking aspect of this era, by the standards of today, was not the revelations in any of these works, but that elected officials felt compelled to address them. To refuse to do so was to risk alienating an angry electorate whose leverage had not yet been stripped away. On January 27, 1975, the United States Senate Select Committee to Study Governmental Operations with Respect to Intelligence Activities—nicknamed the Church Committee after its chair, Senator Frank Church of Idaho—was formed in order to shed light on the secrets of the FBI, CIA, NSA, and other bodies outside the purview of the average American. The research of the committee comprises the most extensive review of intelligence activities ever made available to the public. Among the programs they exposed were MKUltra, COINTELPRO, Family Jewels (assassination operations), HTLINGUAL (illegal monitoring of US mail), Operation Shamrock (spying on domestic telegrams), and Operation Mockingbird (a program designed to shape news media), among others.

The information the committee revealed was both voluminous and selective, a sign of how much internal corruption was at play and a lingering reluctance to reveal it—for it was not only US bureaucracy that was infiltrated, but private institutions as well. Reporter Carl Bernstein, who broke the Watergate story with Bob Woodward, criticized the Church Committee's documentation of Operation Mockingbird, saying that government influence over media was far more insidious than it portrayed, particularly with *The New York Times*. "Top officials of the CIA, including former directors William Colby and George Bush, persuaded the committee to restrict its inquiry into the matter and to deliberately misrepresent the actual scope of the activities in its final report," he wrote in *Rolling Stone* in 1977.[35]

The Church Committee was accompanied by the Pike Committee, a House congressional committee that also investigated the FBI, NSA, and CIA, as well as executive branch abuses committed in the Nixon era. Unlike the Church Committee, which was able to release much of its information to the public, the Pike Committee was stymied by the Ford administration. As a result, most of its information about illicit operations remains classified. In an August 1975 interview, Senator Church warned not only of the dangers of lack of transparency but of changes in technology that laid the groundwork for an American dystopia in the decades to come unless institutions operated with openness and integrity. "If this government ever became a tyranny, if a dictator ever took charge in this country, the technological capacity that the intelligence community has given the government could enable it to impose total tyranny," he said on *Meet the Press*. "There would be no way to fight back because the most careful effort to combine together in resistance to the government, no matter how privately it was done, is within the reach of the government to know. Such is the capability of this technology."[36]

Church's warning was revived in the aftermath of revelations about domestic spying brought forth by Edward Snowden, the NSA employee who leaked documents and then fled to authoritarian Russia, but it is broadly resonant. The dystopia extends beyond state surveillance and into corrupt private technology firms like Facebook that boast authoritarian sympathizers like Peter Thiel on their boards, data mining firms like Cambridge Analytica, built to manipulate the public into backing autocrats, and the general panopticon hellscape of smartphone living, in which everything can be monitored and nothing is revealed. This dystopia will worsen with the emergence of "deep fakes" and Mark Zuckerberg's dehumanizing "metaverse" and the skyrocketing wealth of tech billionaires who are attempting to purchase and monopolize the public sphere. Their ideas, frequently presented as libertarian, are in fact the exact opposite. They are a replication of the worst instincts of government: a surveillance system with even less citizen recourse.

"Facebook in particular is the most appalling spying machine that has ever been invented," Wikileaks founder Julian Assange said in 2011. "Here we have the world's most comprehensive database about people, their relationships, their names, their addresses, their locations, and the communications with each other, their relatives, all sitting within the United States, all accessible to US intelligence."[37] Assange's assessment is prescient, accurate, and ironic, as Assange delivered it in an interview on RT, the state news network of the Kremlin. Since 2011, the Russian government's state surveillance operation has become even more brutal and has benefited greatly from Western social media ventures. Silicon Valley and the state intersect at disturbing inflection points, ones that often involve espionage, like those Danny Casolaro was investigating before he died.

Despite the eventual rollback of many of the policies they inspired, the Church Committee and Pike Committee matter, if only because they present a model for future efforts to enforce accountability. In the 1970s, whistleblowers and reporters brought the truth to light, the public cared and demanded more, and officials complied with their demands. This progress was derailed by the Reagan administration and its operatives, who also learned quite a lot from the two committees. They learned how to make sure this level of accountability never happened again. They gutted the Fairness Doctrine, a 1949 federal act that required that media coverage of controversial political topics be balanced. They created a vast media infrastructure to spread propaganda and repressive laws aimed at preventing internal critique under the guise of national security. They shifted political culture so far to the right that the sensible investigations of the 1970s seem radical in retrospect.

Operatives who sought to block the Church and Pike Committees, like Donald Rumsfeld and Bill Barr, became high-ranking members of future Republican administrations. As frustration with surveillance and corruption arose yet again in the post–Iraq War era, GOP bureaucrats aligned themselves with pseudo-populists bearing deep government connections: Steve Bannon and Erik Prince in the United States, Nigel Farage in the UK, and so forth. These operatives are the worst of the establishment presenting themselves as the establishment's enemy, the dregs of the deep state presenting themselves as the deep state's rivals. They are in the reality-making business, and it's a growth industry when you have a public that has abandoned the expectation of justice but not the illusion of secret saviors waiting for the perfect moment to emerge and set things right. *Do* not *abandon all hope, ye who enter here*, is the motto of the Fake Anti–Deep State Deep State; *your hope is our meat.*

The insights in Marchetti and Marks's *The CIA and the Cult of Intelligence* no longer shock. The greatest gift is the title. For there remains a cult of intelligence, one that our government refuses to examine, one that the public is encouraged to worship—whether in the form of an alphabet agency or an anonymous poster going by the letter Q. It is a cult with all the connotations that word implies: groupthink, excessive secrecy, demands of fealty, and ostracism of anyone who questions its aims.

People cling to the cult out of fear of the toxic mix of autocracy and chaos that has raged during the Trump era and its aftermath. They want to believe there are bureaucratic heroes in wait, and the desperation underlying this belief benefits the deep state operatives whom they claim they want to defeat. The refusal to push for blanket accountability across party lines has allowed institutions to both erode and corrupt. The cults are self-defeating and grotesque, but they endure because the need they serve is more than emotional. Cults of intelligence turn public attention away from the intersection of organized crime with the United States government: an intersection that defines American history as much as wars or racism or the two-party system, but is rarely discussed in frank terms.

To understand why, we need to look at another anomalous era of American accountability: the early 1950s. This was the time of McCarthyism and show trials by the House Committee on Un-American Activities. These hearings, featuring the first face-off between Joseph McCarthy lawyer Roy Cohn and future Attorney General Robert F. Kennedy, remain notorious as an example of abuse of congressional oversight. Their legacy has overshadowed another series of hearings held in that era that are rarely discussed these days, but are more resonant and relevant than ever.

"The week of March 12, 1951 will occupy a special place in history," *LIFE* magazine declared in a cover story in April of that year. "The US and the world had never experienced anything like it. . . . Thousands of people stayed away from their jobs. Department stores and theaters were almost deserted, yet people were not on the streets either. People had suddenly gone indoors—into living rooms, taverns, and clubrooms, auditoriums and back-offices. There, in eerie half-light, looking at millions of small frosty screens, people sat as if charmed. . . . For days on end into the night they watched with complete absorption. . . . Never before had the attention of the nation been riveted so completely on a single matter."[38]

What had caused thirty million Americans—about a fourth of all adults—to remain glued to their television sets all day long? Was it a sporting event, a musical performance, a voyage into outer space? No, it was congressional hearings, aired around the clock, that managed to attract an audience bigger than the 1951 World Series. The hearings were on the menace of organized crime, a phenomenon that J. Edgar Hoover had long denied existed and that had never been revealed to the public as what it was: *organized*. Tabloid tales of gangsters had always attracted public attention—the bandit murders of Bonnie and Clyde, the bootlegging empire of Al Capone—but the perpetrators were portrayed as operating in relative isolation, and certainly as separate from mainstream business and government. In 1951, that myth came to a crashing halt. The exposure of the mafia became America's first must-see TV event.

In May 1950, Congress established the Special Committee to Investigate Crime in Interstate Commerce in response to a resolution introduced in January by Tennessee senator Estes Kefauver. The purpose of the committee was to investigate the influence of organized crime in urban commerce, something major city officials had pleaded with the federal government to do for decades, to no avail. The Special Committee—dubbed the Kefauver Committee—held fourteen hearings in cities across the United States in 1950 and 1951. More than six hundred witnesses gave testimony. Mobsters faced interrogation from senators, including Kefauver, whose plain-spoken southern style and emphasis on the harmful effects of organized crime on ordinary Americans won him fans and transformed the public's perception of gangsters.

Famed mafiosos like Frank Costello, who had once boasted scrappy underdog appeal, were revealed as sophisticated operators primed to navigate a corrupt legal system that until recently had protected them. As Costello dodged incessant Senate inquiries by feigning ignorance and, at one point, laryngitis, irritated Americans saw through his act. Stripped of their tabloid glamour, forced to answer unpredictable questions on live television, the mafia revealed itself as a cold-blooded bureaucracy.

The hearings exposed not only the mobsters themselves, but the complicit officials who enabled them. Crime syndicate members were outed as major donors to political campaigns.[39] Police commissioners, city officials, and other bureaucrats squirmed under the glare of the television spotlight, which in turn emboldened the senators, who were enjoying their sudden fame, to push harder. By the spring of 1951, Americans were throwing "Kefauver block parties" where they reveled in this sudden battle against corruption together.[40] Clarity about organized crime bolstered community: the horror of what was revealed was counterbalanced by the committee's goal of accountability. In 1961, historian Eric Goldman recalled: "Above all, the television proceedings, with their stark portrayal of the practical mayor who might not have been merely practical, of the sinister arrogance of the Costellos and the Virginia Hausers, of the endless shadowy figures that obviously controlled so much, catalyzed the whole vague feeling that corruption was moving through all American life like a swarm of maggots."[41]

The Kefauver hearings confirmed what many Americans already suspected but that had frequently been dismissed as paranoia. They broke the normalcy bias that operated as a chokehold over any discussion of corruption, and did so by mimicking the flamboyant style of the gangsters themselves but combining their rhetoric with rigorous legal inquiry. In the early 1950s, the relatively new medium of television was ideal for draining the power of a media-savvy mafia. The hearings were unscripted interactions that gave sophisticated criminals little opportunity to manipulate the public the way they could the tabloid press. What had been regarded as a conspiracy theory—that a broad syndicate of criminal elites had wrapped its tentacles around business and government, compromising the integrity of institutions through bribes and threats—was revealed as the truth. J. Edgar Hoover, the prime figure behind the canard that "the mafia does not exist," was forced to not only acknowledge it but, at the least, make a pretense that the FBI was going to stop it.

The Kefauver hearings inspired the trials portrayed in *The Godfather* series, classic films that nonetheless convey a selective view of how organized crime operated. Hank Messick, a journalist who covered organized crime throughout the 1960s and 1970s, emphasized that mobs know no ethnic limits.[42] "The Sicilians are just one wing," he said in a 1978 interview. "The most obvious thing about crime in this country is that it's an extension of the free enterprise system. Mobs are just freer in their enterprise."[43] Messick took pains to lay out the extent to which organized crime was misunderstood by Americans in his 1971 biography of National Crime Syndicate head Meyer Lansky: "Organized crime is not the province of any one ethnic group or secret society. Just as no such group has a monopoly on virtue, neither does one have a monopoly on evil. Yet, until this simple truth is accepted, there can be little of lasting value achieved."[44]

Hoover proved Messick's point when he agreed to acknowledge organized crime's existence if they stuck to the misperception that the mafia was primarily an Italian-American operation, instead of a transnational syndicate featuring participants from a multitude of backgrounds. "They had to invent this whole 'Cosa Nostra' notion just to get [Hoover] to take a look at it," Messick recalled. "He was on record as saying there was no such thing. He wanted to stay away from corruption because he knew it would lead to politicians on a local level. . . . You see, things don't change much. It's always an alliance of crime, business, and politics." While Kefauver's hearings were expansive, the follow-up hearings on organized crime, 1963's Valachi hearings, focused exclusively on Italian-American criminal organizations, largely omitting the National Crime Syndicate and its players.

Messick noted that by the late 1970s, the mafia had reverted to a taboo topic unless it fit the cinematic stereotypes of Cosa Nostra. "The golden age for my kind of work was from '61 to '63, when Bobby Kennedy was attorney general. People don't want to hear about organized crime nowadays. They throw mudballs at it. Unless it's *The Godfather*."[45] This was particularly true in regard to Messick's own white whale, Lansky, who had eluded both scrutiny and capture since he began his operation in the 1930s.

A mobster who saw legitimizing criminal activity instead of hiding it as the key to success, Lansky was one of few major mafiosos to avoid testifying publicly to the Kefauver Committee—allegedly because he had acquired blackmail on Kefauver's gambling trips in the good-time town of

Hot Springs, Arkansas.[46] Kefauver had initially held Lansky in contempt for refusing to testify—the closest a congressman had gotten to taking down the head of the National Crime Syndicate—but ultimately allowed him to testify briefly in person with his lawyer, avoiding the televised circus and remaining under the radar.[47] Lansky stonewalled, revealing little, and faced no consequence for his reticence. The Meyer Lansky model of blackmail, media manipulation, and pseudo-respectability was emulated by his protégé, Roy Cohn, who served as an attorney for Joe McCarthy and the Five Crime Families of New York before becoming Donald Trump's mentor in the early 1970s.

The Kefauver hearings produced an 11,000-page report, but their central tenet—that government and corporate entities had been infiltrated by organized crime and could not function without the removal of these elements—did not lead to changes in policy until decades later. In 1970, under direct recommendation from the Kefauver Committee, Congress passed the Racketeer Influenced and Corrupt Organizations (RICO) Act, which created new protocols and penalties in the investigation of organized crime. Lansky, who saw RICO coming, fled to Israel for sanctuary in 1970, using the right of return law as a pretext. But on September 11, 1972, Israel's High Court denied him citizenship due to his four decades of criminal activity, and ordered him to leave. They did, however, grant Lansky a travel document that would allow him passage to any country that would take him.[48] Lansky's tactic was later emulated by a slew of mobsters from the former Soviet Union who abused Israel's right of return law to streamline their criminal operations, most notably Semion Mogilevich, frequently named as the head of today's transnational crime syndicate much as Lansky was in the twentieth century.

In the end, Lansky did not need to hide out in Israel at all. After being ordered to leave Israel in October 1973, he was put on trial for tax evasion in the United States in November, and within four hours was acquitted by a jury.[49] Despite the FBI being fully aware of his criminal network, he was never arrested, and died in 1983 with only $37,000 in cash. This was not an indicator of his financial failure, but of his philosophy, one that is important to grasp when contending with today's criminal elites. "Lansky did not own property—he owned people," Messick stated of his biographical subject. This is the same philosophy that Roy Cohn, and later Donald Trump, emulated. Cohn said he dreamed of dying owing the US government millions of dollars, and in 1986, that is exactly what he did.

Material acquisition is not the goal of the mafia side of the criminal elite, and debt is not a problem. A lifestyle of total impunity, powered by fraud and threat, is the goal. Raw power is not measured in money but by how little you need it. Money is beneath you when you live above the law.

The RICO laws helped eliminate much of the Italian-American mafia throughout the 1970s and 1980s. Rudy Giuliani, appointed US Attorney for the Southern District of New York the year of Lansky's death, clamped down on the Five Families, but this only paved the way for sophisticated mobsters from the Soviet Union to take their place, and as mayor in the 1990s, he raised no objections.[50] Gangsters from the USSR and its successor states took up residence in Trump Tower starting in the mid-1980s and have largely remained impervious to FBI prosecution for decades. The favor granted to them by the FBI, particularly by the New York branch, is understudied and unnerving, particularly given the increasingly open connections between international criminals and the people tasked with stopping them.

As previously noted, two FBI directors from the 1990s, William Sessions and Louis Freeh, went on to work for the Russian mafia after resigning their posts. In 2007, Sessions took on Mogilevich as a client. Freeh, who resigned in June 2001 after being criticized for failing to notice that FBI agent Robert Hanssen had been secretly working for the Russians since 1979, went on to represent Russian companies accused of laundering enormous sums of money for the Russian mafia, including the real estate investment firm Prevezon.[51,52] Freeh continues to represent these companies while, among other ventures, investigating and then refuting allegations of sexual misconduct made against Alan Dershowitz in connection with the Jeffrey Epstein case,[53] and, with Dershowitz, lobbying for Israeli billionaires sanctioned by the US government.[54]

In March 1951, *TIME* magazine put a cartoon of Estes Kefauver on the cover. CRIME HUNTER KEFAUVER: GAMBLERS + POLITICIANS = CORRUPTION, read the title. Next to Kefauver is a masked creature holding a gun and a lead pipe and dollar bills that fall from its tentacles. The creature is an octopus. On August 10, 1963, Estes Kefauver dropped dead at age sixty of a heart attack on the Senate floor—exactly twenty-eight years to the day that Danny Casolaro was found dead in his hotel, and exactly fifty-six years to the day that Jeffrey Epstein was found dead in his prison cell.

In 1951, the New York advertising firm Young and Rubicam, capitalizing on Kefauver fever, ran this ad in American newspapers:

"Across their television tubes have paraded the honest and dishonest, the frank and the furtive, the public servant and the public thief. Out of many pictures has come a broader picture of the sordid intermingling of crime and politics, of dishonor in public life. Suddenly millions of Americans are asking:

What's happened to our ideals of right and wrong?

What's happened to our principles of honesty in government?

What's happened to public and private standards of morality?

Then they can ask the most important question of all: how do we stop what's going on? *Is there anything we can do about it?*"[55]

These are the same questions Americans are asking today. These inquiries know no geographic or partisan bounds, for the problem is pervasive and spans decades. We alternate between having a transnational crime syndicate masquerading as a government and a government that masks a transnational crime syndicate. Either way, it leads to the same outcome: a conspiracy against the American public.

Anomalous Eras of American Accountability are cyclical. Between them are long, destructive eras of gaslighting, censorship, and rebuilding the dark networks of corruption that had been painstakingly exposed and partially dismantled. These maneuvers are not constricted to party lines. The deep corruption of the Nixon, Reagan, and Bush eras would not be possible without the refusal of the Democrats to enforce accountability for prior administrative crimes when they take power. (Additionally, Democratic administrations are rife with their own corruption crises, ones that seem tame only because those of the Republicans are so extreme.) The Democratic Chamberlains of the post-Trump era refuse to bring consequences for even the most severe and blatant of crimes, like orchestrating a coup or letting a fatal plague spread and profiting off the carnage.

The Kefauver hearings and the investigatory committees of the early to mid-1970s provide a road map to a better America. But this road map is not being used. Instead, officials who can enforce accountability alternate between hurtling toward dead ends and driving the country off a cliff.

What changed, starting in the late 1970s, was citizen leverage. Financial leverage, grassroots protest leverage, and the leverage of the vote were all systematically targeted for destruction. Income inequality widened to the point that it outpaced that of the Gilded Age, meaning that billionaires hoard more wealth and have more power than ever before. The repeal of campaign finance regulations and the passing of *Citizens United* allowed corrupt donors to influence politicians at an unparalleled level. The deregulation of Wall Street allowed the merger of organized crime and corporate corruption—always present—to blossom until elite criminals could pack the courts and rewrite the laws in their own favor. The partial repeal of the VRA and the enactment of new voter suppression laws, combined with fealty to donors over the electorate, have drained the American voter of their influence. Elected officials no longer attempt to win you over, they attempt to rewrite laws and district boundaries so that your vote is irrelevant. Their true constituency is the criminal elite.

The media ecosystem that allowed investigative journalism to thrive in the twentieth century has been replaced by a mix of paywalls and propaganda, with little resources for the kind of work journalists like Messick were doing. The culture of censorship that Marchetti and Marks contended with remains in place, strengthened in the aftermath of 9/11.

Most of all, an attack on the political imagination has drained journalists and others involved in politics of their creative spirit. The willingness of writers and artists like Casolaro and Lombardi to forge ahead despite accusations of being a "conspiracy theorist" has eroded in a culture of conformity and careerism—and the loss of a stable income that results from not bowing to these corrosive forces.

This loss of political imagination is not universal—there are brave exceptions, often toiling without the resources of the bot-brained blowhards bleating that all is well—but there is a marked move toward self-censorship. In the unstable period before autocratic consolidation, frightened people want to follow. They do not want to think, and they do not want to be in the line of fire. It is safer not to know.

For they knew: Casolaro and Lombardi, Marchetti and Messick, and so many others who suffered in pursuit of the truth. They knew what was eating away at the heart of America just like the corrupt operatives and complicit officials whom they covered. They knew how infiltration becomes impunity and then immunity. They knew the dangers that ordinary people faced, because they were ordinary people who wanted to protect their country and its citizens, and the only way for that to be possible was for everyone to know the truth. They knew, just like you and I know, and they told everybody.

"Is there anything we can do about it?" Americans asked during the Kefauver hearings, a question that tolls like the metronome of collective conscience. Although the crisis is far worse today than it was in the 1950s or 1970s, there are many things that people can do. Foremost among them is to demand the truth. A problem people deny exists cannot be solved. The great crisis of today is corruption: a crisis that feeds into every other crisis, including the economy, health care, local and state government, freedom of speech, civil rights, foreign relations, technology, and more.

Politicians often refuse to address corruption by claiming that Americans prefer to discuss "kitchen table issues," but corruption *is* a kitchen table issue. The food on the table is rotting because Americans have been served a diet of bullshit for half a century. Occasionally that diet was interrupted by healthier fare—the Kefauver hearings, the Watergate revelations—that they would gather around the kitchen table to consume.

Fighting corruption has always been a popular cause. The main people who cannot stomach it are the criminal elites themselves. This is why they seek to cover up their crimes with scandal or to preemptively invert the narrative by presenting themselves as avatars of justice instead of its destroyers.

Trump and his crime cult understand these tactics very well, but he has rarely received an effective response. The greatest weapon against a reality TV career criminal former president is actual reality. The pathway for those seeking to curtail Trump—not out of a desire for revenge or partisanship, but simply to protect the country from further harm—was always clear. The American fervor for televised trials remains high, and there is a hunger for transparency and justice that is not being met. In 2019, 2020, and 2021, the years of Trump's two impeachment hearings, the national security and public safety of Americans were in grave jeopardy. But many Americans doubted the extent of the danger due to the refusal of officials—particularly Democrats and national security agencies—to act as if we were under severe threat. They reverted to normalcy bias—*"If this were actually dangerous, surely someone would have stopped it long ago!"*—and suffered due to the failure of officials to convey the stakes. The second impeachment hearing, about the worst attack on the Capitol since 1812, lasted only four days.

Kefauver-style hearings laying out not only Trump's impeachable offenses but the broader bipartisan network of corruption and complicity surrounding him would have made the danger clear and possibly contained it. The silos through which Americans receive information would have been shattered, creating a communal camaraderie around battling corruption.

This outcome is still possible. There is no statute of limitations on the truth. Officials only have to try: to remain committed to revealing the horrors of our history in the aim of inaugurating a better and more honest future. And Americans have to be willing to hear it—and there is every indication, given that frustration with elite criminal impunity is the one thing holding this country together, that they are.

Preemptive surrender is permanent surrender. It is better to try and fail than to never try at all. The refusal to try is what is at the heart of current political demoralization in the United States. The refusal to try is what sates the Octopus, what keeps its tentacles gripped tight so that even the slightest movement toward freedom feels futile.

Officials have also refused to investigate institutional corruption in the manner of the Church and Pike Committees, despite overwhelming evidence of institutional corruption in the public domain. They act as though protecting corrupt institutions is more important than protecting America itself. The ordinary Americans whose economic security collapses under the weight of organized crime and white-collar crime—the *real* trickle-down economics—are treated as incidental and disposable. When whistleblowers emerge, as they did on multiple occasions during the Trump administration, they are either imprisoned or threatened with violence as criminal abettors get massive book deals. Narratives are twisted or delayed to the point that they drain the urgency of the crisis, confusing the public as to how much danger they are in. The public lives in suspended animation, in a mix of chaos and inertia intended to agonize.

This, too, can change, but it requires a change in mindset. Rejecting complacency is essential to warding off autocratic encroachment. In a media and political system that tells you that you are either totally screwed or secretly saved, know that you are somewhere in between—and that you have every right to voice your demands, to form your own opinions, to insist that you get what you deserve, and that the criminal elite gets what they deserve too. The radical solution to our problems is to democratize the world's oldest democracy.

The truth is always worth it, no matter the price you pay. Normalcy bias is meant to pacify you out of a state of inquiry. When you continue your inquiry anyway, you may be demonized—called a liar, a conspiracy theorist, an outsider with a bad agenda. This is because you have become a threat to power, a break in the algorithm, a deviation in the plan. Conspiracy theories and actual conspiracies both revolve around questions of preexisting power dynamics and whether they can change. The ability to shift these dynamics is still in your hands—not unilaterally, but in concert with others sharing the same goal, and by acting with integrity and conviction. When everything else collapses, all you have are your principles.

Your only obligation is to the truth, and it is an unbreakable obligation. Everything else stems from it. You are entitled to truth from government as a basic covenant of citizenship. There is no justice without accountability, and there is no accountability without the truth. Insisting that the corruption we witness be acknowledged is never an empty gesture. The very act of this public demand, this uncompromising insistence on exposure of the criminal elite, can set in motion unpredictable events. Americans can learn from the past that we keep repeating. And possibly, in the end, we can break the future.

EPILOGUE

An American Ghost

It is early December 2021, and I am reading the handwritten notes of Danny Casolaro. They are part of the secret history he left behind: files of papers and boxes of files, stacked so high they block the window view of the bare trees outside. The materials date from the 1980s until his sudden death in 1991. I flinch at the familiarity: the names, the dates, the sense of fear as vague as its object. I am hitchhiking on a road to nowhere, not sure if I am ahead or behind. To track the dead leads of a dead man is to grapple with something invasive and elusive at once. You do not know what he considered a fleeting thought or a revelation. Interspersed with investigative reports are personal reflections, scraps of fiction, aphorisms—none meant to be seen, at least not like this. Casolaro was forty-three, the same age I am now, when he drafted a proposal for a book that he thought would expose a conspiracy and in doing so help defeat the conspirators, a book that might have impacted my generation as much as his own.

"Did you find what you were looking for?" the reference librarian asks, and I answer yes even though I have not, because part of what I sought was to feel less alone.

I left St. Louis that morning for the Missouri State Historical Society in Columbia, tracing the path of the Missouri River like so many have done while on a westward expedition based on a bad idea. Manifest Destiny, Bleeding Kansas. This is a cursed route in cursed country. The north side of the river used to be called Little Dixie, because it was populated by white southerners who migrated to Missouri with enslaved human beings. The south side of the river was the Missouri Rhineland, where German-speaking towns still stand, flowing with wine. I moved on and off the highway, wandering into an Ozarkland general store brimming with Bible boxes and velvet Elvises, and then took to the back roads, passing a rotting silo with tree branches breaking through the top and a sign announcing that I had arrived in a town called Kingdom City.

Winter was coming and fields were fallow, leaving spaces so expansive that all I could see was prairie and sky. I wanted to stay and stare at the blue and brown, luring me in like the inverse of an ocean, but I kept going. I drove past remnants of the Berlin Wall on the streets of Fulton, where in March 1946 Winston Churchill made his "Iron Curtain" speech warning of Soviet aggression. Churchill had been invited by President Harry S. Truman, a Missouri native who had dropped atomic bombs on Japan seven months earlier and thought it would be nice for the prime minister of England to support a local college. Many visitors to Missouri do something of great consequence without realizing it at the time, because nothing is supposed to happen here.

Conspiracies are woven into the landscape of American life. They are how Americans reckon with hypocrisy and betrayal, how they feel around the edges of subjects they are not supposed to touch, how they navigate the twilight zone between principles and practice. Conspiracies structure American politics, but they are not called conspiracies when they are wrapped in the flag or stamped with bureaucracy or printed piecemeal in the papers. They are called plans or policies or "just the way things are." When the agendas of elite actors get pushed underground and you have to dig for them—that is when those agendas are called conspiracies, and facts are called theories, and you are called insane for noticing.

In a country this corrupt, the line between a plan and a plot is blurred to the point where you do not know if your interpretation is rooted in insight or paranoia, but you know it is worth pursuing. What the criminal elite want, above all, is for people to stop analyzing these crises, to accept them as normal and leave them alone. This motive is not based in fear of being found out. Instead, it is an attempt at psychic control and retaining the political culture that allows them to operate with impunity. They want you to abandon moral inquiry even more than they want you to abandon the truth.

A blatant conspiracy by the powerful is less likely to be called a crime because people tend to equate getting caught with getting punished. They assume that if an individual is caught committing a crime and nothing happens, it must mean that they did not commit the crime after all. It might even mean that the crime is no longer a crime—at least, not for those people, not for that protected class. The alternate explanation—that the officials who are supposed to curtail the criminals are in on the crime and will let the crime be committed again and again—is too horrifying for many to contemplate, especially when the greatest victim of the crime is the American public.

When the American people push back against this fallacy, and proclaim that all men are truly created equal and therefore all men are subject to equal scrutiny and equal treatment under the law, they are tarred by the powerful as unreliable narrators. This happens both to individuals and to entire ethnic groups whose history of persecution at the hands of the government is normalized to the point of dismissal. The worst myth ever uttered by the powerful is "You deserve it," whether in praise of American exceptionalism or to justify systemic abuse. Who are they to tell us what we are worth, what we deserve?

Who are they? you think as you leaf through the works of a dead messenger, *who are* they? A government of *them*, for *them*, by *them*, against the people, against the people . . .

I live where the Mississippi and the Missouri Rivers meet in the center of the country, a region the people who control the country call the fringes. I inhabit the fringes from the center, because everything has been inverted. I've got fringe theories and fringe fame and a fringe life. I prefer the fringes when the main road is so straight and narrow that it constrains your ability to see the lay of the land. There's a new power dynamic in town, a perverse freedom, the freedom of a living ghost.

A ghost is someone who insists that they are still relevant when others insist that they are dead and gone. A ghost is going to remind you of everything you do not want to know, and they will haunt you until you listen to what they have to say. The longer you pretend ghosts do not exist, the more they will terrify you when you finally see them. History is a ghost, and these days, the future is a ghost too, so what better existence is there than to be a ghost of the present, a shadow of conscience in the dead of night?

"Possession of a secret is no guarantee of its truth," Casalaro wrote in one of many drafts of his book proposal.[1] The institutionalist cult of secrets is the flip side to the brazen impunity of the criminal elite. They feed off each other, making their illusion possible and trapping us inside. A secret is a weapon because it can be hoarded and deployed, but it does not need to be true to matter. A secret can be a veil with nothing under it but power, power rendered invisible by public scrutiny of the veil itself. Strip off the veil and see nothing but *that*—raw, acquisitive power, blazing like a light that never warms—and recoil in horror. It would be so much easier if it meant something.

The things that mean something to you are incidental to them. Life, love, family, freedom, compassion, imagination, individuality—these are not understood in the same way. They are only possessions to steal from you to exert greater control. That is how mafias operate, and you live in a mafia state in a mafia world headed for the mother of all mergers. In a global autocracy, fear and foreboding transcend borders, hovering over the world like a black cloud. The cry of "what is happening?" is as raw in the United Kingdom and Hungary and Turkey and any other country lurching into authoritarian kleptocracy as it is in the United States.

You know you are not supposed to talk about it, not only because you may seem crazy but because it is dangerous. "Don't kill the messenger," you pray, thinking of the kids, but these days the messenger seems less likely to be killed directly by the conspirators than to fall prey to their disaster capitalism along with everyone else. They let the guardrails of society rot into oblivion. As you struggle for daily survival, they target your career, your reputation, your livelihood. They price you out so that they can offer to buy your soul.

You are less surprised by how many fellow travelers sell their souls than by how low the going rate is. *The only way to survive them is to become them*, the respectable people warn. *The only way to elude them is to look in a mirror and not recognize yourself, but see what they want to see.* The respectable ones—they went so far so fast so cheap, there is nothing of them left to see. They are the zombies to your ghost. You have no option but to hang on to the parts of yourself they cannot take. So you destroy your own respectability, annihilate their plausible deniability, tell the truth too early. And you do not regret a thing.

Americans are told they deserve the fruits of conspiracy, but they do not. Americans do not deserve climate change, corruption, or coups. Conspirators lure in accomplices with the promise of belonging, designated by prestige and prizes, but in the end, those are just Potemkin lives. It is better to stand outside the conspiracy and judge it than be a participant. It is better to be labeled a conspiracy theorist, forever orbiting, than inhabit that cold dead sun.

It is better to trust your eyes and ears, not only because official sources are often dishonest but because they are *your* eyes and ears, and the conspirators want to devalue that, to flatten individual perception into something formless and malleable. This was the goal of twentieth-century fascism, and it is easier to attain in the twenty-first, through algorithms and artificial intelligence and whatever else they offer as a replacement for conscience and consciousness.

Where do you hide when the Octopus is everywhere? You can find reprieve inside yourself, in your imagination, in your unwillingness to cede your morality. Or you can hide in plain sight, giving the things that mean nothing to the criminal elite but everything to everyone else: generosity, compassion, unconditional love. There is nothing futile about that kind of life.

It is late December and I am leaving Missouri, driving the back roads south for a trip down the Mississippi River before heading to Texas. It is Christmastime again, the second family Christmas in the Year of Our Plague 2021, a holiday marked with a new variant and new tragedies that people pretend not to see in order to try to avoid. The worst tornadoes in the history of the region hit a week ago but there is no wreckage visible from the highway. If you stay on the main road, it's like the destruction never happened, even though you heard the sirens screeching and the wind roaring and you woke in the morning to photos of bodies buried in rubble and whole towns gone.[2]

There is a record of the American dead in your mind, a list that grows longer each day. It tracks the man-made disasters too, this endless commemoration moonlighting as a rebuttal. It specializes in man-made disasters, in fact, and you vow to remember them all.

When the powerful want you to forget a conspiracy, what they want you to forget most are the victims. The conspirators will try to demoralize you and demonize you. The conspiracy may frustrate and exhaust you. But the injustice the victims endure is straightforward. The victims are why the crime matters. To be human is to care about other people. To seek justice is to honor another's humanity. To destroy elite criminal impunity is to gain equality. The purpose of deciphering a malicious conspiracy is to protect the victims and keep it from happening again.

The victim of this story is America, which sounds wrong, because the villain of this story is America. America is the murderer and America is the dying, America is the betrayer and America is the redeemer. America is all those things, and always was. It is not new to love your country and distrust your government. America was founded on defiance of authority, and as the government only proved itself worthier of distrust, the country never closed off the avenue to a better future. It is still there; you can see it gleaming in your children's eyes.

The backstory of America's betrayal is America's future history. It has not been told in its entirety—how could it?—but it will be, one way or another. For in spite of the complicity and the complacency, the cult mindsets born of fear and favor, it is hard to get Americans to shut up. If we get an American apocalypse, that long-sought focus of fundraisers and fever dreams, it will arrive with its literal meaning of revelation intact.

The truths inside these revelations may not make it into the media. They may be preserved in lore, or conveyed in courts, or spoken in code, safeguarded in lyricism. You have seen this happen in authoritarian states, and you have seen this happen to displaced diasporas. You do not know which category you will end up in, or whether you will get what you want, which is to be an honest writer living on American soil. It is such a small slice of the American dream, but you know who holds the knife—for now.

They knew: the betrayers, the conspirators, the enablers. They knew and they let people suffer and they covered up the evidence and they replaced it with lies. They spurred confusion and dread, but what are those emotions if not internal alarms, signals to start asking questions, to decide for ourselves what we deserve, to shatter their chosen future and replace it with our own? I will watch them as they watch me, but I've got my eyes on something else: a reckoning, a recording, a reordering of past and present and future. They will keep burying and we will keep digging, and planting, because there is a sliver of consolation in the endless grim tide, one that keeps me going. They knew—but I knew, too.

ACKNOWLEDGMENTS

I wrote *They Knew* during a pandemic, which means that I am more grateful than usual for all the people I am about to thank. Anyone with the misfortune of having a writer in their life knows how annoying we are while writing a new book. Now imagine being trapped with that writer, all day long, for two years.

That is why I will first thank my heroically patient husband, Pete, for putting up with me during the writing process, accompanying me on my weird adventures, and being a fantastic husband and father the whole time. Pete read every draft of this book—as I said, he was trapped with me in a pandemic—and offered indispensable editorial advice and encouragement.

Next, thank you to my wonderful readers. My last book, *Hiding in Plain Sight*, came out in April 2020 as the pandemic hit, which meant I relied on word of mouth as events and interviews were canceled. I am grateful to everyone who read and appreciated *Hiding in Plain Sight* and my previous book, *The View from Flyover Country*, which was also a grassroots success. I am very lucky to have such an engaged audience and I am grateful for your feedback.

Thank you to my agent, Robert Lecker, for being steadfast throughout the massive political chaos that ensued after he signed me to his agency in 2016. He has been a great friend to me as well as an excellent agent and I will always be grateful for his support.

It was terrific working once again with Bryn Clark, who also edited *Hiding in Plain Sight*. I am thrilled to have an editor who is as open-minded and sharp-eyed as Bryn, and I look forward to working with her on future projects. Thanks also to everyone at Flatiron Books, especially my publicist Amelia Possanza, Bryn's assistant Ruben Reyes, the copy-editing team, and the production designers who created that amazing cover. Thank you also to Kay Nelson for editorial assistance at the final stages of the book. And thank you to Left Bank Books in St. Louis for your incredible support throughout my publishing career.

I have been in the trenches of the information war with Andrea Chalupa, the cohost of our podcast, *Gaslit Nation*, since we first spoke on the phone on Election Night 2016. These last few years have been rough, but we have soldiered on together, and I am glad to have such a brilliant, passionate, and hilarious friend by my side. Congrats on baby Chloe!

They Knew is the kind of book where I am wary of naming those who I bounced ideas off for the last decade or so on the grounds that it may destroy their reputations, so I'll just say—thank you for listening, friends! You all know who you are and you are all awesome.

Thanks to my mom, Barbara, who was so deeply bored during the pandemic that she read drafts of *They Knew* and corrected the typos. And thanks to my dad, Larry, who occasionally got bored enough to read the early versions as well. I promise I will try to write a "fun book" someday.

Thanks to the other family members—Lizzie, Mike, Jack, Kate, Sally, Phil, Liz, Dave, Julia, and Twizzle the dog. Most of all, thank you to my amazing children, Emily and Alex. You are now old enough to be embarrassed if I gush about how wonderful you are and how proud I am of both of you and how happy you make me. But you are not yet old enough to read this book, so put it down!

Finally, thank you to all the people who, with a pure heart and an inquiring mind, continue to pursue truth and justice—especially the journalists and investigators who paid the ultimate price for that endeavor. The pursuit of truth and justice matters in its own right, and always will, no matter what they tell you.

NOTES

1: Deaths of Deception

1. Mark Twain, *Life on the Mississippi* (New York: Modern Library, 2007), 329.
2. John Killerlane, "Con Man: The Fraud Who Claimed to Have a Cure for Cancer," *History Collection*, October 30, 2017, https://historycollection.com/norman-baker-man-claimed-cure-cancer/2/.
3. "Crescent Hotel History," 1886 Crescent Hotel and Spa, accessed February 11, 2022, https://www.crescent-hotel.com/history.shtml.
4. Killerlane, "Con Man."
5. Ibid.
6. Bill Bowden, "Glass bottles found behind 'haunted' Arkansas hotel date to 1938 cancer elixir," *Arkansas Democratic Gazette*, April 12, 2019, https://www.arkansasonline.com/news/2019/apr/12/glass-bottles-date-to-38-cancer-elixir-/.
7. Brian Mann, "The Sacklers, Who Made Billions from OxyContin, Win Immunity from Opioid Lawsuits," NPR, September 1, 2021, https://www.npr.org/2021/09/01/1031053251/sackler-family-immunity-purdue-pharma-oxcyontin-opioid-epidemic.

2: Theories of Conspiracy

1. Soo Youn, "40% of Americans don't have $400 in the bank for emergency expenses: Federal Reserve," ABC News, May 24, 2019, https://abcnews.go.com/US/10-americans-struggle-cover-400-emergency-expense-federal/story?id=63253846.
2. Jordan Libowitz and Caitlin Moniz, "Jared and Ivanka made up to $640 million in the White House," *CREW | Citizens for Responsibility and Ethics in Washington*, February 8, 2021, https://www.citizensforethics.org/reports-investigations/crew-investigations/jared-and-ivanka-made-up-to-640-million-in-the-white-house/.
3. Mohamad Bazzi, "The troubling overlap between Jared Kushner's business interests and US foreign policy," *Guardian*, July 9, 2019, https://www.theguardian.com/commentisfree

/2019/jul/08/troubling-overlap-between-jared-kushner-business-interests-and-us-foreign-policy.

4. David Cay Johnston, "Wilbur Ross, Cabinet Pick, Has Ties to Putin, Oligarchs," *DCReport .org*, February 25, 2017, https://www.dcreport.org/2017/02/25/another-cabinet-pick-with-secret-ties-to-putin-and-oligarchs/.

5. Kim Masters, "Lawmakers Target Steven Mnuchin over 'Conflict of Interest' in Ties to Hollywood Investor Len Blavatnik," *Hollywood Reporter*, January 29, 2019, https://www.hollywoodreporter.com/news/general-news/lawmakers-target-steven-mnuchin-conflict-interest-ties-hollywood-investor-len-blavatnik-1181129/.

6. Chas Danner, "Trump HHS Aide Michael Caputo Takes Leave of Absence After Facebook Rant," *New York*, September 16, 2020, https://nymag.com/intelligencer/2020/09/trump-hhs-aide-caputo-attacks-cdc-warns-of-insurrection.html.

7. Michael Kruse, "The 'What, Me Worry?' President," *Politico Magazine*, June 8, 2018, https://www.politico.com/magazine/story/2018/06/08/donald-trump-beliefs-what-matters-fatalism-218663/.

8. Sarah Kendzior, "Donald Trump Will Do Anything to Avoid Prosecution—And John Bolton Will Help," *Fast Company*, April 12, 2018, https://www.fastcompany.com/40558314/donald-trump-will-do-anything-to-avoid-prosecution-and-john-bolton-will-help.

9. Donald Trump, "Donald Trump's 2014 political predictions," interview by Brian Kilmeade, *Fox & Friends*, Fox News, February 10, 2014, video, 6:37, https://video.foxnews.com/v/3179604851001#sp=show-clips.

10. Christina Wilkie, "Donald Trump's Brag That He Owned the Tallest Building After 9/11 Wasn't Even True," *Huffington Post*, September 13, 2016, https://www.huffpost.com/entry/donald-trump-911-building-lie_n_57d8017be4b0fbd4b7bb6182.

11. Cox Media Group National Content Desk, "Trump was 'excited' about possible housing-market crash in 2007," *Atlanta Journal-Constitution*, May 24, 2016, https://www.ajc.com/news/national-govt--politics/trump-was-excited-about-possible-housing-market-crash-2007/HZMp8WO7HuCCKazcKcXvVI/.

12. Glenn Plaskin, "The 1990 Playboy Interview with Donald Trump," *Playboy*, March 1, 1990, https://www.playboy.com/read/playboy-interview-donald-trump-1990.

13. Associated Press in Phoenix, Arizona, "Arizona man dies after attempting to take Trump coronavirus 'cure,'" *The Guardian*, March 24, 2020, https://www.theguardian.com/world/2020/mar/24/coronavirus-cure-kills-man-after-trump-touts-chloroquine-phosphate.

14. Ted Johnson, "Bob Woodward Defends Withholding Donald Trump's COVID-19 Comments Until Book's Publication," *Yahoo News*, September 10, 2020, https://www.yahoo.com/entertainment/bob-woodward-defends-withholding-donald-010225111.html.

15. Chris Wilson, "Here's How Often the CDC Has Actually Been Using the 7 Words It Reportedly Banned," *TIME*, December 18, 2017, https://time.com/5069289/cdc-banned-words-trump/.

16. Deb Riechmann, "Trump disbanded NSC pandemic unit that experts had praised," Associated Press, March 14, 2020, https://apnews.com/article/donald-trump-ap-top-news-virus-outbreak-barack-obama-public-health-ce014d94b64e98b7203b873e56f80e9a.

17. Amnesty International, "Forensic Methodology Report: How to Catch NSO Group's

Pegasus," July 18, 2021, https://www.amnesty.org/en/latest/research/2021/07/forensic
-methodology-report-how-to-catch-nso-groups-pegasus/.

18. Shannon Vavra, "Rod Rosenstein is working with NSO Group, the Israeli firm accused
of spying on dissidents," *CyberScoop*, June 1, 2020, https://www.cyberscoop.com/rod
-rosenstein-nso-group-whatsapp/.

19. Reuters Staff, "Fact check: Outdated video of Fauci saying 'there's no reason to be walking around with a mask,'" Reuters, October 8, 2020, https://www.reuters.com/article/uk
-factcheck-fauci-outdated-video-masks-idUSKBN26T2TR.

20. The White House, "Olivia Rodrigo and Dr. Fauci Read Fan (Vaccine) Tweets," YouTube,
July 16, 2021, video, 3:52, https://www.youtube.com/watch?v=o8sHSEtH3L4.

21. Eric Garcia, "CDC director apologises in meeting with disability rights activists after frustration with policy response," *The Independent*, January 14, 2022, https://news
.yahoo.com/cdc-director-apologises-meeting-disability-000542226.html.

22. Ezekiel J. Emanuel, "Why I Hope to Die at 75," *The Atlantic*, October 2014, https://www
.theatlantic.com/magazine/archive/2014/10/why-i-hope-to-die-at-75/379329/.

23. Justine Barron, "Media Elevate Eugenicists, Sideline Disabled Voices in Discussions of
Covid Rationing," FAIR, January 20, 2021, https://fair.org/home/media-elevate-eugenicists
-sideline-disabled-voices-in-discussions-of-covid-rationing/.

24. Chris Prener, "River City Data," accessed February 11, 2022, https://chrisprener.substack
.com/.

25. Danny Wicentowski, "What Tracking Women's Periods Says About Missouri's Anti-
Abortion Scheme," *Riverfront Times*, October 31, 2019, https://www.riverfronttimes.com
/stlouis/what-tracking-womens-periods-says-about-missouris-anti-abortion-scheme
/Content?oid=32487183.

26. Noam Chomsky, "On Historical Amnesia, Foreign Policy, and Iraq," interview by Kirk W.
Johnson, *American Amnesia*, February 17, 2004, https://chomsky.info/20040217/.

27. Elias Canetti, *Crowds and Power* (New York: Continuum, 1960), 281.

28. Hunter S. Thompson, *Better Than Sex: Confessions of a Political Junkie* (New York: Random House, 1994), 6.

29. Nathaniel Hawthorne, "Young Goodman Brown," in *Mosses from an Old Manse* (London: Wiley & Putnam, 1846), http://www.columbia.edu/itc/english/f1124y-001/resources
/Young_Goodman_Brown.pdf.

30. Dan Mangan and Kevin Breuninger, "Judge in Paul Manafort trial says he has been
threatened and is now under US Marshal protection," CNBC, August 17, 2018, https://
www.cnbc.com/2018/08/17/judge-in-paul-manafort-trial-said-hes-been-threatened.html.

31. Joe Heim, "Nancy Pelosi on Impeaching Trump: 'He's Just Not Worth It,'" *Washington Post
Magazine*, March 11, 2019, https://www.washingtonpost.com/news/magazine/wp/2019/03
/11/feature/nancy-pelosi-on-impeaching-president-trump-hes-just-not-worth-it/.

32. William Safire, "Essay; The Patsy Prosecutor," *New York Times*, October 19, 1992,
https://www.nytimes.com/1992/10/19/opinion/essay-the-patsy-prosecutor.html.

33. Igor Bobic and Ryan J. Reilly, "Here Are the 81 People and Entities Close to Trump
Democrats Are Investigating," *Huffington Post*, March 4, 2019, https://www.huffpost.com
/entry/judiciary-democrats-trump-probe-documents_n_5c7d3df8e4b0614614dcfb9c.

34. Marina Fang, "Trump Escalates Attack on Elijah Cummings with Tweet About Baltimore

Burglary," *Huffington Post*, August 2, 2019, https://www.huffpost.com/entry/donald -trump-elijah-cummings-twitter-attacks-burglary_n_5d442994e4b0acb57fcb1db0.

3: Epstein Wasn't the First

1. Matthew Choi, "Biden: QAnon is 'bizarre' and 'embarrassing,' supporters should seek mental health treatment," *Politico*, September 4, 2020, https://www.politico.com/news /2020/09/04/biden-qanon-bizarre-embarrassing-409090.

2. Phil Gailey, "Have Names, Will Open Right Doors," *New York Times*, January 18, 1982, https://www.nytimes.com/1982/01/18/us/have-names-will-open-right-doors.html.

3. Michael Hedges and Jerry Seper, "In Death, Spence Stayed True to Form," *Washington Times*, November 13, 1989.

4. Ibid.

5. Associated Press, "Craig Spence Sent Farewell Message to Friends, Left Suicide Note," November 13, 1989, https://apnews.com/article/df1b0831501317de1d5da1d1252b5279.

6. Paul M. Rodriguez and George Archibald, "Homosexual prostitution inquiry ensnares VIPs with Reagan, Bush 'Call boys' took midnight tour of White House," *Washington Times*, June 29, 1989.

7. Ibid.

8. Joan Mower, "Lobbyist at Center of Capital Vice Case," Associated Press, July 15, 1989, https://apnews.com/article/ae7e4e95320d50fbc28747ac5b87ffaa.

9. Henry W. Vinson with Nick Bryant, *Confessions of a DC Madam: The Politics of Sex, Lies, and Blackmail* (Walterville, OR: Trine Day, 2014), chap. 3, Kindle.

10. William Robbins, "Nebraska Inquiry Is Given File on Sex Abuse of Foster Children," *New York Times,* December 25, 1988, https://www.nytimes.com/1988/12/25/us/nebraska -inquiry-is-given-file-on-sex-abuse-of-foster-children.html.

11. William Robbins, "A Lurid, Mysterious Scandal Begins Taking Shape in Omaha," *New York Times,* December 18, 1988, https://www.nytimes.com/1988/12/18/us/a-lurid -mysterious-scandal-begins-taking-shape-in-omaha.html.

12. Rick Atkinson, "Omaha's Hurricane of Scandal," *Washington Post*, April 1, 1990, https:// www.washingtonpost.com/archive/lifestyle/1990/04/01/omahas-hurricane-of-scandal /f762dad7-c72c-415e-a17c-bd4ece10fa44/.

13. *Conspiracy of Silence*, 1993, uploaded to YouTube November 11, 2011, accessed February 17, 2022, https://www.youtube.com/watch?v=mtstlx96s8M.

14. Jacob Shamsian, "Meet Victoria Toensing and Joseph diGenova, the Republican power couple caught up in the FBI's Rudy Giuliani investigation," *Business Insider*, May 4, 2021, https://www.msn.com/en-us/news/politics/meet-victoria-toensing-and-joseph-digenova -the-republican-power-couple-caught-up-in-the-fbis-rudy-giuliani-investigation/ar -BB1gmf5M.

15. John Mintz, Martha Sherrill, and Elsa Walsh, "The Shadow World of Craig Spence," *Washington Post*, July 18, 1989, https://www.washingtonpost.com/archive/lifestyle/1989 /07/18/the-shadow-world-of-craig-spence/2837e91e-49ce-4121-9416-8e0c7a2debf6/.

16. Michael Hedges and Jerry Seper, "Power Broker Served Drugs, Sex at Parties Bugged for Blackmail," *Washington Times*, June 30, 1989.

17. "New book pictures J. Edgar Hoover as drag queen," UPI Archives, February 6, 1993,

https://www.upi.com/Archives/1993/02/06/New-book-pictures-J-Edgar-Hoover-as-drag-queen/1064728974800.

18. Burton Hersh, *Bobby and J. Edgar* (New York: Basic Books, 2008), chap. 2, Kindle.

19. Nicholas Gage, "Ex-Head of Schenley Industries Is Linked to Crime 'Consortium,'" *New York Times*, February 19, 1971, https://www.nytimes.com/1971/02/19/archives/exhead-of-schenley-industries-is-linked-to-crime-consortium.html.

20. Tom Jicha, "PBS Show Opens Closet Door on Hoover's Sexuality, Mob Ties," *South Florida Sun-Sentinel*, February 8, 1993, https://www.sun-sentinel.com/news/fl-xpm-1993-02-09-9301080563-story.html.

21. Curt Gentry, *J. Edgar Hoover: The Man and the Secrets* (New York: W. W. Norton, 1991), 327–330.

22. Associated Press, "U.S. Official Quits in Escort Service Inquiry," June 30, 1989, https://www.nytimes.com/1989/06/30/us/us-official-quits-in-escort-service-inquiry.html.

23. Joan Mower, "Lobbyist at Center of Capital Vice Case," Associated Press, July 15, 1989, https://apnews.com/article/ae7e4e95320d50fbc28747ac5b87ffaa.

24. Rodriguez and Archibald, "Homosexual prostitution inquiry ensnares VIPs with Reagan, Bush 'Call boys' took midnight tour of White House."

25. *The New York Times*, "Lobbyist Is Arrested in New York," August 10, 1989, https://timesmachine.nytimes.com/timesmachine/1989/08/10/575989.html?pageNumber=21.

26. Eleanor Randolph, "The Bombshell That Didn't Explode," *Washington Post*, August 1, 1989, https://www.washingtonpost.com/archive/lifestyle/1989/08/01/the-bombshell-that-didnt-explode/ff09cdb0-7d64-428b-8415-a6998b9f0c65/.

27. Ibid.

28. Rob Wells, "Why one of the biggest scandals in American history should make us rethink journalism," *Washington Post*, October 30, 2019.

29. Ibid.

30. Paul Rosenberg, "Ronald Reagan 'treason' amnesia: GOP hypocrites forget their hero negotiated with terrorists. He was just really bad at it," *Salon*, June 4, 2017, https://www.salon.com/2014/06/07/ronald_reagan_treason_amnesia_gop_hypocrites_forget_their_hero_negotiated_with_terrorists_he_was_just_really_bad_at_it/.

31. Robert Parry, *America's Stolen Narrative: From Washington and Madison to Nixon, Reagan, and the Bushes to Obama* (Arlington, VA: Media Consortium, 2012), chap 5, Kindle.

32. Robert Parry, "Fooling America," Santa Monica, California, March 28, 1993, https://www.scribd.com/document/132771553/Robert-Parry-Fooling-America-Speech-1993.

33. Jeff Cohen and Norman Solomon, "Robert Parry Still Investigating—in Cyberspace," *Eugene Register-Guard*, January 14, 1996.

34. Randolph, "The Bombshell That Didn't Explode."

35. "[Title Removed]," Associated Press, [date removed], 1989, https://apnews.com/article/b23c2d81176c8d92a2f5069039bdc0b0.

36. Jerry Seper and Michael Hedges, "Spence Arrested in New York; Released Bizarre Interview Is No Night on the Town," *Washington Times*, August 9, 1989.

37. Ibid.

38. John Prados and Arturo Jimenez-Bacardi, eds., "The White House, the CIA and the Pike Committee, 1975," *National Security Archive Briefing Book No. 596*, National Security

Archive, George Washington University, June 3, 2017, https://nsarchive2.gwu.edu/NSAEBB/NSAEBB584/.

39. Jack Anderson and Les Whitten, "CIA Love Trap Lures Diplomats," *Washington Post*, February 5, 1975.

40. Frank Snepp, "Bill Barr: The 'Cover-Up General,'" *Village Voice*, October 27, 1992, https://www.villagevoice.com/2019/04/18/attorney-general-william-barr-is-the-best-reason-to-vote-for-clinton/.

41. Ryan Devereaux, "How the CIA Watched Over the Destruction of Gary Webb," *Intercept*, September 25, 2014, https://theintercept.com/2014/09/25/managing-nightmare-cia-media-destruction-gary-webb/.

42. David Johnston, "Attorney General Makes It Official," *New York Times*, August 10, 1991, https://www.nytimes.com/1991/08/10/us/attorney-general-makes-it-official.html.

43. Seper and Hedges, "Spence Arrested in New York."

44. Jerry Seper and Michael Hedges, "Spence as Much an Enigma in Death as He Was in Life," *Washington Times*, November 13, 1989.

45. Landon Thomas Jr., "Jeffrey Epstein: International Moneyman of Mystery," *New York Magazine*, October 28, 2002, https://nymag.com/nymetro/news/people/n_7912/.

46. Hedges and Seper, "Power Broker Served Drugs, Sex at Parties Bugged for Blackmail."

47. Alexandra Wolfe, "Katie Couric, Woody Allen: Jeffrey Epstein's Society Friends Close Ranks," *Daily Beast*, July 8, 2019, https://www.thedailybeast.com/katie-couric-woody-allen-jeffrey-epsteins-society-friends-close-ranks.

48. Nick Bryant, "Here Is Pedophile Billionaire Jeffrey Epstein's Little Black Book," *Gawker*, January 23, 2015, https://www.gawker.com/here-is-pedophile-billionaire-jeffrey-epsteins-little-b-1681383992.

49. Donald Barr, *Space Relations* (New York: Charterhouse, 1973).

50. Laura Strickler, "Harvard science professors kept meeting with donor Jeffrey Epstein despite his sex offender status," NBC News, July 12, 2019, https://www.nbcnews.com/news/us-news/harvard-science-professors-kept-meeting-donor-jeffrey-epstein-despite-his-n1028536.

51. Emily Steel, Steve Eder, Sapna Maheshwari, and Matthew Goldstein, "How Jeffrey Epstein Used the Billionaire Behind Victoria's Secret for Wealth and Women," *New York Times*, July 25, 2019, https://www.nytimes.com/2019/07/25/business/jeffrey-epstein-wexner-victorias-secret.html

52. James B. Stewart, Matthew Goldstein, and Jessica Silver-Greenberg, "Jeffrey Epstein Hoped to Seed Human Race with His DNA," *New York Times*, July 31, 2019, https://www.nytimes.com/2019/07/31/business/jeffrey-epstein-eugenics.html.

53. John Lockett, "Fake doors and secret underground lairs discovered at Jeffrey Epstein's island," *NZ Herald*, November 1, 2019, https://www.nzherald.co.nz/world/fake-doors-and-secret-underground-lairs-discovered-at-jeffrey-epsteins-island/KM26NDFGN225D53LSNBSZSO4CM/.

54. Vicky Ward, "Jeffrey Epstein's Sick Story Played Out for Years in Plain Sight," *Daily Beast*, August 19, 2019, https://www.thedailybeast.com/jeffrey-epsteins-sick-story-played-out-for-years-in-plain-sight?ref=scroll.

55. Sarah Kendzior, *Hiding in Plain Sight: The Invention of Donald Trump and the Erosion of America* (New York: Flatiron Books, 2020), 84.

56. Lee Brown, "Ghislaine Maxwell possible mistrial a 'punch in the gut': Lisa Bloom," *New York Post*, January 6, 2022, https://nypost.com/2022/01/06/ghislaine-maxwell-possible -mistrial-a-punch-in-the-gut-lisa-bloom/.

57. Bill Chappell, "Ghislaine Maxwell Arrested, Charged in Connection to Jeffrey Epstein Abuse Case," NPR, July 2, 2020, https://www.npr.org/2020/07/02/886537383/fbi-arrests -ghislaine-maxwell-in-connection-to-jeffrey-epstein-case.

58. Kendzior, *Hiding in Plain Sight*, 92–94.

59. Julie K. Brown, *Perversion of Justice: The Jeffrey Epstein Story* (New York: Dey Street Books, 2021), 214, Kindle.

60. Jonathan Stempel, "Jeffrey Epstein estate sued by US Virgin Islands, alleges sex trafficking," *The Age*, January 16, 2020, https://www.theage.com.au/business/banking-and -finance/us-virgin-islands-sues-jeffrey-epstein-estate-alleges-sex-trafficking-20200116 -p53ruf.html.

61. Getty Images, "1,108 Ghislaine Maxwell Photos and Premium High Res Pictures," accessed February 15, 2022, https://www.gettyimages.com/photos/ghislaine-maxwell.

62. Bridget Read, "More Clues That Ghislaine Maxwell's In-N-Out Portrait Was Faked," *New York*, August 20, 2019.

63. David Folkenflik, "How the Media Fell Short on Jeffrey Epstein," NPR, August 22, 2019, https://www.npr.org/2019/08/22/753390385/a-dead-cat-a-lawyers-call-and-a-5-figure -donation-how-media-fell-short-on-epstei.

64. Maxwell Tani, "New York Times Reporter Landon Thomas Jr. Solicited $30,000 for Charity from Jeffrey Epstein," *Daily Beast*, August 23, 2019, https://www.thedailybeast .com/new-york-times-reporter-landon-thomas-jr-solicited-dollar30000-for-charity -from-jeffrey-epstein.

65. Ronan Farrow, *Catch and Kill: Lies, Spies, and a Conspiracy to Protect Predators* (New York: Little, Brown, 2019), 404–405, Kindle.

66. Robert Mueller, "The Evolving Organized Crime Threat," Federal Bureau of Investigation, Citizens Crime Commission of New York City, January 27, 2011, https://archives .fbi.gov/archives/news/speeches/the-evolving-organized-crime-threat.

4: The Cult of the Criminal Elite

1. Olga Lexell, "What exactly are Mike Cernovich and Alan Dershowitz doing in the Epstein case?," *Daily Dot*, July 31, 2020, https://www.dailydot.com/debug/mike-cernovich -alan-dershowitz-jeffrey-epstein/.

2. Aris Folley, "Barr brushes off critics of his reputation: 'Everyone dies,'" *The Hill*, May 31, 2019, https://thehill.com/homenews/administration/446324-barr-defends-reputation -everyone-dies.

3. James V. Grimaldi, Dion Nissenbaum, and Margaret Coker, "Ex-CIA Director: Mike Flynn and Turkish Officials Discussed Removal of Erdogan Foe from U.S.," *Wall Street Journal*, March 24, 2017, https://www.wsj.com/articles/ex-cia-director-mike-flynn-and -turkish-officials-discussed-removal-of-erdogan-foe-from-u-s-1490380426.

4. Ken Dilanian, "Flynn-backed plan to transfer nuclear tech to Saudis may have broken laws, say whistleblowers," NBC News, February 19, 2019, https://www.nbcnews.com /politics/congress/flynn-backed-plan-transfer-nuclear-tech-saudis-may-have-broken -n973021.

5. Aaron Rupar, "Trump national security adviser partnered with KGB-linked business-man to sell mind-reading gear," *ThinkProgress*, December 23, 2016, https://archive.thinkprogress.org/michael-flynn-kgb-mind-reading-equipment-us-government-9741fc0f80c4/.

6. Jackie Flynn Mogensen, "To Celebrate the Fourth, Michael Flynn Posts a Pledge to Conspiracy Group QAnon," *Mother Jones*, July 5, 2020, https://www.motherjones.com/politics/2020/07/to-celebrate-the-fourth-michael-flynn-posts-a-pledge-to-conspiracy-group-qanon/.

7. Donald Trump, transcript of speech delivered in front of the White House, Washington, DC, January 6, 2021, https://www.usnews.com/news/politics/articles/2021-01-13/transcript-of-trumps-speech-at-rally-before-us-capitol-riot.

8. Rob Kuznia, Curt Devine, Nelli Black, and Drew Griffin, "Stop the Steal's massive disinformation campaign connected to Roger Stone," CNN, November 14, 2020, https://www.cnn.com/2020/11/13/business/stop-the-steal-disinformation-campaign-invs/index.html.

9. Dan Mangan, "Trump campaign chief Manafort's associate Kilimnik gave Russia 2016 election strategy, polling, U.S. says," CNBC, April 15, 2021, https://www.cnbc.com/2021/04/15/trump-campaign-chief-paul-manafort-employee-kilimnik-gave-russia-election-data.html.

10. Shanika Gunaratna, "Harry Reid wants deeper FBI probe into possibility of Russian election hack," CBS News, August 30, 2016, https://www.cbsnews.com/news/harry-reid-asks-fbi-do-more-prevent-russian-hack-election-day/.

11. David E. Sanger and Catie Edmondson, "Russia Targeted Election Systems in All 50 States, Report Finds," *New York Times*, July 25, 2019, https://www.nytimes.com/2019/07/25/us/politics/russian-hacking-elections.html.

12. Kenzi Abou-Sabe and Rich Schapiro, "Manafort told Gates not to plead guilty, said Trump's lawyer vowed to 'take care of us,'" NBC News, April 18, 2019, https://www.nbcnews.com/politics/justice-department/manafort-told-gates-not-plead-guilty-said-trump-s-lawyer-n995961.

13. Paul Manafort (@PaulManafort), "Battleground states moving to Trump en masse," Tweet, November 4, 2016, https://twitter.com/PaulManafort/status/794553482330210304?s=20.

14. Devlin Barrett and Philip Rucker, "Trump said he was thinking of Russia controversy when he decided to fire Comey," *Washington Post*, May 11, 2017, https://www.washingtonpost.com/world/national-security/trump-says-fbi-director-comey-told-him-three-times-he-wasnt-under-investigation-once-in-a-phone-call-initiated-by-the-president/2017/05/11/2b384c9a-3669-11e7-b4ee-434b6d506b37_story.html.

15. Rebecca Shabad, "Donald Trump: 'I have nothing to do with Russia,'" CBS News, July 27, 2016, https://www.cbsnews.com/news/donald-trump-denies-he-has-any-ties-to-russia/.

16. Matt Apuzzo and Maggie Haberman, "Trump Associate Boasted That Moscow Business Deal 'Will Get Donald Elected,'" *New York Times*, August 28, 2017, https://www.nytimes.com/2017/08/28/us/politics/trump-tower-putin-felix-sater.html.

17. Sharon LaFraniere and William K. Rashbaum, "Thomas Barrack, Trump Fund-Raiser, Is Indicted on Lobbying Charge," *New York Times*, July 20, 2021, https://www.nytimes.com/2021/07/20/us/thomas-barrack-trump-indicted.html.

18. Ronan Farrow, "Harvey Weinstein's Army of Spies," *New Yorker*, November 6, 2017, https://www.newyorker.com/news/news-desk/harvey-weinsteins-army-of-spies.

19. Tate Delloye, "The Godfather of Tabloid: How childhood friend of Roy Cohn and son of an influential political fixer with ties to Mussolini left the CIA to start the National Enquirer with a loan from mob boss Frank Costello," *Daily Mail*, November 20, 2019, https://www.dailymail.co.uk/news/article-7687673/national-enquirer-roy-cohn-CIA.html.

20. Sarah Kendzior, *Hiding in Plain Sight: The Invention of Donald Trump and the Erosion of America* (New York: Flatiron Books, 2020), 96.

21. Justin Vallejo, "Why some QAnon believers think JFK Jr is still alive—and about to become vice president," *The Independent*, July 22, 2021, https://news.yahoo.com/why-qanon-believers-think-jfk-183333654.html.

22. Jacob Shamsian and Benjamin Goggin, "James Comey's daughter is a lead prosecutor in Ghislaine Maxwell's child sex trafficking case. Here's what we know about her," *Insider*, November 26, 2021, https://www.businessinsider.com/maurene-comey-james-comey-daughter-leading-jeffrey-epstein-case-2019-7.

23. Jan Ransom, "Cyrus Vance's Office Sought Reduced Sex-Offender Status for Epstein," *New York Times*, July 9, 2019, https://www.nytimes.com/2019/07/09/nyregion/cyrus-vance-epstein.html.

24. EJ Dickson, "The FBI Declared QAnon a Domestic Terrorism Threat—and Conspiracy Theorists Are Psyched," *Rolling Stone*, August 2, 2019, https://www.yahoo.com/entertainment/fbi-declared-qanon-domestic-terrorism-181448533.html.

25. Anushka Asthana and Julia Carrie Wong, "The growing influence of the QAnon conspiracy theory," September 20, 2020, in *Today in Focus*, produced by *The Guardian*, podcast, MP3 audio, 32:53, https://www.theguardian.com/news/audio/2020/sep/21/the-growing-influence-of-the-qanon-conspiracy-theory-podcast.

26. Matthew Choi, "Biden: QAnon is 'bizarre' and 'embarrassing,' supporters should seek mental health treatment," *Politico*, September 4, 2020, https://www.politico.com/news/2020/09/04/biden-qanon-bizarre-embarrassing-409090.

27. Ellie Hall, "What Is QAnon? Here's What You Need to Know About the Baseless Mega-Conspiracy Theory," *BuzzFeed News*, August 2, 2018, https://www.buzzfeednews.com/article/ellievhall/qanon-trump-rally-conspiracy-theory.

28. Abraham Lincoln, "The Perpetuation of Our Political Institutions," transcript of speech delivered at the Young Men's Lyceum in Springfield, Illinois, January 27, 1838, https://www.abrahamlincolnonline.org/lincoln/speeches/lyceum.htm.

29. Ralph Blumenthal and Leslie Kean, "No Longer in Shadows, Pentagon's U.F.O. Unit Will Make Some Findings Public," *New York Times*, July 23, 2020, https://www.nytimes.com/2020/07/23/us/politics/pentagon-ufo-harry-reid-navy.html.

30. Tom O'Neill, *Chaos: Charles Manson, the CIA, and the Secret History of the Sixties* (New York: Little, Brown, 2019), 5.

5: Savior Syndrome and Normalcy Bias

1. Bill Kemp, "Environmental issues come of age in the 1990s," *Illinois Times*, April 16, 1990, https://www.lib.niu.edu/1990/ii900413.html.

2. William W. Kellogg, "Is mankind warming the Earth?," *Bulletin of the Atomic Scientists*

(February 1978), https://thebulletin.org/premium/2020–12/1978-is-mankind-warming
-the-earth/.

3. Michael Greshko, "201 Years Ago, This Volcano Caused a Climate Catastrophe," *National Geographic*, April 8, 2016, https://www.nationalgeographic.com/science/article
/160408-tambora-eruption-volcano-anniversary-indonesia-science?loggedin=true.

4. Mary Shelley, *Frankenstein, Or the Modern Prometheus* (London: Lackington, Hughes, Harding, Mavor, and Jones, 1818), 11.

5. Suzanne Goldenberg, "Exxon knew of climate change in 1981, email says—but it funded deniers for 27 more years," *The Guardian*, July 8, 2015, https://www.theguardian.com
/environment/2015/jul/08/exxon-climate-change-1981-climate-denier-funding.

6. George Monbiot, "The denial industry," *The Guardian*, September 19, 2006, https://www
.theguardian.com/environment/2006/sep/19/ethicalliving.g2.

7. Carl Jung, *Psychology and Alchemy* (New York: Bollingen Foundation, 1968), 322–323.

8. John Schwartz, "Overlooked No More: Eunice Foote, Climate Scientist Lost to History," *New York Times*, April 21, 2020, https://www.nytimes.com/2020/04/21/obituaries
/eunice-foote-overlooked.html.

9. Nick Welsh, "John Perlin Rediscovers Feminist Crusader Who Discovered Climate Change," *Santa Barbara Independent*, May 10, 2018, https://www.independent.com/2018
/05/10/john-perlin-rediscovers-feminist-crusader-who-discovered-climate-change/.

10. Clive Thompson, "How 19th Century Scientists Predicted Global Warming," *JSTOR*, December 17, 2019, https://daily.jstor.org/how-19th-century-scientists-predicted-global
-warming/.

11. Robert Kaufman, "Texas governor signs bill prohibiting teaching critical race theory in public schools," *JURIST*, June 17, 2021, https://www.jurist.org/news/2021/06/texas
-governor-signs-bill-prohibiting-teaching-critical-race-theory-in-public-schools/.

12. Robert S. Levine, "Frederick Douglass and the Trouble with Critical Race Theory," *Los Angeles Review of Books*, August 2, 2021, https://lareviewofbooks.org/article/frederick
-douglass-and-the-trouble-with-critical-race-theory/.

13. Alexander Koch, Chris Brierley, Mark Maslin, and Simon Lewis, "European colonisation of the Americas might have caused global cooling, according to new research," World Economic Forum, February 1, 2019, https://www.weforum.org/agenda/2019/02
/european-colonisation-of-the-americas-caused-global-cooling/.

14. Aylin Woodward, "European colonizers killed so many indigenous Americans that the planet cooled down, a group of researchers concluded," *Business Insider*, February 9, 2019, https://www.businessinsider.com/climate-changed-after-europeans-killed-indigenous
-americans-2019-2.

15. Douglas MacMillan, Peter Whoriskey, and Jonathan O'Connell, "America's biggest companies are flourishing during the pandemic and putting thousands of people out of work," *Washington Post*, December 16, 2020, https://www.washingtonpost.com
/graphics/2020/business/50-biggest-companies-coronavirus-layoffs/.

16. "Wealth increase of 10 men during pandemic could buy vaccines for all," BBC, January 25, 2021, https://www.bbc.com/news/world-55793575.

17. "The COVID Racial Data Tracker," COVID Tracking Project, last modified March 7, 2021, https://covidtracking.com/race.

18. Cameron Razieh et al., "Ethnic minorities and COVID-19: Examining whether excess

risk is mediated through deprivation," *European Journal of Public Health* 31, no. 3 (June 2021): 630–634, https://doi.org/10.1093/eurpub/ckab041.

19. Jennifer Rigby, "The least vaccinated countries in the world: The charts showing the scale of inequality," *The Telegraph*, July 23, 2021, https://www.telegraph.co.uk/global -health/science-and-disease/least-vaccinated-countries-world-charts-showing-scale -inequality/.

20. Steven W. Thrasher, "There Is Nothing Normal About One Million People Dead from COVID," *Scientific American*, February 10, 2022, https://www.scientificamerican.com /article/there-is-nothing-normal-about-one-million-people-dead-from-covid1/.

21. Larry Kramer, "An Open Letter to Dr. Anthony Fauci," *San Francisco Examiner,* June 26, 1988, https://aep.lib.rochester.edu/node/49111.

22. Gretchen Gavett, "Timeline: 30 Years of AIDS in Black America," *Frontline*, July 10, 2012, https://www.pbs.org/wgbh/frontline/article/timeline-30-years-of-aids-in-black -america/.

23. Anne Nelson, "The Shadow Network (Council for National Policy) Is Not Going Away," BillMoyers.com, March 24, 2021, https://billmoyers.com/story/the-shadow-network -council-for-national-policy-is-not-going-away/.

24. John Herbers, "Religious Leaders Tell of Worry on Armageddon View Ascribed to Reagan," *New York Times*, October 21, 1984, https://www.nytimes.com/1984/10/21/us /religious-leaders-tell-of-worry-on-armageddon-view-ascribed-to-reagan.html.

25. Ronald Reagan, "We Could See Armageddon," interview by Jim Bakker, *Voices of History,* uploaded to Right Wing Watch, January 17, 2017, video, 1:13, https://www.youtube .com/watch?v=4UUmgKj1oTs.

26. Herbers, "Religious Leaders Tell of Worry on Armageddon View Ascribed to Reagan."

27. Bill Prochnau and Valarie Thomas, "The Watt Controversy," *Washington Post*, June 30, 1981, https://www.washingtonpost.com/archive/politics/1981/06/30/the-watt-controversy /d591699b-3bc2-46d2-9059-fb5d2513c3da/.

28. David Hoffman, "Watt Submits Resignation as Interior Secretary," *Washington Post*, October 10, 1983, https://www.washingtonpost.com/archive/politics/1983/10/10/watt -submits-resignation-as-interior-secretary/84ba758c-03f2-439d-8105-0bab802247b9/.

29. Tom Winter and Ken Dilanian, "Manafort associate is Russian spy, may have helped co- ordinate e-mail hack-and-leak, report says," NBC News, August 18, 2020, https://www .nbcnews.com/politics/national-security/manafort-associate-russian-spy-may-have -helped-coordinate-e-mail-n1237121.

30. David D. Kirkpatrick, "Who Is Behind Trump's Link to Arab Princes? A Billionaire Friend," *New York Times*, June 13, 2018, https://www.nytimes.com/2018/06/13/world /middleeast/trump-tom-barrack-saudi.html.

31. Erica Orden, "Trump ally Tom Barrack jailed on charges of acting as an agent of a foreign government," CNN, July 20, 2021, https://www.cnn.com/2021/07/20/politics/tom-barrack -arrested/index.html.

32. Ron Kampeas, "Michael Flynn's lies to FBI included one about Israel," *Jerusalem Post*, November 27, 2020, https://www.jpost.com/american-politics/michael-flynns-lies-to -fbi-included-one-about-israel-650427.

33. Vicky Ward, *Kushner, Inc.: Greed. Ambition. Corruption. The Extraordinary Story of Jared Kushner and Ivanka Trump* (New York: St. Martin's Press, 2019), 117.

34. TBashII (@RukhnamaLives), "It's like those logic puzzles," Tweet, February 21, 2019, https://twitter.com/RukhnamaLives/status/1098601200986009601?s=20.

35. Andrew Brown, "Bush, Gog, and Magog," *The Guardian*, August 10, 2009, https://www.theguardian.com/commentisfree/andrewbrown/2009/aug/10/religion-george-bush.

36. Jim Sciutto and Nicole Gaouette, "CIA chief met with sanctioned Russian spies, officials confirm," CNN, February 2, 2018, https://www.cnn.com/2018/02/01/politics/pompeo-russian-spies-meeting/index.html.

37. Edward Wong, "The Rapture and the Real World: Mike Pompeo Blends Beliefs and Policy," *New York Times*, March 30, 2019, https://www.nytimes.com/2019/03/30/us/politics/pompeo-christian-policy.html.

38. TOI Staff, "New Pentagon adviser said Pompeo, senior officials made rich by 'Israeli lobby'," *Times of Israel*, November 14, 2020, https://www.timesofisrael.com/top-pentagon-advisor-said-pompeo-senior-officials-made-rich-by-israeli-lobby/.

39. Tracy Wilkinson, "Secretary of State Pompeo's RNC speech from Israel shatters norms, spurs investigation," *Los Angeles Times*, August 25, 2020, https://news.yahoo.com/secretary-state-pompeo-shatter-political-191012502.html.

40. Sam Sokol, "Pompeo may visit Israel during Blinken trip," *Haaretz*, May 25, 2021, https://www.haaretz.com/israel-news/.premium-pompeo-may-visit-israel-during-blinken-trip-1.9841373.

41. TOI Staff, "Mossad head could join Mnuchin fund, possibly violating waiting period—report," *Times of Israel*, May 26, 2021, https://www.timesofisrael.com/mossad-head-could-join-mnuchin-fund-possibly-violating-waiting-period-report/.

42. Karen DeYoung, "Trump picks a supporter of West Bank settlements for ambassador to Israel," *Washington Post*, December 15, 2016, https://www.washingtonpost.com/world/national-security/trump-picks-a-supporter-of-west-bank-settlements-for-ambassador-to-israel/2016/12/15/1a50c03c-c32e-11e6-9a51-cd56ea1c2bb7_story.html.

43. Michael Schwartz and James Masters, "David Friedman photograph sparks Jerusalem controversy," CNN, May 23, 2018, https://www.cnn.com/2018/05/23/middleeast/david-friedman-jerusalem-illustration-intl/index.html.

44. Matthew Lee and Bradley Klapper, "Trump declares Jerusalem Israeli capital, smashing US policy," Associated Press, December 6, 2017, https://apnews.com/article/north-america-donald-trump-ap-top-news-tel-aviv-jerusalem-1d4e1824283f41eaa8422227fa8e6ea7.

45. Yosi Birnbaum, "Sheldon Adelson 7–2–2010.wmv," recording of speech by Sheldon Adelson, February 10, 2010, video, 8:42, https://www.youtube.com/watch?v=2EGgCdChPOw.

46. Associated Press, "Convicted U.S. spy Pollard is greeted by Netanyahu as he arrives in Israel," *Politico*, December 29, 2020, https://www.politico.com/news/2020/12/29/jonathan-pollard-spy-israel-452235.

47. Connie Bruck, "The Influencer," *New Yorker*, May 3, 2010, https://www.newyorker.com/magazine/2010/05/10/the-influencer.

48. Israeli-American Council IAC, "Chuck Schumer (D-NY) & Nancy Pelosi (D-CA) with Haim Saban—2018 IAC National Conference," recording of 2018 Israeli American Council National Conference, December 12, 2018, video, 07:40, https://www.youtube.com/watch?v=zvi3O9NkhQI&t=3s.

49. Marcy Oster, "In secret recording, Lev Parnas and Igor Fruman draw parallel between

Trump and the Messiah," Jewish Telegraphic Agency, January 6, 2020, https://www .jta.org/quick-reads/in-secret-recording-lev-parnas-and-igor-fruman-draw-parallel -between-trump-and-the-messiah.

50. Robert Parry, "How Roy Cohn Helped Rupert Murdoch," *Consortium News*, January 28, 2015, https://consortiumnews.com/2015/01/28/how-roy-cohn-helped-rupert-murdoch/.

51. Roy M. Cohn to Edwin Meese III, James A. Baker III, and Michael K. Deaver, Washing-ton, DC, January 27, 1982, https://trumpfile.org/wp-content/uploads/2021/03/Murdoch -Reagan-Cohn-letter.pdf.

52. "Testimonial Dinner in Honor of Roy M. Cohn," May 2, 1983, uploaded to Consor-tium News in January 2015, https://consortiumnews.com/wp-content/uploads/2015/01 /Cohn-Dinner.pdf.

53. Margot Hornblower, "Roy Cohn Is Disbarred by New York Court," *Washington Post*, June 24, 1986, https://www.washingtonpost.com/archive/politics/1986/06/24/roy-cohn-is -disbarred-by-new-york-court/c5ca911-3245-48f0-ab01-c2c0f3c3fc2e/.

54. Nicholas Gage, "Rosenstiel Link to Crime Denied," *New York Times*, March 12, 1971, https://www.nytimes.com/1971/03/12/archives/rosenstiel-link-to-crime-denied-but -schenley-aide-concedes.html.

55. Emma Margolin, "'Make America Great Again'—Who Said It First?," NBC News, Sep-tember 9, 2016, https://www.nbcnews.com/politics/2016-election/make-america-great -again-who-said-it-first-n645716.

56. Tom Nichols, "Five Ways Nuclear Armageddon Was Almost Unleashed," *National Inter-est*, August 9, 2014, https://nationalinterest.org/feature/five-ways-nuclear-armageddon -was-almost-unleashed-11044?page=3%2C1.

57. Nate Jones and J. Peter Scoblic, "The Week the World Almost Ended," *SLATE*, April 13, 2017, https://slate.com/news-and-politics/2017/06/able-archer-almost-started-a-nuclear -war-with-russia-in-1983.html.

6: Memory-Holing a Coup

1. Twitter Safety (@TwitterSafety), "After close review of recent Tweets," Tweet, January 8, 2021, https://twitter.com/TwitterSafety/status/1347684877634838528.

2. George Orwell, *Nineteen Eighty-Four* (New York: Alfred A. Knopf, 1949), 222.

3. Trump Twitter Archive, https://www.thetrumparchive.com/.

4. Janice Williams, "National Archives to Make All of Donald Trump's Tweets Publicly Available," *Newsweek*, January 20, 2021, https://www.newsweek.com/donald-trump -national-archive-tweets-1563149.

5. Shannon Bow O'Brien, "Trump wants the National Archives to keep his papers away from investigators—post-Watergate laws and executive orders may not let him," *The Conversation*, October 22, 2021, https://news.yahoo.com/trump-wants-national -archives-keep-123857309.html.

6. Allan Smith, "CNN president Jeff Zucker has a framed Donald Trump tweet in his office," *Insider*, August 2, 2016, https://www.businessinsider.com/jeff-zucker-cnn-donald-trump -tweet-2016-8.

7. Jack Brewster, "Jan. 6 Rally Organizer Ali Alexander Reappears and Urges Followers to 'Gather Together Once Again to Fight'," *Forbes*, June 14, 2021, https://www.forbes.com

/sites/jackbrewster/2021/06/14/jan-6-rally-organizer-ali-alexander-reappears-and-urges
-followers-to-gather-together-once-again-to-fight/?sh=10cf30e23bc2.

8. Mark Hosenball and Sarah N. Lynch, "Exclusive: FBI finds scant evidence U.S. Capitol attack was coordinated—sources," Reuters, August 20, 2021, https://www.reuters
.com/world/us/exclusive-fbi-finds-scant-evidence-us-capitol-attack-was-coordinated
-sources-2021-08-20/.

9. Ryan J. Reilly, "'Sedition Hunters': Meet the Online Sleuths Aiding the FBI's Capitol
Manhunt," *Huffington Post*, June 30, 2021, https://www.huffpost.com/entry/sedition
-hunters-fbi-capitol-attack-manhunt-online-sleuths_n_60479dd7c5b653040034f749.

10. Martin Pengelly, "Republican mega-donor buys stake in Twitter and seeks to oust Jack
Dorsey—report," *The Guardian*, February 29, 2020, https://www.theguardian.com
/technology/2020/feb/29/paul-singer-elliott-management-twitter-jack-dorsey.

11. Ali Breland, "Twitter's New Privacy Policy Is Making It Harder to Spread Warnings
About Online Fascists," *Mother Jones*, December 3, 2021, https://www.motherjones.com
/politics/2021/12/twitter-privacy-policy/?utm_source=twitter&utm_campaign
=naytev&utm_medium=social.

12. Chris Kahn, "Nearly 80% of Americans say Biden won White House, ignoring Trump's
refusal to concede: Reuters/Ipsos poll," Reuters, November 10, 2020, https://www.reuters
.com/article/us-usa-election-poll/nearly-80-of-americans-say-biden-won-white-house
-ignoring-trumps-refusal-to-concede-reuters-ipsos-poll-idUSKBN27Q3ED.

13. "Poll: One-fifth of voters, almost half of Republicans, agree with storming of US Capitol," ABC News 10, January 8, 2021, https://www.news10.com/news/us-capitol-coverage
/poll-one-fifth-of-voters-almost-half-of-republicans-agree-with-storming-of-us
-capitol/amp/.

14. "Ipsos/Reuters Poll: The Big Lie," *Ipsos*, May 21, 2021, https://www.ipsos.com/sites/default
/files/ct/news/documents/2021–05/Ipsos%20Reuters%20Topline%20Write%20up-%20
The%20Big%20Lie%20-%2017%20May%20thru%2019%20May%202021.pdf.

15. Tatishe Nteta, "Toplines and Crosstabs December 2021 National Poll: Presidential Election
& Jan 6th Insurrection at the US Capitol," University of Massachusetts Amherst, last modified December 28, 2021, https://polsci.umass.edu/toplines-and-crosstabs-december-2021
-national-poll-presidential-election-jan-6th-insurrection-us.

16. Ben Collins, "QAnon falsehoods move to text message chains," NBC News, January 12,
2021, https://www.nbcnews.com/tech/internet/qanon-falsehoods-move-text-message
-chains-n1253962.

17. Aaron Keller, "Pro-Trump Woman Shot and Killed at U.S. Capitol Retweeted Attorney Lin Wood's 'Must Be Done' List Before She Died," *Law & Crime*, January 6, 2021,
https://lawandcrime.com/2020-election/pro-trump-woman-shot-and-killed-at-u-s
-capitol-retweeted-attorney-lin-woods-must-be-done-list-before-she-died/.

18. Nick Visser, "CBS Chief Les Moonves Says Trump's 'Damn Good' for Business," *Huffington Post*, March 1, 2016, https://www.huffpost.com/entry/les-moonves-donald
-trump_n_56d52ce8e4b03260bf780275.

19. Andrew Dention, "X-Files Uncovered: An Interview with Chris Carter," *Rolling Stone*
724/725 (December 28, 1995), http://howie.gse.buffalo.edu/effilno/interests/xfiles/rstones
/rscc.html

20. Mark Memmott, "It's True: 'Mistakes Were Made' Is the King of Non-Apologies," *The*

Two-Way, NPR, May 14, 2013, https://www.npr.org/sections/thetwo-way/2013/05/14/183924858/its-true-mistakes-were-made-is-the-king-of-non-apologies.

21. George W. Bush, transcript of press conference held at the White House, Washington, DC, September 16, 2001, https://www.nytimes.com/2001/09/16/national/text-of-bushs-press-conference.html.

22. Joel Roberts, "9/11 Chair: Attack Was Preventable," CBS News, December 17, 2003, https://www.cbsnews.com/news/9-11-chair-attack-was-preventable/.

23. Donald Rumsfeld, Joseph Biden, and Henry Hyde, "Text: Rumsfeld on NBC's 'Meet the Press,'" interview by Tim Russert, *Meet the Press*, NBC, September 30, 2001, text transcript, https://www.washingtonpost.com/wp-srv/nation/specials/attacked/transcripts/nbctext_093001.html.

24. Lawrence Wright, *The Looming Tower* (New York: Random House, 2007).

25. Michael Ausiello, "The Sept. 11 Parallel 'Nobody Noticed'," *TV Guide*, June 21, 2002, https://www.tvguide.com/news/sept-11-parallel-41409/.

26. Bob Graham, *Intelligence Matters: The CIA, the FBI, Saudi Arabia, and the Failure of America's War on Terror* (New York: Random House, 2004), introduction, Kindle.

27. Abigail Tracy, "Explosive Declassified Report Details Saudi Ties to 9/11," *Vanity Fair*, July 15, 2016, https://www.vanityfair.com/news/2016/07/declassified-report-saudi-ties-september-11.

28. Laura Sullivan, "Biden Declassifies Secret FBI Report Detailing Saudi Nationals' Connections to 9/11," NPR, September 12, 2021, https://www.npr.org/2021/09/12/1036389448/biden-declassifies-secret-fbi-report-detailing-saudi-nationals-connections-to-9-.

29. Ron Suskind, "Faith, Certainty and the Presidency of George W. Bush," *New York Times*, October 17, 2004, https://www.nytimes.com/2004/10/17/magazine/faith-certainty-and-the-presidency-of-george-w-bush.html.

30. Rick Rouan, "JFK files: What we know about another delay in the release of assassination records," *USA Today*, October 25, 2021, https://www.msn.com/en-us/news/us/jfk-files-what-we-know-about-another-delay-in-the-release-of-assassination-records/ar-AAPWbIX?ocid=uxbndlbing.

31. "Report: Netanyahu Says 9/11 Terror Attacks Good for Israel," *Haaretz*, April 16, 2008, https://www.haaretz.com/1.4970678.

7: America Is Purple, Like a Bruise

1. Donald Trump, "Donald Trump's 2014 political predictions," interview by Brian Kilmeade, *Fox & Friends*, Fox News, February 10, 2014, video, 6:37, https://video.foxnews.com/v/3179604851001#sp=show-clips.

2. Ronald Radosh, "Steve Bannon, Trump's Top Guy, Told Me He Was 'a Leninist,'" *Daily Beast*, August 22, 2016, https://www.thedailybeast.com/steve-bannon-trumps-top-guy-told-me-he-was-a-leninist.

3. Alan Gilbert, "The Far-Right Book Every Russian General Reads," *Daily Beast*, February 26, 2018, https://www.thedailybeast.com/the-far-right-book-every-russian-general-reads.

4. Ibid.

5. Jeremy W. Peters, "Bannon's Worldview: Dissecting the Message of 'The Fourth Turning,'" *New York Times*, April 8, 2017, https://www.nytimes.com/2017/04/08/us/politics/bannon-fourth-turning.html.

6. Casey Michel, "Bob Dole's biggest impact may have come post-retirement. And not in a good way," NBC News, December 8, 2021, https://www.msn.com/en-us/news/politics /bob-dole-s-biggest-impact-may-have-come-post-retirement-and-not-in-a-good-way/ar -AARBEmr.

7. Casey Michel, "Want to Break Up the United States? The Kremlin Is Ready to Help," *Daily Beast*, March 11, 2020, https://www.thedailybeast.com/want-to-break-up-the-united-states -the-kremlin-is-ready-to-help.

8. T. S. Eliot, *Four Quartets*, "The Dry Salvages" (New York: Harcourt Brace, 1943), 35.

9. Sarah Silverman (@SarahKSilverman), "Maybe we should break up," Tweet, September 12, 2021, https://twitter.com/SarahKSilverman/status/1437236890885754880?ref_src =twsrc%5Etfw.

10. "After Newsom recall fails, Ben Shapiro says secession may be 'the best hope' for conservatives," *Media Matters*, September 15, 2021, https://www.mediamatters.org/ben -shapiro/after-newsom-recall-fails-ben-shapiro-says-secession-may-be-best-hope -conservatives.

11. Glenn Beck, "A 'National Divorce' is coming one way or another. Here's why," *Glenn Beck*, October 21, 2021, https://www.glennbeck.com/radio/a-national-divorce-is-coming -one-way-or-another-here-s-why.

12. Brian Stelter, "With Book, Buchanan Sets His Fate," *New York Times*, February 26, 2012, https://www.nytimes.com/2012/02/27/business/media/with-book-buchanan-set-his -fate.html.

13. Alex Griffing, "Marjorie Taylor Greene Again Pushes for 'National Divorce,' Praises 'Second Amendment Rights' as Means of Defense," *Mediaite*, January 11, 2022, https:// www.mediaite.com/politics/marjorie-taylor-greene-again-pushes-for-national-divorce -praises-second-amendment-rights-as-means-of-defense/.

14. Annika Neklason, "The Conspiracy Theories That Fueled the Civil War," *The Atlantic*, May 29, 2020, https://www.theatlantic.com/politics/archive/2020/05/conspiracy-theories -civil-war/612283/.

15. Kevin Roose, "Silicon Valley's Secessionist Movement Is Growing," *Intelligencer*, October 21, 2013, https://nymag.com/intelligencer/2013/10/silicon-valleys-secessionists.html.

16. Barack Obama, "Keynote Address," transcript of speech delivered at the 2004 Democratic National Convention in Boston, Massachusetts, July 27, 2004, https://web.archive .org/web/20080403144623/http:/www.barackobama.com/2004/07/27/keynote_address _at_the_2004_de.php.

17. Bradford Betz, "Obama says controversy over infamous 'bitter' comments about small-town America still 'nags at me,'" Fox News, November 18, 2020, https://www.foxnews .com/politics/obama-controversy-infamous-bitter-comments-small-town-americans -still-nags-me.

18. Casey Michel, "How a Ukrainian tycoon became Cleveland's commercial real estate kingpin," *ThinkProgress*, August 21, 2019, https://archive.thinkprogress.org/how-did-this -ukrainian-tycoon-become-clevelands-commercial-real-estate-kingpin-7c58f789fc8e/.

19. Laura Meckler and Josh Dawsey, "Republicans, spurred by an unlikely figure, see political promise in targeting critical race theory," *Washington Post*, June 19, 2021, https://www .washingtonpost.com/education/2021/06/19/critical-race-theory-rufo-republicans/.

20. Lachlan Markay, "Scoop: FEC lets foreigners finance U.S. ballot fights," *Axios*, Novem-

ber 2, 2021, https://www.axios.com/fec-foreign-money-referendum-dcc92322-05ad
-4093-8bb8-35446ef6c964.html.

21. Casey Michel, "U.S. Politicians Can't Stop Taking Len Blavatnik's Money," *Bellingcat*,
    October 21, 2019, https://www.bellingcat.com/news/2019/10/21/u-s-politicians-cant-stop
    -taking-len-blavatniks-money/.

22. Young America's Foundation, "Lieutenant General Michael T. Flynn," November 14,
    2016, video, 33:15, https://www.youtube.com/watch?v=W0CThXL37Jk.

23. Candace Rondeaux, "The Digital General: How Trump Ally Michael Flynn Nurtured—
    and Profited From—the QAnon Conspiracy Theory," *The Intercept*, June 27, 2021,
    https://theintercept.com/2021/06/27/qanon-michael-flynn-digital-soldiers/.

24. Thomas R Beveridge, *Geologic Wonders and Curiosities of Missouri* (Jefferson City: Missouri Department of Natural Resources, 1990), 334.

25. Bruce L Cline, *History, Mystery, and Hauntings of Southern Illinois* (Marion: Illinois
    History, 2014), 161–162.

26. Bruce McMillan, "Tower Rock: Sentinel of the Mississippi," *Living Museum* 56, no. 2
    (Summer 1994): 19–21, https://www.academia.edu/3546739/Tower_Rock_Sentinel_of
    _the_Mississippi.

27. Ibid.

28. Mark Twain, *Life on the Mississippi* (New York: Modern Library, 2007), 57–59.

8: The Octopus

1. Steve Ditlea, "In New French Best-Seller, Software Meets Espionage," *New York Times*,
   June 20, 1997, https://archive.nytimes.com/www.nytimes.com/library/cyber/week
   /062097loeil.html.

2. Brian Prince, "Data Search Technology Used by FBI Makes Its Way to Enterprises,"
   eWeek, April 29, 2009, https://www.eweek.com/news/Data-Search-Technology-Used-by
   -FBI-Makes-Its-Way-to-Enterprises/#sthash.FkDBOZiS.XaJRMNZk.dpuf.

3. Ibid.

4. Dana Kennedy, "Jeffrey Epstein 'Friend' Ghislaine Maxwell Has More Skeletons in Her
   Family Closet Than a House of Horrors," *Daily Beast*, August 18, 2019, https://www
   .thedailybeast.com/jeffrey-epstein-friend-ghislaine-maxwell-has-more-skeletons-in
   -her-family-closet-than-a-house-of-horrors?ref=scroll.

5. Danny Casolaro, "The Octopus: A Proposal," State Historical Society of Missouri,
   Columbia.

6. Ibid.

7. David Corn, "The Dark World of Danny Casolaro," *The Nation*, October 28, 1991,
   https://ia601305.us.archive.org/32/items/Danny-Casolaro/corn.pdf.

8. Ron Rosenbaum, "The Strange Death of Danny Casolaro," *Vanity Fair* (December 1991),
   https://archive.vanityfair.com/article/1991/12/the-strange-death-of-danny-casolaro.

9. Richard L. Fricker, "The INSLAW Octopus," *WIRED*, January 1, 1993, https://www.wired
   .com/1993/01/inslaw/?topic=&topic_set=.

10. Danny Casolaro, unpublished manuscript draft, State Historical Society of Missouri,
    Columbia.

11. Ibid.

12. Rosenbaum, "The Strange Death of Danny Casolaro."

13. Emilia Díaz-Struck et al., "Pandora Papers: An offshore data tsunami," International Consortium of Investigative Journalists, October 3, 2021, https://www.icij.org/investigations/pandora-papers/about-pandora-papers-leak-dataset/.

14. Danny Casolaro, "Octopus: Proposals and Drafts," personal notebooks, State Historical Society of Missouri, Columbia.

15. "The 'Conspiracy' Art of Mark Lombardi," *Weekend Edition Saturday*, NPR, November 1, 2003, audio, 5:02, https://www.npr.org/2003/11/01/1487185/the-conspiracy-art-of-mark-lombardi.

16. Patricia Goldstone, *Interlock: Art, Conspiracy, and the Shadow World of Mark Lombardi* (Berkeley, CA: Counterpoint, 2015), introduction, Kindle.

17. Patricia Goldstone, "The Mysterious Death of an Artist Whose Drawings Were Too Revealing," interview by Jeff Schechtman, *Radio WhoWhatWhy*, December 4, 2015, audio, 36:13, https://whowhatwhy.org/podcast/the-mysterious-death-of-an-artist-whose-drawings-were-too-revealing/.

18. Ibid.

19. Joshua Glenn, "Conspiracy so immense," *Boston Globe*, December 7, 2003, http://archive.boston.com/news/globe/ideas/articles/2003/12/07/conspiracy_so_immense/.

20. David Leigh, "Bush, the Saudi billionaire and the Islamists: The story a British firm is afraid to publish," *The Guardian*, March 31, 2004, https://www.theguardian.com/media/2004/mar/31/pressandpublishing.saudiarabia.

21. Goldstone, *Interlock*.

22. Ibid., Part Two "Clinton—Marc Rich—Bruce Rappaport—BNY—Graham—Bliley."

23. "Philadelphia Fugitive Placed on FBI's 'Ten Most Wanted Fugitives' List," Press Releases, FBI, last modified October 21, 2009, https://archives.fbi.gov/archives/philadelphia/press-releases/2009/ph102109a.htm.

24. Robert Mueller, "The Evolving Organized Crime Threat," Federal Bureau of Investigation, Citizens Crime Commission of New York City, January 27, 2011, https://archives.fbi.gov/archives/news/speeches/the-evolving-organized-crime-threat.

25. Goldstone, "The Mysterious Death of an Artist Whose Drawings Were Too Revealing."

26. Anthony Lewis, "Security and Freedom," *New York Times*, May 22, 1975, https://www.nytimes.com/1975/05/22/archives/security-and-freedom.html.

27. John Marks, "On Being Censored," *Foreign Policy*, no. 15 (Summer 1974): 93–107.

28. Victor Marchetti and John Marks, *The CIA and the Cult of Intelligence* (New York: Dell, 1980), xi.

29. Ibid., 321.

30. Beverly Gage, "What an Uncensored Letter to M.L.K. Reveals," *New York Times*, November 16, 2014, https://www.nytimes.com/2014/11/16/magazine/what-an-uncensored-letter-to-mlk-reveals.html.

31. "The Watergate Story—Timeline," *Washington Post*, last modified April 25, 2008, https://www.washingtonpost.com/wp-srv/politics/special/watergate/timeline.html.

32. "Time | American magazine," Encyclopaedia Britannica, last modified December 29, 2021, https://www.britannica.com/topic/Time-American-magazine.

33. Frank Merrick, "The CIA: Time to Come In from the Cold," *TIME*, September 30, 1974, http://content.time.com/time/subscriber/article/0,33009,908779-3,00.html.

34. Seymour M. Hersh, "Huge C.I.A. Operation Reported in U.S. Against Antiwar Forces,

Other Dissidents in Nixon Years," *New York Times*, December 22, 1974, https://www.nytimes.com/1974/12/22/archives/huge-cia-operation-reported-in-u-s-against-antiwar-forces-other.html.

35. Carl Bernstein, "The CIA and the Media," *Rolling Stone*, October 20, 1977, http://www.danwismar.com/uploads/Bernstein%20-%20CIA%20and%20Media.htm.

36. Frank Church, "The Intelligence Gathering Debate," interview by Ford Rowan, *Meet the Press*, NBC, August 17, 1975, https://www.youtube.com/watch?v=YAG1N4a84Dk.

37. Don Reisinger, "Assange: Facebook is an 'appalling spy machine,'" *CNET*, May 3, 2011, https://www.cnet.com/home/smart-home/assange-facebook-is-an-appalling-spy-machine/.

38. *LIFE Magazine*, "It Is Positively the Most Wonderful Thing I Ever Saw," April 2, 1951.

39. "The Kefauver Hearings 1950–1951," *Pop History Dig*, https://www.pophistorydig.com/topics/kefauver-hearings-1950-1951/.

40. Gilbert King, "The Senator and the Gangsters," *Smithsonian Magazine*, April 18, 2012, https://www.smithsonianmag.com/history/the-senator-and-the-gangsters-69770823/.

41. Eric F. Goldman, *The Crucial Decade—and After: America, 1945–1960* (New York: Alfred A. Knopf, 1960), 198.

42. Hank Messick, *Lansky* (New York: Berkeley Publishing Corporation), 11.

43. Paul Hendrickson, "The Mob Chaser as Country Boy"," *Washington Post*, May 20, 1978, https://www.washingtonpost.com/archive/lifestyle/1978/05/20/the-mob-chaser-as-country-boy/0f94b6c1-afba-4e74-93c3-e0f5c8655ba6/.

44. Hank Messick, *Lansky* (New York: Berkley, 1971), 11.

45. Paul Hendrickson, "The Mob-Chaser as Country Boy," *Washington Post*, May 20, 1978, https://www.washingtonpost.com/archive/lifestyle/1978/05/20/the-mob-chaser-as-country-boy/0f94b6c1-afba-4e74-93c3-e0f5c8655ba6/.

46. Ben Montgomery, "Spoiled by mobsters, Meyer Lansky's daughter recalls family men, not killers," *Tampa Bay Times*, June 13, 2014, https://www.tampabay.com/features/humaninterest/spoiled-by-mobsters-daughter-of-meyer-lansky-recalls-family-men-not-killers/2184266/.

47. Messick, *Lansky*, 154.

48. "Israel Refuses Citizenship to Lansky, But Offers Him Special Travel Papers," *New York Times*, September 12, 1972, https://www.nytimes.com/1972/09/12/archives/israel-refuses-citizenship-to-lansky-but-offers-him-special-travel.html.

49. "Lansky Acquitted of Evading Taxes," *New York Times*, July 26, 1973, https://www.nytimes.com/1973/07/26/archives/lansky-acquitted-of-evading-taxes-reputed-underworld-figure-wins.html.

50. Sarah Kendzior, *Hiding in Plain Sight: The Invention of Donald Trump and the Erosion of America* (New York: Flatiron Books, 2020).

51. Natasha Bertrand, "Former FBI director represented Russian firm at center of major money-laundering probe," *Insider*, November 16, 2017, https://www.businessinsider.com/fbi-director-louis-freeh-russia-prevezon-money-laundering-2017-11.

52. Paul Radu, Dmitry Velikovsky, and Olesya Shmagun, "Prevezon Holdings: The Black Money Collector," *Organized Crime and Corruption Reporting Project*, November 17, 2020, https://www.occrp.org/en/the-fincen-files/prevezon-holdings-the-black-money-collector.

53. Wiley Rein, "Investigation by Former FBI Director Louis Freeh Concludes That the

Totality of the Evidence Refutes Allegations Made Against Professor Dershowitz," *PR Newswire*, April 8, 2016, https://www.prnewswire.com/news-releases/investigation-by -former-fbi-director-louis-freeh-concludes-that-the-totality-of-the-evidence-refutes -allegations-made-against-professor-dershowitz-300248841.html.

54. Brian Schwartz, "Trump ally Alan Dershowitz and ex-FBI Director Louis Freeh are lobbying for an Israeli billionaire the US has accused of corruption," CNBC, November 5, 2019, https://www.cnbc.com/2019/11/05/alan-dershowitz-ex-fbi-director-louis-freeh -lobbying-for-israeli-billionaire-dan-gertler.html.

55. Goldman, *The Crucial Decade—and After: America, 1945–1960*, 198.

Epilogue: An American Ghost

1. Danny Casolaro, "The Octopus: A Proposal," State Historical Society of Missouri, Columbia.

2. Gabrielle Borter, "'I've got towns that are gone,' Kentucky Governor Beshear says," Reuters, December 12, 2021, https://ottawasun.com/news/world/ive-got-towns-that-are -gone-kentucky-governor-beshear-says/wcm/18d7dc6e-850f-4bb0-b7a0-de8eafd2d68f.

INDEX

ABOUT THE AUTHOR

Sarah Kendzior is the *New York Times* bestselling author of *Hiding in Plain Sight* and *The View from Flyover Country*. She has a Ph.D. in anthropology from Washington University in St. Louis. She has reported for the *Guardian*, the *Atlantic*, and the *New York Times*. She lives in St. Louis.